Becoming **Teachers of Inner-cit**

STUDIES IN INCLUSIVE EDUCATION
Volume 22

Series Editor
Roger Slee, *Institute of Education, University of London, UK*

Editorial Board
Mel Ainscow, *University of Manchester, UK*
Felicity Armstrong, *Institute of Education – University of London, UK*
Len Barton, *Institute of Education – University of London, UK*
Suzanne Carrington, *Queensland University of Technology, Australia*
Joanne Deppeler, *Monash University, Australia*
Linda Graham, *University of Sydney, Australia*
Levan Lim, *National Institute of Education, Singapore*
Missy Morton, *University of Canterbury, New Zealand*

Scope
This series addresses the many different forms of exclusion that occur in schooling across a range of international contexts and considers strategies for increasing the inclusion and success of all students. In many school jurisdictions the most reliable predictors of educational failure include poverty, Aboriginality and disability. Traditionally schools have not been pressed to deal with exclusion and failure. Failing students were blamed for their lack of attainment and were either placed in segregated educational settings or encouraged to leave and enter the unskilled labour market. The crisis in the labor market and the call by parents for the inclusion of their children in their neighborhood school has made visible the failure of schools to include all children.

Drawing from a range of researchers and educators from around the world, Studies in Inclusive Education will demonstrate the ways in which schools contribute to the failure of different student identities on the basis of gender, race, language, sexuality, disability, socio-economic status and geographic isolation. This series differs from existing work in inclusive education by expanding the focus from a narrow consideration of what has been traditionally referred to as special educational needs to understand school failure and exclusion in all its forms. Moreover, the series will consider exclusion and inclusion across all sectors of education: early years, elementary and secondary schooling, and higher education.

Becoming Teachers of Inner-city Students

Life Histories and Teacher Stories of Committed White Teachers

James C. Jupp
Georgia Southern University, USA

SENSE PUBLISHERS
ROTTERDAM/BOSTON/TAIPEI

A C.I.P. record for this book is available from the Library of Congress.

ISBN: 978-94-6209-369-0 (paperback)
ISBN: 978-94-6209-370-6 (hardback)
ISBN: 978-94-6209-371-3 (e-book)

Published by: Sense Publishers,
P.O. Box 21858,
3001 AW Rotterdam,
The Netherlands
https://www.sensepublishers.com/

Printed on acid-free paper

To *Jim Ingman* –

Who lived ethically, *alternatively*

TABLE OF CONTENTS

ACKNOWLEDGMENTS

First and foremost, I need to thank my wife María Elvia who seventeen years ago said "yes" to my marriage proposal. I don't know what I would do without her or my sons, Octavio and Alfonso. *Son los amores de mi vida.*

Besides my family who believes in me and follows me on this crazy adventure, I'm grateful for the teachers in this study who openly and honestly provided their life and teacher stories. I can't list your real names but I'm continually astounded and humbled by the time we spent together in schools and what we accomplished (and failed to accomplish) teaching in re-segregated and unequal savage inequalities. Thanks for letting me tell your stories. And thanks for other public school colleagues and students too many to list here. I have tried to do justice to your stories and narrate them in compelling and critical ways.

Besides family, research respondents, and public school colleagues and students, there are so many people to thank. There is Lisa Cary, a great scholar and my Dissertation Chair who came up with the idea for this study in the first place while we were both at the University of Texas at Austin. There is Patrick Slattery, my friend, confidant, and mentor who first encouraged and then taught me how to make the move to higher education where I work today preparing teachers. There are colleagues and co-conspirators everywhere too many to name, but I'll list a few who have been particularly supportive in this project and in helping me along this pathway (in no particular order) – Tony Miele, Tim Lensmire, Raffy Vizcaino, Peter Appelbaum, Laura Jewett, Miryam Espinosa, Ugena Whitlock, Petra Hendry, Seungho Moon, Brandon Sams, Jenn Job, Jenn Milam, Jenny Sandlin, Jake Burdick, Mingui Gao, Diane Prince, and Ryan Kelly. I also need to add Bill Pinar to the list of acknowledgements, as he read and provided invaluable feedback on an early manuscript of this project.

Recently, I began working at Georgia Southern, and there I've found an excellent group of colleagues for sharing ideas. Among them, I need to thank Missy Bennett, Yasar Bodur, Michelle Reidel, Greg Chamblee, Lorraine Gilpin, Scott Beck, Julie Maudlin, Kym Drawdy, Christine Draper, Lina Soares, Bill Reynolds, Ming Fang He, Bill Schubert, Bob Lake, Chris and Katie Brkich, Ronnie Sheppard, and others.

To everyone listed above and others still: *I'm wishing you well, and I'm grateful for our conversations and support over the years.*

SERIES EDITOR'S FOREWORD

In a recent research colloquium at The Victoria Institute where I work in Melbourne, Australia, Allan Luke, Jean Phillips and James Ladwig presented from a comprehensive longitudinal evaluation of *The Stronger Smarter Learning Communities*. *The Stronger Smarter Learning Communities* was a project that aimed to improve the educational experiences and outcomes for Aboriginal and Torres Strait Islander students across Australia by building cultural awareness and educational leadership in indigenous education. The research is significant in that it employed an omnibus design that was qualitative and quantitative, cross-sectional and longitudinal to provide a very rich empirical database from which to interrogate key issues and challenges for leadership in Indigenous education in this country.

I raise this because in his prefatory remarks to the research colloquium on pedagogy and learning Professor Luke observed the penchant of education policy-makers and researchers in the west to attempt to build school improvement programmes that can be grafted upon schools and jurisdictions globally. We export and import education policy sanctioned by international comparisons such as PISA and TIMMS. This trend reveals both a chronic case of cultural amnesia and worse still geopolitical blindness.

The catch-cry of *evidence-based policy making* is more precisely characterised as policy-based evidence making. I lived and worked in England where there was an abundance of evidence that demonstrated the ways in which race could be seen as a marker of educational underachievement and disproportionate exclusion and referral to special education. Sally Tomlinson alerted British educators to this in the early 1980s (Tomlinson, 1982). Seventeen years later Dave Gillborn and Deborah Youdell's (1999) book, *Rationing Education* documented the systematic operation of educational triage where students whose academic prognosis looked bleak were streamed into terminal education tracks. Gillborn's (2008) application of critical race theory illustrates the persistence of *whiteness* in education.

Of course, for many years we have been reading of unequal cultural relations as they are played out in North America (Kozol, 1991). Not only have African-American and Latino children been left behind, we know that Sally's observations in the UK about the correspondence of disproportional over (and under) representation in special education applies (Parrish, 2002). Critical Race Theory offers us a way of interrogating *whiteness* and of understanding the micro-aggressions that are played out in the minutiae of intercultural exchanges. Put simply, teaching is political work and teachers are political operatives. Accordingly we need to consider the politics we enact in our classrooms, staffrooms, playgrounds and community halls. Teaching is difficult work and teachers need to consider the choices they make that frame the world their students come to know. Julie Allan (2005) drew from Foucault to remind us of the transgressions of inclusive education and that, above all, inclusive education is an ethical project on ourselves.

James Jupp does just that. From the early description in this book of his decision to opt for teaching as a realistic employment opportunity, we encounter an educator who is constantly situating and resituating himself and his work. The level of political engagement and reflexivity in this book speaks of integrity, commitment and a will to embrace the transformative power of teaching and learning in our schools. In his book *Possible Lives,* Mike Rose (1995) described public education as America's boldest democratic experiment. *Becoming* Teachers of Inner-city Students: Life Histories and Teacher Stories of Committed White Teachers is an instruction on how to keep the experiment on the workbench. This book is a valuable addition to the series, *Studies in Inclusive Education.* More precisely James Jupp exemplifies the frame of mind of an inclusive educator.

Roger Slee
Series Editor
Studies in Inclusive Education

REFERENCES

Allan, J. (2005). Inclusion as an ethical project. In S. Tremain (Ed.), *Foucault and the government of disability* (pp. 281–297). Ann Arbor, The University of Michigan Press.

Gillborn, D. (2008). *Racism and education: Coincidence or conspiracy?* London, Routledge.

Gillborn, D., & Youdell, D. (2000). *Rationing education: Policy, practice, reform and equity.* Buckingham, Open University Press.

Kozol, J. (1991). *Savage inequalities: Children in America's schools.* New York, Crown Publishers.

Parrish, T. (2002). Racial disparities in the identification, funding and provision of special education. In D. Losen & G. Orfield (Eds.), *Racial inequality in special education.* Cambridge, Harvard Education Press.

Rose, M. (1995). *Possible lives: the promise of public education in America.* Boston, Houghton Mifflin Co.

Tomlinson, S. (1982). *A sociology of special education.* London, Routledge and Kegan Paul.

INTRODUCTION

To Becoming Teachers of Inner-city Students

LIFE HISTORY ORIENTATION

Capacitating White Teachers

This book aims to capacitate an overwhelmingly White teaching force for teaching diverse students attending *de facto* segregated inner-city schools. My life history, as a White teacher from a middle class background who taught first in rural poor and then inner-city schools, tells a story of struggling with and working to bridge differences in teaching and learning with students whose background were different from mine. As many other White teachers, my life history and teacher stories, intertwined as they are, have taken place under conditions in which I was frequently the *only* White person in the classroom. As a public school teacher of eighteen years turned professor and writer, I write about and present my own and other committed White male teachers' life histories and teacher stories as a resource for preservice and professional teachers to read, think about, and reflect on in developing their own professional identities. In *Becoming Teachers of Inner-City Students*, I present a series of essays based on committed White male teachers' life histories and teacher stories that seek to understand what it means to become teachers who teach across borders of race, class, culture, language and other differences in exceedingly difficult social and economic times for public education. My aim, as I write and hope to be read in good faith, is to help professional and preservice teachers find ways to understand their students and themselves, dwell in classrooms and stay in education, develop commitments to students and communities, and ultimately, connect with students, families, communities and other agencies in taking up the ordinary heroics that take place in classrooms everywhere every day. My life history and teacher stories, important as positionality and credibility supporting this book, are narrated in Chapter One.

Challenging Historical Conditions

As I take up the writing of *Becoming Teachers of Inner-City Students*, I realize preservice and professional teachers face challenging historical conditions in the present. Up until the end of the 20th century, the function of public schools was to "Americanize" immigrant students and to sort other students toward occupation or college (Spring, 2000; Tozer, Senese, Violas, 2009; Tyack, 1974). Increasingly in the 21st century, public schools designed with Industrial Era concerns of Americanizing or sorting are required to take up quite a different task: the *academic achievement* of diverse and immigrant students. In taking up the academic achievement of diverse

1

and immigrant students, an understanding of teachers' professional identities and ability to cross borders of race, class, culture, and language all take on increasing importance.

In current data on the teaching profession, White teachers make up 88.6% of the combined elementary and secondary public teaching force (National Center for Educational Statistics [NCES], 2004) while the number of White students enrolled in public elementary and secondary students trends downward to 55.8% (NCES, 2010). White teachers, the vast majority of public school teachers, are increasingly required to cross borders of race, class, culture, language and other differences in classrooms. In inner-city schools where teachers in this study and I worked, this broad statistical disproportion of White teachers became even more pointed. Inner-city schools overwhelming represent *majority-minority* schools. This majority-minority status in inner-city schools is reflected in recent statistical data that indicate increased concentrations of minority students who attend schools with an enrollment of over 75% minority populations. In the case of the most sizeable minorities in the US, 57% of Hispanic students attend schools with an enrollment of over 75% minority populations (NCES, 2009). Similarly, 52% of African-American students attend schools with an enrollment of over 75% minority populations (NCES, 2009). Increasingly, students historically categorized as minorities paradoxically represent majorities in elementary and secondary school settings (NCES, 2009), and more broadly speaking in national trends, minority students are quickly trending to become the majority of elementary and secondary students enrolled in public schools as they currently constitute 44.2% of total students (NCES, 2010). In contrast, only 3% of White students enrolled in public schools attend schools with enrollment of over 75% minority populations (NCES, 2009). Like Kozol (2005), my lived experience of teaching and working in majority-minority inner-city schools led me to the conviction that an ugly *de facto* re-segregation now aggressively accompanies savage inequalities in schools.

Challenging historical conditions include 1) a persistent majority of White teachers, 2) increasing numbers of diverse students, 3) and an ugly *de facto* re-segregation in inner-city schools. I recognize the need for increased attention on social justice in education as that is an important subtheme of this book, though I insist social justice represent an interactionist project (Ellsworth, 1989; Pinar, 2011) rather than just declaring injustices. Additionally, I recognize that the development and retention of a diverse teaching force also represents a key educational priority and accompanying component of social justice in schools. In recognition of these and other broad currents, *Becoming Teachers of Inner-City Students* seeks to deal explicitly and specifically with one component of a larger social justice project: *the development and capacitation of White teachers' professional identities to cross borders of race, class, culture, language and other differences in classrooms*. In taking up the development and capacitation of White teachers' professional identities to cross borders, this research narratively focuses on the study of teachers' lives and professional identities inherent in life history and teacher story research.

Life History and Teacher Story Research

Becoming Teachers of Inner-city Students employs life history and teacher story research for studying and representing committed White male teachers' professional identities. Life history and teacher story research come from the practical, pragmatic, and democratic tradition in educational research that seeks to articulate teachers' complex professional identities and knowledges (e.g., Connelly & Clandinin, 1988; Clandinin & Connelly 1992, 1995; Cole & Knowles, 2000; Dewey, 1902; Eisner, 1985; Goodson & Sikes 2001; Henderson & Gornik, 2007). Against the grain of top-down policy mandates and prescriptive administrative reforms, life history and teacher story research provides up-from-below stories of teaching, learning, and identities in schools. Life history and teacher story research carries with it an understanding of teachers' professional identities, knowledges-in-contexts, and curriculum wisdom forged in practice with students. Emphasizing what is lacking in top-down mandates or prescriptive reforms, life history and teacher story research recognizes professional and preservice teachers' tacit position of power in that any and all mandates or reforms pass through and must be reconstructed in very practical ways by teachers and students in schools. Quite literally, all and any reforms or changes that reach students involve teachers' willing it *not* merely political mandates, administrative directives, or other control fantasies typical in the history of education. Following the feminist dictum *the personal is political*, life history and teacher story research recognizes that teachers are in fact very powerful, even when the use of this power is against-the-odds and against-the-grain. Though some teachers know they are powerful, too few teachers act individually or collectively on these understandings, nor do they recognize the power associated with their positions and practical expertise.

Emphasizing this tacit position of professional power, life history and teacher story research begins with an understanding that teaching is private, public, and practical intellectual work developing over teachers' lives (Pinar, 2012). Teaching is *private* intellectual work in that teachers recover their interior experiences and understandings, subject area knowledges, curriculum and pedagogy, likes and dislikes, strengths and weakness, and then take these into their work with students in classrooms every day. Teaching is *public* in that these interior inclinations and understandings play out over time in public and political spheres and have enormous consequences to students, families, communities, and beyond. Teaching is *practical* in that it requires that teachers develop not only subject area knowledge but hands-on know-how regarding what curriculum materials to represent subject area knowledge, what teaching models to adapt to reach students, and how subject area knowledge, curriculum materials, and teaching models might be artfully combined (Dewey, 1902; Eisner, 1985; Schwab, 1978, 1983; Shulman, 1987). Beginning with teaching as private, public, and practical intellectual work, studying teachers' life histories and teacher stories allows us to valorize teachers' professional processes of *becoming* as a means of understanding professional identities along with teaching and learning, particularly here, teaching and learning in classrooms that cross borders of race, class, culture, language, and other differences.

Very briefly, *life history* as taken up here refers to committed White male teachers' identities recovered in life story interviews and reconstructed in social and historical bounds, and *teacher stories* refer to professional story interviews recovered and reconstructed in practical teaching narratives. Understood in first person narrative, these definitions mean I learned-to-teach and taught-to-learn as part of my broader life story. I crossed borders of race, class, culture, language, and other differences, and my life became intermingled with students' life stories and communities' social and historical contexts. I learned to tell and re-tell my life story as it related to students' stories, subject areas taught, and surrounding milieus, and in doing so, I developed teacher stories about my and students' work together. My life history and teacher stories contained contextualized understandings and knowledges about who I have become along with how to work with Mexican immigrant, Mexican-American, Latino, and African-American students in inner-city schools. My life history and teacher stories very much articulate and constitute my professional identity as teacher. *When I change roles to researcher and tell teachers' and my own stories within historical, social, community, and other contexts, I transform life and teacher story interviews into life history and teacher story research.* Life history and teacher story research comes from a specific line of educational research that narrates, constitutes, and proliferates teachers' identities and professional knowledges in educational contexts (Connelly & Clandinin, 1988; Clandinin & Connelly, 1992, 1995; Cole & Knowles, 2000; Goodson, 1992, 1995; Goodson & Sikes, 2001). Important in life history and teacher story research is that it *valorizes* rather than diminishes teachers' identities, understandings, and knowledges developed in their life and teacher stories.

Critical-Intercultural and Intersubjective "Identifications" and "Readings"

In briefly describing life history and teacher story research, I begin to articulate critical-intercultural and intersubjective understandings of identity taken up in this book and called *identifications*. As teachers' life history and teacher stories demonstrate, cultural identities are malleable, changeable, and draw on historical and social resources in which they are bound (Bruner, 2002; Butler, 1999; Hall, 2003). Beginning with narrative notions of identity-malleability and -changeability, I emphasize critical-intercultural and intersubjective understandings of cultural identity, though I understand that these concepts imply arduous shared cultural labor. *Critical-intercultural* understandings of cultural identity emphasize that cultures living in close proximity in institutions like schools might and quite often do learn from each other. *Intersubjective* understandings of cultural identity emphasize that distinct cultural groups like Whites and people of color can share understandings in conversation or collaboration. Critical-intercultural and intersubjective understandings of identity are expressed throughout the entire text and texture of this book *both* in teachers and my life histories and teaching stories *along with* the scholars and researchers that I work with to support the research. Though neither critical-intercultural nor intersubjective understandings are "guaranteed" in *a priori* ways, intercultural and intersubjective understandings represent important positions for teachers who work across borders of race, class, culture, language, and other differences as they allow for co-penetrating identities.

In taking up intercultural and intersubjective understandings of identity in this study, I emphasize multicultural and diversity education (Appelbaum, 2002) that recognizes group identities but also understands identity complexities. I emphasize that cultural identities, including identities of Whites, are constructed in relationally-bounded performances (Bruner, 2002; Butler, 1999) that focus on *who-we-are-becoming* (Hall, 2003), a phrase that references the first word in the title of this book. In emphasizing that identities represent processes of who-we-are-becoming, I reconceptualize cultural identity as narrative, process-oriented, and relational identifications. *Identifications*, as definition, refer to *narrative process identities within historical and social boundedness.* The notion of identifications, reviewed and explained in Chapter One and used through this book, provides a key starting point for further developing recent discussions of progressive White identities in education (Asher, 2007; McCarthy, 2003; Perry & Shotwell, 2009; Raible & Irizarry, 2007). These recent discussion on progressive White identities in education recognize yet grapple with and critically interrupt White privileges and hegemonic whiteness without evasions or facile "White ally" solutions. Identifications, as critical-intercultural and intersubjective concept, necessarily inform the essays that come.

Identifications, as starting point for progressive White identities in education, also suggest possible critical-intercultural and intersubjective readings of this book, even for students from diverse non-White backgrounds. That is, even though this book is about White male teachers in inner-city settings, its educative value for preservice and professional teachers is *not* limited to one specific group or professional setting. Just as I learned to negotiate my identity from teachers of color with whom I worked and scholars of color whom I studied, critical-intercultural and intersubjective understandings developed in this book provide resources for discussions on preservice and professional teacher identities that are useful for other groups' discussions on identities as well. Even though this book is about the development of committed White teachers' identifications, these discussions, in a generous critical-intercultural and intersubjective reading, also provide resources for broader discussions of preservice and professional teachers' identities writ large.

THE ESSAYS TO COME

An Overview

This book, based on life history and teacher story research, provides a series of reflective essays on *Becoming Teachers of Inner-city Students.* These research essays unfold as laid out below, and they can be read individually, sequentially, or non-sequentially, though I provide an overview of concepts appearing throughout the book in Chapter One.

Chapter One, "Capacitating Concepts," uses my life history and teacher stories as a vehicle for narratively scaffolding, presenting, and explaining concepts appearing throughout the book. Capacitating concepts are especially directed toward White preservice and professional teachers' understandings yet serve to inform any critical-intercultural and intersubjective understanding of teachers' professional identity (Appelbaum, 2002). Of key importance with capacitating concepts are narrative process-oriented notions of professional identity that I call professional identifications. *Professional identifications*, as definition, refer to *narrative process identities within discursive contexts that understand and enact curriculum wisdom in classrooms*. Professional identifications within discursive contexts, explained further in Chapter One, help narrate teachers' professional becoming. Other concepts presented and explained in Chapter One are White privilege and White teachers' race-evasive identities as these concepts provide background for discussions of *capacitating concepts* that follow. I narratively scaffold, present, and explain capacitating concepts in Chapter One, and each of these concepts will receive further explanation as they help me narrate teachers' stories in subsequent chapters. Of equal importance in Chapter One are notions of *culturally relevant teaching* (Ladson-Billings, 1995; 2009) and *curriculum wisdom* (Davis, 1997; Schulman, 1987; Henderson & Gornik, 2007). In synthesizing culturally relevant teaching and curriculum wisdom, I narratively present and explain these concepts with examples of practical curriculum development from my teaching stories in order to support transferability of these concepts to preservice and professional teachers' classrooms.

Chapter Two, "Teachers' Race-Visible Professional Identifications," narrates life histories and teacher stories of committed White male teachers of inner-city students focusing on their understandings of teaching across borders of race, class, culture, and language. Narrating committed White male teachers' life histories and teacher stories, I discuss discursive contexts of teachers' work such as historical inequality, *de facto* re-segregation in schools, and accountability pressures, and I narrate professional identifications of three committed White male teachers. Teachers' life histories and teacher stories narrate motivations and commitments, show public teaching as linked to private lives and aspirations, articulate understandings of race and class in their teaching, and finally provide practical examples of curriculum wisdom for transferability to preservice and professional teachers' practice. I end this chapter with a discussion of narrative patterns that emerged across all teachers' stories. These narrative patterns demonstrate teachers' understandings of *race-visible professional identifications*, *difference within difference*, and *relational-experiential teaching*.

Chapter Three, "On Teachers' White Double-Consciousness," discusses committed White male teachers' structural *and* deficit understandings of student differences along with their tensions and exhaustions as career teachers. After further defining and explaining structural and deficit understandings of student difference,

I reveal contradictory understandings in teachers' professional identifications that paradoxically narrate student differences understood as *both* structural oppression *and* deficits of family and character. As I interpret these contradictions through W.E.B. Du Bois's (1903/1995) notion of Black double-consciousness, teachers' professional identifications reveal a contradictory split-half view on student differences I call teachers' White double-consciousness. In their professional identifications, White double-consciousness clearly recognizes structural oppression in students' lives, yet paradoxically, teachers' meliorist understandings retain strong residues of individualistic notions such as "family commitment" and "personal effort" inherent in their students' educational chances very much pronouncing a White middle class ethic. White double-consciousness, as it emerged in teachers' professional identifications, underscored teachers and students' negotiated identities in inner-city schools that, as part of the institution of school, require teachers and students' good faith efforts through relationality. Finally, this chapter concludes by revealing, as part of professional identifications, on-going frustrations and exhaustions related to career teachers' stories. Working across borders of difference, professional identifications embrace "the grind" (Jackson, 1968/1990, p. 1) and avoid self-congratulatory or facile "victory narratives" (Cary, 1999, p. 414).

Chapter Four "What are Progressive Masculinities?" provides a discussion focusing on teachers' life histories as they relate to masculinities (Beynon, 2002; Connell, 1987, 1995; Tolson, 1977). Reviewing literatures on masculinities and male teachers, I narrate teachers' alternative masculinities as driving component behind other alternative identifications. Several themes, across teachers' interviews, emerged as manifestations of alternative masculinity. These manifestations of alternative masculinities, embedded in respondents' life histories, emerge as counternarratives (Bamberg, 2004; Bamberg & Andrews, 2004; Peters & Lankshear, 1996) to the Conservative Restoration's straight, clean-cut, upwardly mobile, and instrumental professional White male identities. Paradoxical, oppositional, and tension-filled, teachers' progressive masculinities grounded respondents' progressive commitments to teaching. This chapter ends by analysing the second split-half view of committed White male teachers' personal and professional identifications.

Chapter Five, "Toward Second Wave White Teacher Identity Studies," draws together main conclusions developed in previous chapters and emphasizes the following:

> White teachers in this study forged *race-visible professional identifications* that, articulated especially in Chapters One and Two, provided specific and contextualized understandings of teaching and learning through race, class, culture, language, and other differences that I call *race-visible curriculum wisdom*. Race-visible professional identifications and curriculum wisdom strive to add to conversations on preservice and professional teacher understandings of specific-and-practical curriculum development lacking in theoretical discussions of multicultural education.

White teachers' personal and professional identifications provided complicated *split-half views* manifest both in their *White double consciousness* and *progressive masculinities*. Taking life and teacher stories in this study seriously, these concepts developed in Chapters Three and Four, provide for destabilization and critique of teachers' personal and professional identifications. Even though White teachers in this study developed race visible professional identifications, these identifications did *not* provide final identity "solutions" for preservice and professional teachers to simply "adopt," as if such a thing were possible. Rather, race-visible professional identifications emerged as problematically negotiated with students in schools and even in broader historical and social contexts. Split-half views that came from this research provided *not* administrated identity "solutions" *but rather* narrated and problematized in-process identity work that might serve as resources for preservice and professional teachers' *becoming*.

White teachers' race-visible identifications and split half views suggest a need for *second wave White teacher identity studies*. Second-wave White teacher identity studies extend previous work on whiteness and White identity in education but do so in ways that look deeply into lived White identities and teachers' racial understandings and teaching practices that teach through race, class, cultural, language, and other differences. Even so, second wave White teacher identity studies, as developed here, do *not* prescribe final "identity solutions" for pre-service and professional teachers' adoption but instead suggest on-going critique, process, and *becoming*. Second wave identity studies, as this book demonstrates, emphasize an on-going grappling with race, class, culture, and language as part of teaching and learning.

In short, second wave White teacher identity studies drive at *complex conversations on White identity in education for preservice and professional teachers.* In this last emphasis – *complex White identity in education* – I return to an important and under-elaborated discourse on White teacher identity initiated, but not fully articulated, by Joe Kincheloe and Shirley Steinberg (1998). Complex progressive White identifications might:

> generate a sense of pride in the possibility that White people can help transform the reality of social inequality and reinvent themselves around the notions of justice, community, social creativity, and economic political democracy. ...The importance of antiracist, positive, creative and affirmational White identity in this teaching context cannot be overstated. (p. 21)

It is in this spirit that *Becoming Teachers of Inner-City Students* proceeds, along the lines of complex progressive yet not-finished, incomplete, and tension-filled understandings of White teachers and their work with diverse students.

CAPACITATING CONCEPTS

In Becoming Teachers of Inner-city Students

INTRODUCTION

Narratively Presenting and Explaining Capacitating Concepts[1]

Chapter One narratively presents and explains capacitating concepts in *Becoming Teachers of Inner-city Students*. As capacitating concepts emerged narratively in my professional understandings, I present and explain these concepts narratively from both teaching and aesthetic standpoints.

As I recount my life history and teacher stories in Chapter One, I narratively present and explain capacitating concepts for developing teachers' intercultural and intersubjective professional identifications. *Capacitating concepts*, as definition, refer to *concepts that inform and capacitate teachers' professional identifications as teachers work across borders of race, class, culture, language, and other differences.* The capacitating concepts, presented and explained in my life history and teacher stories below, narratively unfold as follows: 1) *boundedness* and *identifications*, 2) *discursive contexts* and *professional identifications*, 3) *race-visible professional identifications*, 4) *deficits versus structures* for understanding student differences, and 5) *progressive masculinities* and *counternarratives*. This chapter concludes with a practical discussion of the capacitating concepts from my teacher stories that illustrate *race-visible curriculum wisdom*. Each capacitating concept is narratively presented and explained through my life history and teacher stories in this chapter, and these capacitating concepts are the concepts readers should take away as they appear in the chapters to come. I also provide further discussion of capacitating concepts in chapters in which the concepts are used and emphasized.

In developing capacitating concepts, I emphasize narrative explanation and presentation for both teaching and aesthetic reasons. From a teaching standpoint, I narratively present and explain capacitating concepts to create scaffolded understandings for preservice and professional teachers. Narratively scaffolded understandings, rather than present prescriptions for preservice and professional teachers to "adopt," support narrative and constructivist teaching. From an aesthetic standpoint, I narratively present and explain capacitating concepts so as to perform understandings of struggle, discomfort, and personal growth inherent in teachers' professional identifications. Professional identifications along with commitments are not easily attained, represent achievements, and often professional identifications require trauma, challenge, re-invention and the shedding of previous identities for new ones. I hope to represent the struggle inherent in professional identifications usually overlooked in prescriptive "best-practice dispositions" put forth in teacher education and professional development. Following teaching and aesthetic reasoning, I narratively perform capacitating concepts through my life history and teacher stories. But in doing so, I narrate struggle, discomfort, growth, renewal, and self-narrativization inherent in professional identifications providing lived experiences behind professional dispositions. Through my life history and teacher stories, I perform an example of process-oriented professional identifications that valorize teachers' *becoming* while simultaneously teaching capacitating concepts used in the chapters that come.

Value Positionality: A Deadly Serious Make-Or-Break Moment

In valorizing my and other teachers' *becoming*, life history and teacher story research requires an understanding of the researcher's positionality in classrooms, schools, communities, and the research itself. With life history and teacher story research, the researcher's life history and teacher stories represent a *deadly serious make-or-break moment*. Very directly, the research's stories – *my stories* – inform how the research might be read, how it might be understood, and how readers construct *transferability* of meaning to their own teaching and professional lives in classrooms. Though quantitative and even some qualitative research emphasizes emotional distance, life history and teacher story research pushes in the opposite direction. Instead of emphasizing distance, life history and teacher story research valorizes the researcher's involvement, commitments to schools and children, and lived experiences as integral to the research. In the same way I needed my life story and teacher stories as background in classrooms to have *cred* with students in inner-city schools, life history and teacher story research posits the centrality of researchers' life history and teacher stories to the research's *credibility* and possible impact with preservice and professional teachers. Though many education professors shy away from practical discussions of their (sometimes thin) involvement in classrooms, Title I schools, or diverse communities, life history and teacher story research here emphasizes that the researcher's experience counts as key experiential knowing. I narrate my life history and teacher stories in this chapter *not only* from teaching and aesthetic standpoints *but also* as a means to create narrative *credibility* for capacitating concepts along with the stories in subsequent chapters. It is with teaching and aesthetic reasoning along with the make-or-break-moment of narrative credibility that I present my life history and teacher stories below.

MY LIFE HISTORY AND TEACHER STORIES

Boundedness

Very much echoing the present conditions of many, many of my present students, I entered teaching out of sheer necessity of finding paid work in a depressed economy bereft of opportunity for young people. In the midst of a recession, I needed a job first and foremost and was having no luck finding anything at all let alone work for someone with a university degree in the College of Liberal arts at the University of Texas. In the wake of the Savings and Loan Crisis, Black Monday of 1989, and the financial bailout under President Bush, Sr., there were no new jobs available during that period, and those who had jobs held on for dear life. That certainly sounds familiar to students in my classrooms nowadays.

Privileged through whiteness and middle class status though not feeling or understanding it at that time, I distinctly remember the day riding my bicycle up Guadalupe Street several blocks north of the Drag in Austin where I saw a convenience store with a *help wanted-apply within* sign posted. Excitedly, I entered and asked for a job application, and the attendant responded, holding a huge pile of applicants in his hand, "OK, but we already have thirty applicants." Then, *precisely then*, I realized I was not going to get a job in Texas doing anything anytime soon much less apply my, what appeared at the time to be useless, degrees in English, Spanish, and sociology.

Exasperated with myself, my education, and the economic boondoggle that left shiny and new office buildings standing vacant in Houston, Dallas, and Austin, I understood, perfectly well, why I was not finding any work. I realized, quite clearly because of my critical education, that an elite class of investors had frivolously driven up the market values of stocks, corporate earnings, investments, and especially commercial real estate beyond any reasonable expectation of returns very much preceding the "casino capitalism" (Giroux, 2012, p. 2) of today. Eyes opened to the false promises of the Reagan Presidency and its aftermath, I felt repulsion for official corporate and financial "success" belied by my jobless condition yet maintained in the hegemonic masculinity of many others my age studying MBAs and sporting business suits, power ties, and Ray-Bans®. In all of this, I knew that I was going to have to try something different. Shortly afterward, I decided to leave the United States, and I got on a bus to Mexico City understanding that there were jobs teaching English. That's how my teaching career began, out of sheer joblessness.

Boundedness, as capacitating concept, refers to contexts of my life such as privileged whiteness and middle class status identities ostensibly at odds with the economic boondoggle in the aftermath of the Reagan Presidency. All teachers in this study mentioned the Reagan Presidency and its aftermath as semiotic anchor in their life and teacher stories that emerged during the Conservative Restoration (Apple, 2000). *Boundedness*, as definition, refers to *structured contexts that, by degrees, shape and call identities into being*. Boundedness is a capacitating concept because it suggests that, on the structured contexts of lives, it is possible to change ourselves and the contexts by identifying resources, options, and alternatives.

Identifications

Life as a teacher began for me in Mexico in 1990 when I finally found a job teaching English as a Foreign Language in Mérida. In Mérida, there were several language institutes, and studying English was especially important in Mexico at the time of deliberations on the North American Free Trade Agreement. I found work at *El Instituto Benjamín Franklin* in Mérida.

Suddenly working as a teacher in Mexico, I had a lot to learn. I knew English, and I continually worked on my Spanish through reading. I learned Mexican national, regional, and local cultures first out of interest, respect, and love for where I was, but I also realized, professionally, that understanding students' cultures, identities, and experiences was important for being able to teach them well, I enthusiastically took it upon myself, as I took up many projects of my youth, to learn about my students and their lives in every way possible. In mastering Spanish and immersing myself in Mexican cultures, I sought, through a privileged gringo-expatriate frame, a total view and was allowed to move across many sectors of society as an interesting anomaly who could report on life in the United States. Teaching, both in the *Instituto* and moonlighting in private classes, gave me access across social strata. I learned through teaching and interacting socially with businessmen and government officials, and alternately, the clerks, secretaries, and employees who worked for them. These relationships led to others, and I counted among my friends several mechanics at the Coca Cola plant, the Secretary of the Department of Communication, and a Cuban exile teaching at *La Universidad Autónoma de Yucatán* along with many teachers and students whom I worked with daily.

Additionally, I sought out the social-historical literatures getting guidance from my students, co-workers, and friends regarding, for example, historians of the Mexican Revolution or the trajectory of modernist and magical realist literary traditions. With this guidance, I read voraciously from these traditions and continue to do so today, with the increasing feeling of reading over someone's shoulder. In striving for this total view, I experienced a strange *déjà vu*, seeing the hierarchies of Houston and Austin that I grew up in take a different form with a new cast of players. Most importantly, what I began understanding during my first five years living and working in Mexico was the full extension of "realties" that existed both within and beyond the possibilities of my understanding. Only after more reading and experience was I able to fully comprehend the hopes, yearnings, short-comings, and inherent White privilege (McIntosh, 1988) in this experience: *I* was the one who could freely cross borders, find work in Mexico, and become useful because of my education. Through both firsthand experience and reading, I came to understand that about thirty percent of the Mexican people live in conditions that citizens in the United States consider destitute, and about half of Mexican children receive little more than a primary school education.

Identifications, as capacitating concept, refer to processes of self-narrativization (Hall, 2003) through which I and others form and reform identities including, in my case, transgressing boundedness, developing relationships across cultures, engaging in formal education and self-study, and learning a second language and culture as examples. Special to boundedness narrated above, I found cultural resources through self-narrativization. I formed and reformed myself within boundedness, and through these processes of self-narrativization, I developed identifications very different from many of my childhood friends and classmates who simply reproduced White middle class identities in West Houston. Teaching in Mexico and later in Title I rural and inner-city schools provided me with identifications very different from those my age who went to work for their family business or got entry level corporate jobs.

Recognizing that identifications provide conditions special to life stories and take place always within bounded duress, identifications importantly recover narrative processes of self-inscription as at once historical, cultural, and political (Butler, 1999). Identifications recognize race, class, gender and other historical and social bounds (Appelbaum, 2002) as I have attempted to do above; nonetheless, identifications recover complicated notions of lived-experience and exigencies of existential choice in phenomenological traditions that insist, ultimately, that *I* am ethically accountable for the reality I create and engage in. All teachers in this study demonstrated, in their life and teacher stories, processes of life-altering and -enabling self-narrativization I call identifications. *Identifications*, reviewing the definition from the Introduction, refer to *narrative process identities within historical and social boundedness*.

Discursive Contexts

After having worked in Mérida for four years, I moved to Matamoros, Tamaulipas just south of Brownsville, Texas along the United States-Mexican border in 1994. After having moved to Matamoros, I landed a job teaching in Los Fresnos, Texas, a small town about ten miles from the Mexican border and Matamoros. Christmas of that year traveling on a bus to Mexico City, I met my wife María Elvia Hernandez Peralta from Córdoba, Veracruz. We fell in love and were married six months later. Due to my wife's immigration status and job in Matamoros, we took up residence in Matamoros where for the next six years I found more permanent work in Raymondville, Texas about forty miles north of the border. We have now been married for sixteen years and have two sons, Octavio and Alfonso, who are six and nine years old at the time I write this.

Teaching public school in rural poor settings starting in 1994 was a big change. In Los Fresnos and Raymondville, I taught in a new setting, and my students were no longer adults in language classes but rather rural, Title I, Mexican immigrant, and Mexican-American students. The public school context in South Texas presented a whole different set of concerns for me as a classroom teacher. These concerns included how to keep students on-task, how to develop curriculum materials and projects, how to discipline students' fairly, and how to get results on the Texas Assessment of Academic Skills (TAAS) of the 1990s. As a teacher of predominantly rural poor Mexican immigrant and Mexican-American students in South Texas along with a few White students, I began to see the flip-side of the social conditions I observed teaching in Mexico. Teaching in South Texas (and later in Austin), I taught students from many Mexican immigrant families mixed in with longstanding Mexican-American lineages along with small numbers of White and African-American students in predominantly Mexican-American communities.

At that time, accountability had already begun to predominate administrative concerns. Administrators directed me to link my lessons to the Texas Essential Elements (EEs), and my students, at the end of my first year, took the TAAS test that later became the Texas Assessment of Knowledge and Skills (TAKS) in the early 2000s. I also worked on the committee for Raymondville ISD that stayed after school four times to review and provide "feedback" to Texas Education Agency about the new standards or Texas Essential Knowledge and Skills (TEKS). The TEKS, modified between their first release and the present, nonetheless provided the curriculum standards through the present. What was most disturbing about working with TAAS and later TAKS testing in Texas was the increasing pressure to narrow the curriculum away from authentic academic tasks such as essay writing, research, and projects toward multiple choice items and writing formulas similar to the test itself (Valenzuela & McNeil, 2000), and as I worked first in regionally- and later in community-segregated Title I schools, administrators with jobs on the line placed enormous focus on "bubble students" or those students who were barely failing or passing practice tests rather than on the most needy or academically proficient students. As a curriculum maker and planner, I mostly ignored pressures to teach *Book or Brain?* strategies for TAKS reading passages or formulaic writing of *1-2-3 essays* and reflections, yet under pressure from the administration, I didn't always engage students in library research or do as much independent study as I wanted because of administrative emphasis on testing. In staff development I was presented "quick fix" curriculum and pedagogy to get results on tests in Raymondville and also in "progressive" Austin ISD. It's important to note that this trend toward testing, especially in Title I schools, created incrementally greater and greater curriculum management pressures as the years went by. Before I left Austin ISD in 2008, standardized tests – including practice tests, six weeks tests, TAKS "boot camps," and finally the TAKS itself – took up, if added together in consecutive days, more than six weeks of the year! Indeed, schools had become "cram schools" (p. xii) that William Pinar (2012) referred to in his recent book. < right more

Discursive contexts, another capacitating concept I narrate in my teacher stories, refer to the way that schooling is shaped by historical, social, and institutional discourses. In my case, discursive contexts meant geographically- or community-segregated Title I schools focused on classroom discipline, state standards, and TAKS testing – all of which very much influenced and constituted teachers and students' experiences. Discursive contexts provide a capacitating concept because, as they relate to discourse in the word "discursive," they serve as a reminder that working conditions are very much constituted in historical, social, and political languages. Therefore, the term discursive contexts suggests *malleability* regarding the "realities" that teachers and students face in schools. Because discursive contexts emphasize historically, socially, and politically *constructed professional contexts*, teachers might understand such conditions as changeable in both personal and collective identifications. *Discursive contexts*, as definition, refer to *historical and social boundedness in schooling of particular teachers and students.*

Professional Identifications

As an English teacher in public schools, I was reborn twice: once in South Texas and again in inner-city Austin. When I started teaching in South Texas through the Alternative Certification Program, I gravely struggled to "hold" students attention, "control" their behavior, and "teach" the Texas Essential Elements. My *holding* attention, *controlling* behavior, and *teaching* standards without reference to my students' lives was quickly turning out to be a disaster. After one very long month, I contemplated quitting and returning to Mexico. In short, I was crashing and burning, but I was lucky enough to have several mentors including Rigo García[2] and Dr. José Luís Pérez who saw something in me worth salvaging.

Regarding teaching and learning, I found a mentor in Dr. José Luís Perez who gave me a copy of *Stories That Must Not Die*, a book of South Texas legends by Juan Sauvageau (1989). That insightful gift, from a great teacher (I'll add), represented the beginning of my *professional identifications* as a public school teacher. Sauvageau's (1989) book, a bi-lingual edition of oral legends from South Texas, helped me to leverage students' cultures and languages toward academic learning. Leveraging students' cultures and languages toward academic learning, hastened by my mentor's selection of curriculum, provided me with one basic insight greatly supported by research on teaching, learning, identity, and culture that is convincingly documented in Gloria Ladson-Billings' (2009) *The Dreamkeepers*. Later during my masters at the University of Texas at Brownsville, I read Ladson-Billings (1995, 2009), who demonstrates the importance of leveraging students' backgrounds, respecting home cultures, developing mainstream cultural competencies, insisting on students' academic success, and activating students' critical thinking on social issues. I also read John Dewey's (1902/1990) *The Child and the Curriculum* that suggests the integration of subject area knowledge and students' experience in ways that create personal and social growth. John Dewey, who represents the practical and democratic traditions in education, and Ladson-Billings, who represents the tradition on teaching, learning, culture, and identity, both influenced my teaching more than any other historical or contemporary educators, and they had a profound effect on what I tried to accomplish in the classroom in subsequent years as the experimentation continued. Reading Ladson-Billings and Dewey lead me to an on-going practical experimentation with culturally relevant teaching with my students in language arts and social studies that, in adapting a term from Henderson and Gornik (2007) and others (e.g., Clandinin & Connelly, 1992, 1995; Davis, 1997; Shulman, 1987), I narratively present and explain as *curriculum wisdom* in the next section. Yet, even with these insights developed in South Texas, my professional learning wasn't over yet.

After having lived in Mérida and Matamoros and taught in Mexico and in South Texas for ten years, my wife and I left Matamoros in the summer of 2000 and headed to Austin where I entered the PhD program in curriculum and instruction at the University of Texas. Upon leaving Raymondville, I started to work for Austin ISD.

Immediately after entering my first classroom, I was astonished to be assigned new teacher status by students, faculty, and administrators. I again struggled to re-create myself and my curriculum for Mexican immigrant, Mexican-American, and African-American middle school students in inner-city Title I settings. Despite having taught for ten years, I was surprised to find myself starting over again in an unfamiliar context, and once again, I was in an out-and-out fight for my professional life. For the first three months, I was bewildered and distraught at how poorly things were going for me and others in Southside Middle School.

My students in Austin presented different needs, interests, and family backgrounds from the ones I previously experienced despite demographic "similarities" or belonging ostensibly to the same ethnic-racial groups. Much to my dismay (though perhaps unsurprising in retrospect), my experiences in Raymondville were not completely transferable to inner-city discursive contexts that had different demands, learning expectations, and student identities. Again, I found a mentor in the Department Head, Victor Rodríguez, who met with me almost daily and coached me through the transition by teaching me how to develop lessons that balanced students' backgrounds, cultures, identities, and interests toward social learning in intricately structured cooperative lessons. These cooperative lessons teetered precariously between wrongly executed "discovery" lessons, which degenerated into chaos in my new setting, and teacher-centered lessons, which had functioned more in South Texas but resulted in big discipline problems in Austin ISD.

Working in an inner-city setting, succeeding but always re-creating myself and re-inventing my teaching, I became aware of the limits of culturally relevant teaching in schools, and I also experienced the excitement of making connections amidst the difficulties and exhaustion of being a career teacher. It's important to discuss making connections because, as this book will reveal, the teachers and I experimented with culturally relevant teaching in leveraging students' backgrounds, cultures, identities, and interests toward academics in a number of ways along the lines of critical pedagogy (Freire, 1970/2002) specific to our contexts. For example, I developed curriculum on *de facto* re-segregated schools, the gentrification of students' neighborhoods, civil rights movements in the United States, Fredrick Douglas's *Narrative of a Life of Slave*, indigenous genocide in Bartolomé de Las Casas' *A Short Account of the Destruction of the West Indies*, all representing critical counternarratives (Peters & Lankshear, 1996).

Amidst reporting on making connections and successes, it is important to emphasize that this curriculum wisdom was continually re-created in my professional identifications. I did not find sure-fire formulas nor silver bullets for developing authentic relationships or "best practices," even from one year to the next. Instead, I continually struggled and re-created my professional identifications in developing practical *pedagogical content knowledge* (Shulman, 1987): "that special amalgam of content and pedagogy" (p. 8) including teachers' academic knowledge, students backgrounds and characteristics, specific curriculum materials, community contexts, and knowledge of educational purposes. In this narrative of struggle to reach my students, sometimes succeeding and sometimes failing, my professional identifications articulate the character of what is described, often in context-free and facile ways in teacher education, as *reflective professionalism* (Schön, 1983; Shulman, 1987). Reflective professionalism, when taken up authentically by preservice and professional students *is not* just "writing reflections." Rather, reflective professionalism is geared toward digging deep, asking personal and social questions, overcoming challenges, and solving personal and professional problems in ways that result in private and public intellectual growth and personal development (Pinar, 2012). Shulman (1987) calls this type of reflective professionalism *reflection-in-action* because it makes authentic lived experience forged in professional practice the centerpiece. It is important to note for preservice and professional teachers, even though the work got easier and more routine, I would never say "I got it down." The teachers in this study along with my stories all represent on-going struggle and frustration yet rewarding connections in our professional identifications.

In my teacher stories, the notion of *professional identifications* becomes evident. *Professional identifications*, as capacitating concept, relate to identifications' self-narrativization and refer to process-oriented remaking of professional identity under the duress of unequal and segregated historical and social conditions. Professional identifications, in my case, meant re-creating myself, re-inventing pedagogical content knowledge, and engaging in reflective professionalism in on-going ways, especially when I changed schools. Professional identifications meant a constant re-narrativization of my professional self in practical curriculum experimentation. In developing professional identifications, I found mentors, developed curriculum resources, and came to understand students and contexts. Nonetheless, the private and public intellectual labor of professional identifications never seemed over, always seemed to start anew (Pinar, 2012). *Professional identifications*, as defined previously in the Introduction, refer to *narrative process identities within discursive contexts that understand and enact curriculum wisdom in classrooms.*

Race-Visible Professional Identifications

Being twice re-born as a teacher, professional identifications represented an on-going project. Working in South Texas while living in Matamoros, Tamaulipas, I became sensitized toward and learned to negotiate intersections of border culture in which race, class, language, culture, and other differences marked visible power relations that simply did not allow for "color-blind" or White race-evasive identities. In Matamoros and South Texas, identity sensitivity was sharpened, especially along the lines of race, class, language, and culture, and who is allowed to speak and represent those intersections is carefully negotiated. As an example of sharpened identity sensitivities, many of my Mexican-American friends almost never crossed over to Matamoros from the antipathy they felt (and accompanying shame I think) because their Spanish stuck out in Matamoros as *agringado* or whitened, and according to their stories, this occasioned problems. Mexicans in Matamoros and

17

in other towns along the Mexican side of the border *les pendejeaban* or hassled my Mexican-American friends because of "whitened" Spanish. Because of these sharpened sensitivities of race, class, culture, and language, simply taking the position that we are all deep down the same or just essentialized "individuals" was not a position that found affirmation along the United States-Mexican border much less in communities, schools, and classrooms.

It is important to interject at this point that existing understandings of White teacher identity emphasize White teachers' race-evasive identities (e.g., Howard, 2006; Marx, 2004, 2008; Marx & Pennington, 2003; McIntyre, 1997, 2002, Sleeter, 1992, 1993). That is, existing understandings on White teacher identity demonstrate White teachers' insistence on erasing or evading "group" identities, especially those signifying historical or social oppression like race, class, culture, and language. White teachers' race-evasive identities diminish or dismiss group identity and social historical oppression and instead emphasize "individuals," "personalities" "characteristics," "abilities," and by doing so, race-evasive White teacher identity, often unconsciously, reinstates over-simplified understandings of "individualism," "personal merit," and "success" understood differently and more complexly within marginalized groups. Christine Sleeter (1992, 1993, 1995, 2001), whose work is foundational in describing White teachers' race-evasive identities, summarizes this extensive body of research:

> Faced with the paradox of liking and helping students of color while explaining away the subordination of people of color and adhering to social structures that benefit themselves and their own children, the White teachers I studied responded in patterned ways. Many simply refused to "see" color. Others searched for "positive" associations with race by drawing on their European ethnic experience…. Discussing race or multiculturalism meant discussing "them," not the social structure. (1993, p. 168)

My research, expanding Christine Sleeter's research (though taking quite a different tack), focuses *not* on describing White teachers' race-evasive identities *but rather* on articulating, generating, and proliferating White teachers' *race-visible professional identifications.*

Teaching in South Texas, I first learned a patient, open-ended, border pedagogy as the means of crossing cultures and finding intersections of lived experience with my students and community members. Despite this patient and personal practice of border pedagogy, race-visible professional identifications did not come all at once. I too remember reading Peggy McIntosh's (1988) "White Privilege: Unpacking the Invisible Knapsack" during my masters degree and rankling with "objections" described in White teachers' race evasive identities (e.g., Howard, 2006; Marx, 2004, 2008; Marx & Pennington, 2003; McIntyre, 1997, 2002, Sleeter, 1992, 1993). Nonetheless, after more personal and professional experience, McIntosh's main points appear obvious to me: White middle class culture occupies the hegemonic center in the United States through notions of individualism, merit, and success – concepts very relevant and

18

simplistically understood in schools of the past and present. Since White middle class culture occupies the hegemonic center, White identities receive privileges. More recent research emphasizes that White teacher identity is unstable (Lensmire, 2011) complicated (Asher, 2003; McCarthy, 2003; Raible & Irizarry, 2007), and can take contradictory oppositional forms (Jupp & Slattery, 2010, 2012; Jupp, 2013). This new research begins to suggest that White privileges differ depending on one's relation to the hegemonic center. Due to sharpened identity sensitivities, I came to realize that White privilege was extremely visible in South Texas and Matamoros. This fact was underscored by multinational corporations' *maquiladoras* located in Matamoros where five hundred plus factories and plants with highly paid White professionals supervised other Mexican administrative staff and Mexican workers. Mexican workers, at the bottom of the hierarchy, made ten dollars a day. This transnational context heightened rather than diminished understandings of hegemonic whiteness and White privilege.

Put simply, as someone who lived in Matamoros and crossed the international border to South Texas every day, I learned race-visible identifications in communities and schools that in my teaching became *race-visible professional identifications.* Only through repeated forays into communities, schools, and students' lived experiences, could I ultimately gain (or fail to gain) others' confidence, and the interactions and contexts were complex and required patient understandings of students' cultural codes and my own positionality as teacher. Race-visible professional identifications, developed through border pedagogy, allowed me to "see" students' identity intersections and differences within difference and to develop professional identifications that, through intercultural and intersubjective understandings, could cross-over, take on authority, and speak with my students with the necessary authority to teach. As a new teacher, I think it's always important to ask yourself and carefully contemplate the question: *Why would my students listen to me?*

As a teacher in inner-city Austin, race-visible professional identifications became even more important. I began to actively study students' cultures, experiences, and interests through questionnaires and life writing assignments at the beginning of the year to accelerate understandings of students' identities. Using "data" I collected, I developed curriculum that incorporated what I learned into units of study I narrate in the next section. Briefly, as examples, I developed curriculum that integrated song lyrics (mostly hip hop and R&B lyrics) for close reading, Mexican-American and urban legends for literary analysis, neighborhood stories and essays in writing workshops, and studies of masculinity in pop culture using what I learned in questionnaires and life writing. For independent reading, I surveyed for what my students were interested in, and in doing much of the reading on-line, I delivered content links they requested yet insisted on carefully written summaries of their readings to document academic skills. For research, I collaborated with social studies emphasis on inalienable rights and created structured choice through menus in which students might select Thomas Jefferson or Miguel Hidalgo, Martin Luther King or Pancho Villa, Elizabeth Cady Stanton or Dolores Huerta. Not surprisingly, many of my Mexican immigrant and Mexican students chose Miguel Hidalgo or Pancho Villa as research topics, though many also chose Thomas Jefferson or Martin Luther King. *Race-visible professional identifications,* as definition, *refer to professional identifications developed over time that recognize race and other identities in ways that inform teaching and learning in classrooms across borders of difference.*

Structural and Deficit Understandings of Student Differences

Besides emphasizing race-visible professional identifications in Austin ISD, I also learned to negotiate intersections with gang cultures embedded in neighborhoods surrounding the schools. Gang cultures, though certainly present in Raymondville ISD[3], took on a more prominent role in inner-city Austin. I also observed the deep ambivalences (Valenzuela, 1999) and learning resistant identities (Ogbu & Simmons, 1998; Willis, 1977) my students had regarding school and school learning, though present in South Texas, became harder to negotiate in inner-city settings.

Many teachers, especially ineffective White teachers but also some teachers of color I worked with, displayed great disdain for students and their families who represented gang associations, demonstrated ambivalences, or performed learning resistance. Wrapped up in this disdain was the teachers' perceived "values conflict," and students I worked with often identified teachers they considered "haters" in informal conversations with me. Haters, as I understood my students' stories, were the teachers who exclusively focused on values conflicts and expressed resentments (Reynolds & Webber, 2009) against their students in self-righteous ways. Inherent and implied in haters' thinking were deficit understandings (Katz, 1989; Valencia & Solórzano, 1997; Valenzuela, 1999) of students, families, and communities. Deficit understandings, *not* a capacitating concept (rather an incapacitating one necessary for this discussion), refer to teachers' understandings of student differences as deficiencies or pathologies of genetics, character, work ethic, values, or culture. Especially in inner-city Austin ISD, I learned to walk away or sometimes contest "private" conversations in the lounge degrading or belittling students, families, and communities, and I openly contradicted deficit understandings in meetings or public forums.

Contrasting with deficit understandings, capacitating concepts in this narrative emphasize *structural understandings* of teachers and students' identities. *Structural understandings,* as definition, *refer to recognizing teachers and students' identifications as bounded in social and historical conditions that shape yet do not determine lives.* Structural understandings push back against deficit understandings of students and their families and imagine other possibilities for teaching and learning. When contesting deficit understandings in the lounge or in meetings, I registered structural understandings of student differences similar to the teachers in this study. All teachers in this study narrated pages upon pages of structural understandings in their life and teacher stories.

Nonetheless, as historical and sociological literatures on educational institutions demonstrate (e.g., Apple, 1993; McNeil & Valenzuela, 2000; Spring, 2000; Tyack, 1974), deficit thinking is more complicated than simply *what's in teachers' heads,* and in fact, deficit understandings are implicitly tied to schooling institutions. Discursive contexts, historically and socially embedded as discussed above, such as Title I, accountability, standardized testing achievement "gaps," students "below grade level," tracking "bubble students," and notions of "merit" are inherent in schools as institutions and *all* represent deficit understandings. Contradictorily, teachers in this study – including myself, at times – exhibited both structural *and* deficit understandings of student differences in life and teacher stories. Teachers' structural and deficit understandings, the focus of Chapter Three on *White double-consciousness* (which pulls no punches), is designed to elicit capacitating and reflective discussions on student differences from preservice and professional teachers.

Reflecting: Progressive Masculinities and Counternarratives

In concluding this section, I see that my life history and teacher story narrates a type of progressive masculinity. My story emphasized a contradictory middle-class White masculinity. This masculinity, which narrated contesting received identifications, searching for alternatives, opposing hegemonic representations, and engaging in self-narrativizations, demonstrate what I term *progressive masculinities* notably studied by Raewyn Connell (1995) and Alan Tolson (1977) in gender studies on male identity. *Progressive masculinities,* as definition, *refer to contradictory and, at times, utopian distantiation from hegemonic instrumental, technical, and goal-oriented masculinity.* Progressive masculinities, the topic of Chapter Four, expand existing understandings on male teacher identity and seek to capacitate understandings of male teachers. Important in committed White male teachers' progressive masculinities are *counternarratives* (Lankshear & Peters, 1996) that, defined and explained in more detail in Chapter Four, refer to oppositional identifications that push back against yet, in a paradoxical way, closely reflect instrumental and goal-oriented hegemonic masculinities of the Reagan Era through the present.

RACE-VISIBLE CURRICULUM WISDOM

Race-Visible Professional Identifications In-Action

I conclude Chapter One with stories of race-visible professional identifications in-action that demonstrate capacitating concepts I call *race-visible curriculum wisdom.* Synthesizing traditions on teaching, learning, culture, and identity along with practical democratic traditions in education, I story a few examples of race-visible curriculum wisdom recovered and reconstructed from my teaching with inner-city students that are also reflected in all teachers' life and teacher stories. *Race-visible curriculum wisdom,* as definition, refers *to personally recovered and professionally reconstructed curriculum knowledge and expertise developed for teaching and learning across differences in specific contexts.* I narrate examples of curriculum wisdom from my practice *not* to provide a victory story of my practices *but rather* to modestly provide a few examples of curriculum wisdom inherent in race-visible professional identifications. Narratively presenting and explaining race-visible curriculum wisdom in context, I recover and reconstruct over-arching themes that synthesize the tradition on teaching, learning, culture, and identity with the democratic practical tradition[4]. These overarching themes I synthesize from both traditions include: *deliberative dialogue, relationality, synthetic teaching,* and *socio-political critique*. In their life histories and teacher stories, all teachers in this study engaged these themes in their teaching, and in fact, my engagement in the traditions is deeply tied to my role as narrator of teachers' life and teacher stories. Race-visible curriculum wisdom, as it relates to my research on teaching and learning *and* my efforts to narrate teachers' stories, provides an over-arching way of representing life-history-and-teacher-story-based capacitating themes.

Deliberative Dialogue

Deliberative dialogue refers to deliberately introducing dialogue with students as part of curriculum development. Deliberative dialogue can take many forms including discussions, teacher observations, K-W-L charts, student letters, neighbourhood maps, formative evaluations, student responses, student surveys, or questionnaires. The important thing in deliberative dialogue is that preservice and professional teachers integrate students' backgrounds, cultures, identities, and interests into subsequent lessons in substantive ways.

In my professional identifications, I focused on the use of a questionnaire (see Appendix B, Figure 1) to help direct curriculum design, though I used other methods to gather data about the students as well. The questionnaire, from Angela Vasquez in my first period class, was fairly representative of the eighth grade students I had across my comprehensive classes. In using the questionnaire for curriculum development, I distributed the questionnaire, and the students worked on it in class and finished it for homework. Over the weekend, I studied the questionnaires as qualitative "data," and I looked for thematic patterns in students' responses that could inform my future lesson planning. In my study, the questionnaire yielded several patterns that I later included in my curriculum including students' emphasis on family, hip hop, and sports. The pattern I'll story here is about sports.

After reviewing the questionnaires, I immediately realized that most students in my classes had seventh period athletics indicated in Angela's on-going comments about sports:

What was an activity you enjoyed?

I loved playing sports a lot. My favorite sports I loved doing were basketball, softball...[5]

One activity I really enjoyed at school was?

Playing volleyball for the school and making the A team. Also basketball and being able to start in the game. (Figure 1, p. 2)

From this pattern articulated in Angela's questionnaire, I developed curriculum addressing standards for an expository writing unit that focused on the differences between college basketball and street basketball.

Directed at many students who imagined themselves future professional or college athletes, I intended the unit to provide awareness of the intensity of such an undertaking and a critique of corruption in college and professional sports. As part of this unit, I played clips from the movie *Blue Chips*, and on a separate day I had several boys on the basketball team play an exposition game using street rules as part of class activities. As part of pre-writing, students summarized movie clips, and took notes on the rules of street basketball. After discussing the differences between college and street basketball, I had students write similarities and differences on sentence strips which I later stapled to the wall. Students drafted their essays in class, and they wrote final copies in the computer lab. Here is an excerpt from Angela's paper:

> The difference between college and street ball is that they play on different kinds of courts. College basketball plays on a wooden gymnasium court. Street basketball plays on a concrete court. College ball has a coach that tells them what plays to run. Street ball is freestyle. Players do what they want. In college games, they are organized. In college basketball they use a lot of strategies.
>
> In college ball mostly money influences the sports and makes the players want to win. It also makes them play very bad on purpose. The sports become very complicated, because if a team wins then they get rewarded. Money makes gamblers want to gamble. Then a gambler might be the coach or the player of a team. It also makes players want something back if they play or coach a team. Money can make players go bad.
>
> I think that money can be negative in sports. It's negative for all these reasons I wrote down above. Money in sports is good for one reason; it's good to buy equipment for the team. This is what I do think of money's influences on sports.

I conceived of this assignment as a bridge between personal narrative essays required in middle school and expositional writing required in high school. The purpose of writing like this, as it addresses standards on expositional writing in ways that approach social critique, is to recover and reconstruct students' interests and experiences in order to inform future experiences (Dewey, 1902), yet at the same time, I was working directly with academic standards on expositional writing.

Relationality

Relationality refers to an understanding that curriculum requires the careful cultivation of professional and personal relationships. Related to deliberate dialogue, an understanding of relationality is tied to an incident that occurred a few months after taking a job in Austin ISD.

I was having a really hard time with discipline having just started at Austin ISD, especially in my second and seventh period classes. As I had started a few weeks after the school year, my classes required students to be pulled from a previously established schedule. The fact that my schedule removed several students from their electives made those students angry, and as I was working with seventh graders, quite a bit of that anger ended up being directed at me.

Despite that difficulty, my first month or so had been good, but when they gave me another teacher's class to avoid her resignation from her own discipline problems, things got worse for me in a hurry. I had been managing students through keeping them working, beginning to adapt my lessons, and calling home when students were misbehaving, but after I inherited the problems in a new seventh period class, I was suddenly struggling very publicly. My second period, when I first had them, had been confrontational but manageable, but now, things were deteriorating in seventh and second period as students in both classes knew each other. My second period became more challenging to work with, and Traci Rodriguez had been particularly difficult. This went for several weeks, until one day Traci was jumped by a group of girls in the hall near my room, and one of the girls bit Traci in the face, trying to disfigure her because of her beauty and radiant skin. During the assault, I stepped in and separated the girls. The girls who had assaulted Traci ran off, and I was left with Traci in my arms crying with very deep purple incisions above her left cheek. She looked at me with hurt and scared eyes and exclaimed "That bitch *bit* me!" And she started crying again. I have always been surprised, even in recalling this, that deep bite marks did not bleed.

I yelled at astonished onlookers "Go to class!" I sent another kid from my class to get the Assistant Principal. After the incident was over, I walked into a speechless classroom, and all of us were shaken. I said, "What is going on here?" What followed was one of the most informative and well-participated discussions I had that year. *Right then* I stopped being a ghost in the hallways and started to be a teacher in that school. Even though more challenges awaited me, I had turned an important corner. Traci now respected and defended me, and when I returned the next year, she appeared at my door just after the bell rang. She gave me a hug and a radiant smile with a scar just over her left cheek. She was checking to see if I had come back.

Synthetic Teaching

Synthetic teaching refers to explicitly considering students' cultures and background knowledges when designing lessons and assignments. When Luís Pacheco entered my room as a sixth grader, he hardly spoke English at all though he had been in bilingual education for fourth and fifth grade in elementary school. He was relieved when he realized I could speak Spanish to him as he learned English, and the entire class was taught in English the entire time. I allowed him to respond to assignments in Spanish and English during this transition period which has now become a standard practice for English language learners (e.g. Bomer, 2011; Freeman & Freeman,

2004; Lighbown & Spada, 2006). In seventh grade, Luís was lucky to have Roberto Guanajuato as his English teacher, and he made gains in that class that I would later benefit from. When I was moved to eighth grade in my fourth year at Southside, I was happy to find Luís on my list. Luís was still, for the most part, in a silent period in eighth grade for social purposes, but he could write in English. By this time, he handed in all his work written in English, which, as any language learner knows, is a big jump in just the two years between sixth and the beginning of eighth grade.

But where Luís finally really shined was on the eighth grade research paper that, as an eighth grade team, we had themed along social studies work with inalienable rights in the Declaration of Independence and the US Constitution's Bill of Rights. In this assignment, students did biographical research choosing from a menu of preselected freedom fighters (Appendix B, Figure 2). In this assignment, I also provided a space for students to choose their own freedom fighter, if they had their own topic idea. I structured the assignment this way because I wanted students to have choice, but I also wanted to engage students in established disciplinary knowledge and skills in the state standards: specifically social studies knowledge, library research, and (again) expositional writing necessary for high school. The topic choices included familiar names like Thomas Jefferson, George Washington, and John Adams, but topics also included other names positioned to leverage background knowledge of Mexican immigrant, Mexican-American, and African American students such as Miguel Hidalgo, Pancho Villa, Emiliano Zapata, Martin Luther King, or Rosa Parks. The topics also included freedom fighters from different women's movement such as Elizabeth Cady Stanton, Betty Friedan and Lucrecia Mott. I worked on the freedom fighter menu with the librarian to make sure there were a range of books for all of these topics available. I also provided, for students below grade level, a scaffolding outline (Appendix B, Figure 2) that helped students know what to look for and how to organize their writing. Most of the students had never done library research or written a research paper beyond a few notecards in seventh grade.

Nevertheless, it is Luís's paper that makes the best argument for synthetic teaching. Many of the African-American students chose topics such as Martin Luther King or Rosa Parks that related to their culture, background knowledge, and previous classroom learning in Eastside classrooms. Nonetheless, Luís's paper turned out to be a good paper, and certainly it represented his best work in eighth grade in my class. Here is an excerpt from Luís's paper:

> This report is about Miguel Hidalgo. Miguel Hidalgo was born in 1753. Through his childhood, he studied at the Jesuit College of San Francisco Javier. He already knew how to read and write already. He was educated in Valladolid now Morelia.
>
> He was an enthusiastic and hard-working man, always worried about the well-being of his community. To help the indigenous, he built an estate where he established a pottery shop, a tanning shop, a blacksmith stable, a carpentry store, and a loom.

When he became a priest he was not able to marry and did not have any children. He went to the priests and became a religious leader. On September 16th of 1810, Miguel Hidalgo started the Grito de Dolores. Hidalgo took the banner with the image of the Virgen of Guadalupe, ringing the church bells. He gathered many faithful Catholics from his parish to listen to his speech. He talked to them about Spanish oppression and about the need to free themselves.

Father Hidalgo fell in an ambush staged by Felix María Calleja and after was relieved of his duties as a priest. He was sentenced to death. His fight was not in vain, as Mexico would gain its Independence on September 21st 1821. Mexico would never have gained its independence had it not been for Hidalgo's calling on the people. His Grito brought about the birth of Mexico.

His head with Allende, Aldama, and Jimenez' was carried to Guanajuato and were put in cages of iron and hanged on the four corners of the Alghóndiga de Grana until Independence in 1812. Today, the rests [remains] of his body are in Mexico [Federal District] in the Independence Angel or Angel of Independence.

During the assignment, Luís commented to me that he had studied Miguel Hidalgo in Mexico, and when he was doing his research, he printed out and read from a few on-line sources in Spanish. When Luís was writing, he would often consult a dictionary and my knowledge about a word or phrase he didn't know how to translate. Luís's paper, beginning with knowledge he learned in Mexico along with reading in Spanish, is an argument for synthetic teaching that combines standards, students' culture, students' background knowledge, and valued academic knowledge. Luís's paper, like many of the good papers written by African American students on Martin Luther King or Rosa Parks, started being written in his rural school in Mexico where he had already studied Father Miguel Hidalgo. Synthetic teaching seeks to recognize previous learning and experiences (Dewey, 1902/1990, Ladson-Billings 1995, 2009) students bring to the classroom.

Socio-Political Critique

Socio-political critique refers to including critical reflection or conscientization into lessons and assignments. As part of teaching through deliberative dialogue, my last year teaching I began the year with neighbourhood maps as pre-writing for a personal essay on neighborhoods. Taken from Colleen Fairbanks' (1998a) elaborate description of neighborhood writing, I had students make maps of their neighborhood. I printed out zip codes from Google Maps, and I provided several examples of student work. I also had students list major avenues, smaller streets, and important places in their community that would appear on the map. Students created maps that served as a basis for two subsequent writing assignments. Key in the first assignment was the discussion of neighborhood "issues" that appeared in students' table talk as they worked on the maps in class, and during this talk, I was able to learn a lot about students, families, and their neighborhoods. Issues that emerged in informal discussions on neighborhoods included violence, drugs, gangs, and the invasion of "outsiders" into the neighborhood, known in more critical language as gentrification.

Coordinated with these discussions and the assignment, the Principal invited a speaker from the Hispanic Bar Association of Austin (HBAA) to visit the classroom and discuss neighbourhood issues. Guided by the critical direction of Ms. Gomez from the HBAA along with my suggestions, gentrification dominated the discussions. Students discussed family members losing property to developers and Mexican-American businesses with generations in their neighbourhood being "closed" when properties were "sold" to commercial real estate developers. The following interactions were typical of these discussions:

Ms. Gomez: So what happens when developers put condos and mansions all over the place?

S1: My *tía* had to sell her house because she could pay *las taxas*.

S2: People come from outside the neighbourhood, and they tear down places and put in expensive shops that we don't even go to. They tore down *El Mercado* [popular restaurant] and put in condos with a hair salon and *Urban Outfitters.* We don't shop there! That's for White people [laughter].

S3: They take over everything nice. It sucks, then the people who move in don't come to our churches and the kids don't come to Eastside Middle....

Ms. Goméz: It seems like the Eastside is now farther East, like in *Del Valle.*

S2: Yeah, everyone is moving farther East, past 183.

Ms. Goméz: What race are those who buy the condos and go the pricey shops?

S2: They're White. It's the Mexicans who are losing their houses, businesses, and the neighborhoods as they were.

Working on the topic of neighborhoods, students critiqued the encroachment on their neighborhood and identified other issues like developers' greed, the "push out" of families from East Austin, and increasing inequality in their neighborhood. In this unit, students' engage in socio-political critique. Here is an excerpt from David Gutierrez's essay:

The people who actually end up buying these houses have a lot of money. For some reason, they now think this neighborhood is nice, but not long ago that was a different story. People not from the same neighborhood used to think and say it is the "ghetto" or "who would want to live there?" Well, I guess things change when you have all that money.

What do these rich people do? From what I see they have to do a lot of work. Frist they knock down the house then build it again but in different version and lastly they live in it for a while and then sell it for a much higher price. The question is: Why knock down a house that's just fine and been there a long time? The answer is, they want to make a whole pile of money. What about the Mexican people who live in the neighborhood their whole lives? Who pay more taxes? Who can't afford to live in the neighborhood anymore? Some of them have children and some of them are old. What about them? I don't see why rich Whites should be allowed to take over something they used to consider "ghetto."

Important in this discussion is that that socio-political critique is not special or unusual, and lessons like this continued after I left by many socially conscious teachers who view surroundings and inequalities as resources for teaching. In my experience, teaching social political critique was best when it related directly to students' backgrounds or neighborhoods, so in that way, students took an immediate interest in such discussions rather than understanding them only as more academic learning.

NOT A VICTORY STORY BUT RATHER A GRIND

Having introduced capacitating concepts in this chapter, in concluding it is important to recover on-going struggles in teachers' life and teacher stories in the rest of *Becoming Teachers of Inner-City Students*. It becomes important to narrate teachers' in this study and my on-going challenges and exhaustion because neither the teachers nor I recounted teaching as a facile victory narrative of prescriptive "best practices" that other teachers should simply adopt for "success." Life histories and teaching stories, narrativized and contextualized in practical detail, are *not* felicitous "victory narratives" (Cary, 1999, p. 414) waiting to be made into feel-good Disney® movies nor are they think-tank propaganda to support crass versions of charter school "reform" like KIPP™ schools which really represent another form of tracking that sorts the meritorious poor from the undeserving through "choice." Unlike commercially-driven victory narratives in best practices or propaganda, life histories and teaching stories very much drive at curriculum theory and practice as "a form of autobiographically informed truth-telling that articulates the educational experience of teachers and students as lived" (Pinar, 2012, p. 35). Life histories and teaching stories, drawing on and embodying curriculum theory and practice, contrast with commercialized media representations that define the "crisis" or "problem" *historically* as students, families, or communities and *presently* as teachers, their unions, or public schools themselves. Life history and teaching stories, contrasting with commercialized media representations or propagandistic reforms, reject the notion that students, families, and communities *or* teachers, unions, and schools simplistically represent "the problem" – both positions, by now, that wreak of shallow corporate interest, cheap political claptrap, and sound-bite media exchanges that are worthy only of educators, intellectuals, and serious citizens' scorn.

While earning respect and sometimes love of students, colleagues, and community, the teachers in this study and I do not recount a victory story as becoming a teacher is a messy, unfinished, and partial task, and though at times it is extremely rewarding, critical, and deeply engaging, I remain modest in my claims, narrating my and other teachers' stories within the context of what Philip Jackson (1968/1990) appropriately called "the daily grind" (p. 1). I refuse a victory story, not because I think the teachers in this study and I were "unsuccessful" in reaching and changing many students' lives. I think that committed teachers *can* and *do* change students' lives in classroom every day. As life history evidence, I am in continual communication with many, many of my ex-students today who are now university students and who recall the time spent in my and other teachers' classrooms as important to their education. Nonetheless, I emphasize the daily grind because, as the essays that follow are about teaching, learning, culture, and identity, I refuse to consider the teaching as a simple "solution" to complex social realities that require greater investments in the public sphere, structural changes in how schooling is conducted, and most of all, an emphasis on public investment (Giroux, 2011, 2012) so missing in today's political discussions. Even so with these considerations and limits, I offer the essays that follow in hopes of providing identification resources for preservice and professional teachers' discussion and development of professional identifications as they become teachers of diverse inner-city students.

NOTES

1   For a research essay on evidence-based capacitating concepts, see Appendix A. Appendix A provides a detailed expository discussion on capacitating concepts.
2   All names are pseudonyms. Place names, with the exception of respondents' schools, are actual place names.
3   In the first month I worked in Raymondville, I broke up two boys who were fighting only to find out that one of them had been stabbed by a third boy.
4   See the brief reading list below to substantiate the over-arching themes that I drive at in this subsection. For further reading in traditions on teaching, learning, culture, and identity, researchers and interested students might see Bruner (1995), Cummins (1986), Gay (2000), Gonzales, Moll, & Amanti (2005), or Nieto (1999). This tradition drives at the notion that teaching and learning are culturally mediated and interactive. For further reading in practical democratic traditions, interested students might see Cole and Knowles (2000), Connelly & Clandinin (1988), Clandinin & Connelly (1992, 1995), Davis (1997), Dewey (1902/1990), Eisner (1985), or Henderson & Gornik (2007). This tradition drives at the notion that teaching and learning are mediated through students' interests, experiences, and social contexts. Each of these traditions provides evidence-based approaches to what I call *race-visible curriculum wisdom*. Appendix A provides a research essay that documents evidence and integrates both traditions outlined in this note.
5   Student writing, in the samples below, has been modestly "corrected" for mechanics for publishing purposes.

RACE-VISIBLE PROFESSIONAL IDENTIFICATIONS

And Curriculum Wisdom

INTRODUCTION

Lead-In Story Clip

David McGrady, fourteen year journeyman teacher, signals the race-visible professional identifications described in Chapter Two.[2]

JJ: Tell me about being a White teacher?

David: One of my goals is to be a White man in their [students'] lives, older, straight [Al Anon] again because I went straight, uh, who's not a cop, a lawyer, a bill collector, a probation officer, a guard, a salesman, uh, what other jobs can I think, you know, the banker, lawyer, uh yeah, whatever, that I'm their teacher and I've gotten better and better at it over the years …I mean I think not recognizing race as a fact or an issue is discounting the values and experiences of what the kids bring to the classroom. Uh… And what I bring to it. (Interview 6b, pp. 1–2)

McGrady's teacher story signals *not* race-evasive identity in existing understandings of White teachers (e.g., Marx, 2004, 2008; Marx & Pennington, 2003; McIntyre, 1997, 2002, Sleeter, 1992, 1993), *but rather* it emphasizes race-visible professional identifications that "recognize race as a fact or issue" (David McGrady, Interview 6b, p. 2). In recognizing race as a fact or issue, McGrady recognizes "what kids bring to the classroom" (David McGrady, Interview 6b, p. 2) as resources for teaching and learning. McGrady's story clip, signaling the direction that race-visible professional identifications take, provides a lead-in for Chapter Two.

Chapter Two Overview

Developing race-visible professional identifications briefly exemplified above, Chapter Two narrates notions of committed White male teachers' race-visible professional identifications and curriculum wisdom. In developing these notions, Chapter Two 1) further elaborates on professional identifications 2) provides greater detail on discursive contexts of teachers' in this study; 3) recounts three life histories and teacher stories that narrate and develop race-visible professional identifications and curriculum wisdom; and, 4) reveals three narrative patterns that cut across all teachers' professional identifications including *race-visibility, difference-within-difference*, and *relational-experiential teaching.* Chapter Two, in summary, narrates teachers' life histories and teacher stories articulating race-visible professional identifications and curriculum wisdom within specific discursive contexts.

PROFESSIONAL IDENTIFICATIONS AND DISCURSIVE CONTEXTS

Recovering and Reconstructing Meaning

Before narrating race-visible professional identifications in Chapter Two, I begin by further detailing professional identifications and discursive contexts. Professional identifications and discursive contexts, narratively presented and explained in Chapter Two, represent over-arching capacitating concepts for reading and understanding this chapter. Professional identifications and discursive contexts, as I discuss and explain them, recover and reconstruct notions from Jean Clandinin and Michael F. Connelly's (1992, 1995) research on practical teaching and learning. It is important to note that, as I recover Clandinin and Connelly's research, I provide not on an exhaustive review adopting their "framework," but rather I reconstruct narrative concepts from their research *adapting them* for my purposes.[3]

As a reader of Clandinin and Connelly's research, I follow their Deweyan understanding that I must personally *recover and reconstruct meaning* from within rather than adopting, prescribing, or assigning meaning from without. Connelly and Clandinin (1988) summarize what it means for learners to recover and reconstruct meaning:

> As always...we can only provide narrative fragments. As a reader of the text, one of your purposes is to *recover* the meaning, as best you can, as it is expressed by the storyteller. The significant meaning, of course, is yours, and so you need to *reconstruct* a meaning for yourself. (p. 198)

The notion that learners recover and reconstruct meaning, besides suggesting the role for preservice and professional teachers' professional identifications, serves to frame Chapter Two in two ways.

First, and relevant to the first half of this chapter, I recover and reconstruct professional identifications and discursive contexts from Clandinin and Connelly's notions of teachers-as-curriculum-makers and professional knowledge landscapes. Professional identifications seek to recover and reconstruct teachers-as-curriculum-makers (Clandinin & Connelly, 1992; Connelly & Clandinin, 1988), and similarly, discursive contexts seek to recover and reconstruct teachers' professional landscapes (Clandinin & Connelly, 1995, 2000). Second, and relevant to the second half of this chapter, teachers in this study, through life histories and teacher stories, recover and reconstruct childhood concerns and preoccupations as components in their professional identifications. Teachers in this study, as the stories demonstrate, recover private concerns and preoccupations from childhood, and these private concerns and preoccupations, reconstructed in their professional identifications, provide the basis for what is understood in common sense terms as "commitment" in their *becoming* public school teachers. A fruitful metaphor for preservice and professional teachers as well as researchers' self-study, I recover and reconstruct meaning as narrator of teachers' stories in the same way teachers in this study recover and reconstruct meaning in telling their stories in interviews. Teachers' and my recovery and reconstruction of meaning provide central themes for this chapter that I return to in the final section.

Professional Identifications and Teachers-as-Curriculum-Makers

As particularly relevant to Chapter Two, professional identifications recover and reconstruct the notion of teachers-as-curriculum-makers (Clandinin and Connelly 1992; Connelly & Clandinin, 1988; Craig, 2008). Professional identifications, recovering and reconstructing teachers-as-curriculum-makers, cultivate images of teachers as *competent* and *democratic* along with understandings of curriculum as *multistoried process*. Professional identifications, recovering teachers-as-curriculum-makers, reconstruct teachers' contextualized competencies (Clandinin & Connelly, 1992; Connelly & Clandinin, 1988; Craig, 2008). Professional identifications, in reconstructing competencies, "strengthen the view of teachers as knowledgeable human beings" (p. 283) engaged in humanizing teaching and learning (Craig, 2008).[4] Further, professional identifications, strengthening competent and humanizing images, recover and reconstruct teachers-as-curriculum-makers' aspirations to enable students' personal and social growth.

> ...the teacher as curriculum maker means more than the reconstruction of social heritage and student experiences for student growth. Through this reconstruction, it means the growth of society itself. Social and personal growth are intimately connected in an 'organic' venture in which the teacher is the central curriculum maker. (Clandinin & Connelly, 1992, p. 379)

Professional identifications, recovering and reconstructing an enabling ethic for preservice and professional teachers, drive at rekindling teachers' democratic identifications seemingly lost in technical-expert discussions of standards, accountability, and standardized tests. Teachers' democratic identifications, reconstructed in professional identifications, move beyond "filling students' heads" with standardized objectives toward recovering an ethic of enabling their own and students' freedom (Dewey, 1902/1990). Finally, professional identifications, besides reconstructing teachers' competency and democratic identifications, emphasize that teaching and learning in the practical tradition unfold as a "multistoried process" (Olson, 2000, p. 169; Craig, 2008, p. 286). Further described in the next subsection on discursive contexts, professional identifications understand enacted curriculum as students and teachers' stories taking place within larger social, historical, personal, and professional histories. *Against-the-grain* of technical-expert viewpoints in policy and administrative understandings of teaching and learning, teachers' race-visible professional identifications recovered and reconstructed – in their storytelling – understandings of teachers-as-curriculum-makers.

In this recovering and reconstructing, professional identifications advance teachers-as-curriculum-makers (Clandinin & Connelly, 1992; Connelly & Clandinin, 1988; Craig, 2008) in new directions. Professional identifications, in advancing teachers-as-curriculum-makers, locate Clandinin and Connelly's concepts within discussions of cultural identity seemingly diminished in previous understanding of "experience." Following Xu, Connelly, He, and Phillion (2007), professional identifications move beyond experience and integrate notions of teachers-as-curriculum-makers into historically and socially bounded yet "self-narrativized identifications" (Bruner, 2002, Butler, 1999; Hall, 2003) defined and discussed in Chapter Two. Professional identifications, beginning with self-narrativized identifications, move beyond experience to recognize and make visible teachers and students' race, class, culture, language, and other differences for engagements in teaching and learning.

Discursive Contexts and Professional-Knowledge-Landscapes

In addition to professional identifications' that recover and reconstruct teachers-as-curriculum-makers, discursive contexts recover and reconstruct professional-knowledge-landscapes (Clandinin & Connelly, 1995, 2000; Craig, 2008). *Discursive contexts*, as definition, refer to *historical and social boundedness in schooling of particular teachers and students.* Discursive contexts, in recovering and reconstructing professional landscapes, emphasize that teachers' professional identifications emerge from within larger social and historical narratives. Clandinin & Connelly (2000) explain lives as personal stories within larger historical and social narratives that discursive contexts seek to recover and reconstruct:

> Just as we found our own lives embedded within a larger narrative of social science inquiry, the people, schools, and educational landscapes we study undergo day-to-day experiences that are contextualized within a longer-term historical narrative. (p. 19)

More specifically, recovering and reconstructing professional-knowledge-landscapes (Clandinin & Connelly, 1995, 2000), discursive contexts emphasize that professional identifications and curriculum wisdom emerge from and are contextualized within local communities which, in turn, come into being within historical and social narratives. Discursive contexts, recovering and reconstructing professional knowledge landscapes,

> …draw on individual biographies, on the particular histories of the professional landscape in which they find themselves, on how they are positioned on the landscape, and on the form of everyday school life that the professional landscape allows. (Clandinin & Connelly, 1995, p. 27)

Discursive contexts, recovering and reconstructing what is valued in professional landscapes (Clandinin & Connelly, 1995, 2000) provide the multistoried contexts for teachers' day-to-day experiences. In recovering and reconstructing, discursive contexts also advance professional knowledge landscapes (Clandinin & Connelly, 1995, 2000) toward broader interpretations of social and historical context.

Several Discursive Contexts of this Research

Professional identifications, the ones developed by teachers in this study, emerge within particular discursive contexts. Historical inequality, school failure, deficit understandings of student achievement, community racial sensitivity, and negative views of poor children's families provide multistoried discursive contexts.

First, historical inequalities and persistent segregation in American schooling (Kozol, 2005; Spring, 2000; Tyack, 1974) provide a discursive context. Teachers' inner-city Central Texas schools very much reflect the social order Kozol (1991) described when he visited San Antonio in writing *Savage Inequalities* yet such schools are further deteriorated in the present (Giroux, 2012). Kozol (1991) describes, very precisely, the discursive contexts surrounding teachers' work in this study.

Seven minutes from Alamo Heights [rich neighborhood]…is Cassiano—a low income housing project. Across the street from Cassiano, tiny buildings resembling shacks, some of them painted pastel colors shades, house many of the children who attend the Cooper Middle School, where 96 percent of the children qualify by poverty for subsidized hot lunches and where 99.3 percent are of Hispanic origin. (p. 224)

Kozol's (1991) description, updated only by further school deterioration within patches of downtown gentrification, provides an on-going discursive context. Teachers in this study and I worked in Title I inner-city schools with diverse populations including predominantly immigrant, Mexican-American, and African-American students along with very few White students. Contrasts between Teachers' schools, who served South and Eastside students, and schools serving middle class and wealthy students on the West and Northside represented drastic differences both in surrounding neighborhoods and in school conditions.

Second, racially charged communities provide a discursive context. In 2008 when teaching 8th grade English, I collected this homework reflection from Nubia Mortíz. The reflection emerged, not in a discussion on undocumented workers, but rather within a unit on US primary documents. Nonetheless, it is easy to see the day-to-day preoccupations and hurt of children who live or are associated with large communities of undocumented workers:

No we [Mexican immigrants] are really not free in the US. It's a big lie… Even the White citizens here are not free. Sure their rights are stretched out a lot more while those who are not legal have to deal with the same laws yet get punished cruelly. Our inalienable rights include Life, Liberty, and the Pursuit of happiness yet here in Texas alone, hundreds have those rights taken away in a matter of minutes even if they have been loyal and good residents here in the US. They [immigrants] come here to pursue a better job for a better life, ready to work and to help yet they are just sent back to the life they left behind in the first place. Not a hint of freedom there. (Researcher Journal, p. 37)

In an inner-city school, racial identities, far from evasive or "false," become sharpened, and community members and students articulate these understandings in lessons and in learning resistance. Teachers in this study and I, sensitized to students and community members' understandings, learned from students and communities as part of work routines, and as part of this learning, developed race-visible professional identifications narrated below.

Third, the National Commission on Excellence in Education's (NCEE) *A Nation at Risk* (1984/1994) provides a discursive context. *A Nation at Risk* (NCEE, 1984/1994) casts a long shadow over standards and accountability discourses that frame teachers' work in this study. *A Nation at Risk* (NCEE, 1984/1994), reframing educational discussions around state (now national) standards, school choice, accountability, high stakes testing, performance pay, and other "marketizing" measures, articulates the educational agenda of the Conservative Restoration (Apple, 2000; Giroux, 2009, Giroux, 2012). Standardized skills and knowledge reassert historically White disciplinary expectations (Bloom 1987; Hirsch, 1988) and ignore or aggressively diminish student identities and communities' knowledge resources for teaching and learning. Re-doubled accountability measures reflect White cultural anxieties in the face of a changing nation (Slattery, 2006; Pinar, 2004). Accountability, with its roots in *A Nation at Risk* (NCEE, 1984/1994), presses down on teachers and students' identities, teaching, and learning, and even as it currently mandates content in testing and accountability, it also unfairly labels teachers and students as failures, low performing, and below grade level.

LIFE HISTORIES AND TEACHER STORIES

Amplifying and Pluralizing

Having further developed professional identifications and discursive contexts, this section narrates life histories and teacher stories. First, Mike Taymes' life history and teacher stories recount professional identifications as "a gift" recovering and reconstructing his father's abandonment during his childhood. Second, Jack Springman's life history and teacher stories recount professional identifications as "separateness" recovering and reconstructing White-centric cultural norms of his youth. Third, Bennett Ferris' life history and teacher stories recount professional identifications as "activist stance" recovering and reconstructing his working class background in critical ways. In the section that follows the life histories, I present narrative patterns that emerged in all teachers' professional identifications in this study. These narrative patterns include *race-visibility*, *understanding-difference-within-difference*, and *relational-experiential teaching*. When understood together, teachers' life histories and teacher stories along with narrative patterns, provide an outline for race-visible professional identifications and curriculum wisdom.

A Gift

Mike Taymes' professional identifications recover and reconstruct his earliest family memories. Mike Taymes teaches in the "emotionally disturbed" unit at Eastside Middle School in Austin, Texas.

When Taymes was three months old, his Dad left his mother and him stranded on the side of the highway in San Antonio. As Taymes recounts,

> I was born in Dallas, Texas. My father left when I was three months old, left my mom and I stranded in San Antonio, took her car, drove it back to Dallas, said he didn't want to be a part of the family. So they were soon divorced and he gave away all parental rights so I did not meet him until I was in college, and that will come later. (Interview 1a, p. 1)

This hardship, sending his mom and him into rural poverty, provides the central and recurrent theme reconstructed in Taymes' professional identifications.

Taymes, living in his grandfather's house, recalls "happy days" (Interview 1a, p. 2) growing up in a rural conservative family. His family, influenced by White supremacist rural Texas, used "the N word quite frequently, and you know it was always, a put-down" (p. 5), and his grandmother kept a framed "picture of Ronald Reagan up in her bedroom" (Interview#1a, p. 6) as Taymes narrated his family background. He recounted, for the greater part, being happy and oblivious to his family's poverty and internalizing their racism.

Overtime, his mom became a reading teacher, and she remarried. Taymes had a mixed relationship with his stepfather that "because of some alcoholism, you know, often would escalate into physical altercations" (Interview 1a, p. 2). With his mother as a teacher, Taymes was successful in school and labeled gifted and talented. Additionally, he received rewards and recognitions from peers and teachers including a trip to Washington DC in middle school. Nonetheless, in high school and early college, he started to realize his values and beliefs "did not mesh with the [family's] status quo" (Interview 1a, p. 6). He recounted befriending Black peers because he "was really into hip hop, had always been" (Interview 1a, p. 5), and he reported, in late high school and university settings, developing a progressive outlook based on veganism, green politics, revisionist history, and liberation Buddhism, all of which continue to represent important identifications as they emerged in his life history and teacher stories.

Nonetheless, he majored in business following his original expectations of simply "getting ahead" in college. Although he reported wanting to switch majors to

science education midway, Taymes recounted he could not afford "starting over...
financially" (Interview 1a, p. 10) as an education major. Taking his last electives
before graduation, Taymes took a course on human sexuality, and when the professor
read a short story about rape, Taymes flashed back to when he was "sexually
molested by an older step cousin, and all of a sudden it all came flooding back to
me. And it was very difficult for me to deal with" (Interview 1a, p. 11). Critically
reconstructing his family's rural conservative and White supremacist background
along with coming to terms with sexual abuse of his childhood provided the bases of
his professional identification.

Graduating in the late 90s, Taymes received lucrative job offers from Sears and
Bacardi but turned them down with the intention of trying to give back. He began a
series of jobs working with "emotionally disturbed" children including a therapeutic
wilderness camp, Houston ISD's experimental program for juvenile offenders, and
eventually, a halfway house in East Texas. In these settings, Taymes came into
contact with predominantly poor White and Black youths in which "there's one or
two White kids for every six Black kids on probation, whereas it's the exact opposite
in foster care and the sexual abuse that we were seeing" (Interview 1a, p. 21). As
he began his career trying to give back, he found himself feeling "almost guilty for
getting paid because of the therapy I was receiving" (Interview 1a, p. 18), especially
in the years of the Wilderness Camp program. Taymes' professional identifications
critically recovered and reconstructed his father's abandonment, his resultant
childhood poverty, physical altercations with his step father, and abuse by his step
cousin. This therapeutic recovery and reconstruction indirectly paralleled many
of his students' experiences in the "emotionally disturbed" unit where he teaches
now. Like many of his students, Taymes grew up without his father around, lived in
an extended family arrangement, and experienced abuse, in his case, physical and
sexual abuse.

In narrating his present inner-city work setting, Taymes described the "emotionally
disturbed" unit where he teaches:

> The – I'm just gonna talk about my current class. "Intro Scene," it's about 75
> percent African American in a school that's about 20 – well, I guess, roughly
> 20 to 30 percent African American [and 70–80 percent Hispanic], so again
> there's a disproportionate number of African American students in our class as
> opposed to the outside population. Also all the students in the unit are males, so
> that's another disproportion relative to the outside. (Interview 1b, p. 5)

Conscious of racial and gender identities of his students, Taymes' directly recognized
the disproportion of African American male students. This recognition, along with
the recognition of the broader school's demographics, narrated discursive contexts
of continued inequality and segregation both within the school and in the broader
community context. Even within heavily segregated discursive contexts discussed
above, further segregation and inequality marginalized many African American
males within the walls of the school.

In narrating his understanding of classroom discipline, Taymes emphasized matter-of-fact disciplinary structures that make students responsible for their actions. Taymes narrated insights regarding his structured classroom.

> So I have been in out and out power struggles, and you know, something that sat with me, there was a young African American kid, Frank Jefferson, he was from Barns, Texas. And he had been adopted, and he refused to do what we wanted him to do eighty percent of the time. And at one point I'm screaming at him. ...And, and the Director [of the wilderness camp], the one I spoke of earlier, comes to me, pulls me to the side and he says have you met, you know, Frank's dad. And I said no. And he said, well he's a cop, for one thing. And he's a 6'6 African American man. And James doesn't listen to him. That's why he's here. You've known him for a month. What makes you think that he's gonna listen to you if he won't listen to him? You know, it's up to James. It's not up to, it's not up to us. All we can do is role model and show him another way to go about it. ...So, you know, so I didn't engage, when I was in the social behavior skills classroom, I didn't engage in these power struggles. The systems were in place with the rewards, and here's what you need to do, at this point, when you don't choose to do it, and then there will be consequences. (Interview 1a, pp. 25–26)

Regarding discipline, Taymes relied, not on "winning confrontations" with students but on setting up disciplinary systems and focusing on students' development of choice.

In narrating his teacher stories, Taymes described what I called synthetic teaching and socio-political critique as curriculum wisdom described in Chapter Two. Taymes draws on his love of hip hop in order to engage his students in academic standards and critique Hip-Hop's commercialized trajectory.

> Yeah, definitely cultural factors come into lesson planning in regards to the – the – the readings that we do, the pieces that I bring in, you know, I – I like to introduce metaphors by bringing in this rap record or rapper from Chicago, and he sings this song and – and you think it's about a woman and then at the end you find about that it's really a song about a critique of hip hop and how it's commercialized, but he's – but he's personified it and so there's – there's a lesson on personification and metaphors. You know, alliteration, any time that I can bring in something, especially culturally relevant, musically so, it goes over better; you know, reading a poem that Tupac wrote versus something by Shakespeare is gonna be a lot more relevant and generate a lot more discussion because it's something familiar and then that's the jumping off point for, you know, it's okay to read poetry, 'cause we're reading Tupac and then you slide in, you know, you slide in something else. (Interview 1b, p. 3)

Taymes' teacher stories, as narrated in this clip, provide an example of curriculum wisdom through synthetic teaching. Taymes recognizes and introduces students'

39

cultural identities, but he also goes beyond indulging students in "their" cultures. Instead, Taymes engages in socio-political critiques of hip hop, a resource recovered and reconstructed from his youth, not just to celebrate it but also to show "how it's commercialized" (Interview 1b, p. 3). Important here, though, is the malleability of academic standards such as "personification and metaphors" (Interview, 1b, p. 3) in ways that are informed by his life story and students' identities. This clip articulates sophisticated curriculum wisdom, namely, synthetic teaching, that provides a contextualized example of pedagogical content knowledge (Schulman, 1987) in which language arts curriculum is taught in context. This curriculum wisdom synthesizes students and teacher's identities, subject area standards, cultural milieus, and it recovers meaning yet moves beyond celebrating "students' cultures" toward reconstructing them in more sophisticated ways for students' understanding.

Taymes' professional identification, as it emerges in his life history and teaching narratives, is not *only* cultural relevance (Ladson-Billings, 1995, 2009) for academic success, though it contains those elements. Taymes, although he integrates students and the teacher's identities, subject area standards, and cultural milieus (Schwab, 1978; 1983), also critiques and reconstructs, professionally, the identifications represented in *his* life story. Taymes, in member checking sessions after his life and teaching story interviews, remarked:

> Well, I almost look upon, you know my father walking out, also the abuse almost as gifts because you know I know firsthand, I didn't have to read a book to learn how this affects you. I lived it every day. And then when I'm working with my students whose fathers are incarcerated or who have endured some kind of abuse and you know they're displaying these behaviors that I used to see in myself, self-medicating, inappropriate choices, a distorted view of sexuality and people's roles in society, especially in regards to the African American men, and that kind of you know, just being so tough and you know, not letting the world get you down, you know having to be put in positions where they're the man of the house and they're thirteen years old, and I can relate. I was there. Dealing, interacting with step-parents. You know, I did that. I had to, you know I was in fights with my step-father. Physical ones, had to be broken up by people as I got older. You know I understand that mentality and the control issues so that allows me to interact with my students, I think on a, on a better, just, I just, inherently I know, you know how to do it. I've been there, they can relate. They can't say that you don't know what you're talking about because I *do* know what I'm talking about. And so that was, you know my, my biological father, that was a gift that he gave me. (Interview 1b, pp. 28–30)

In Taymes' life history and teacher stories, I see his personal and therapeutic recovery and reconstruction as interwoven within his professional identifications and commitments. For Taymes, the personal therapy in the professional identification represents his "commitment." In the end, Taymes says that "it all boils down to helping myself" (Interview 1b, p. 13).

A Separateness

Jack Springman, eighth grade English and media studies teacher in Southside Middle School in Austin ISD, recalled growing up in conservative Orange County, in retrospect, as "very difficult" (Interview 5a, p. 1). From a conservative middle class background, Springman narrates prescriptive and narrow value hierarchy of achievement, competition, pop culture, and sports that, "if you were at all different in any way, you were basically shunned" (Interview 5a, p. 4). In narrating this prescriptive and narrow value hierarchy, Springman recounts that his family insisted he study "to be a doctor or some other professional degree," and that when he wanted to be anything else, "It was not, to them, it was not success" (Interview 5b, p. 14). Several times during the interviews, Springman refers to this narrow value hierarchy as "White" (Interview 5a, p. 4) or "White-centric" (Interview 5a, p. 19; Interview 5b, p. 1). In recalling high school, Springman recounts "I think there was one African-American in my high school, like *one*" [respondent's emphasis] (Interview 5a, p. 4). With Springman, the discursive contexts on historical inequality and persistent segregation provided him with White privilege as later exemplified in his master's degree, middle class social status, and description of attending an all-White and middle to upper-middle class school.

Paradoxically, this discursive context was reversed as he entered the teaching profession; nonetheless, Springman reported on being entrenched – quite uncomfortably – in hegemonic and meritocratic notions of achievement and competition. Elaborating on this value hierarchy, Springman described it as "White-centric" (Interview 5a, p. 19). When I asked him to explain that term, Springman responded:

> Ah, it's almost like a superiority thing it's almost like, you know, that we, the world revolves around dead White guys as I refer to school, you know, the literature that we read in our schools in an English class, the history, the laws of our government were enacted by dead White guys so, you know, the White-centric attitudes that, not so much overt racism, but the kind of position that, like okay, well the White man is the top and everything *trickles down* from him. [Researcher's emphasis] (Interview 5b, p. 1)

In narrating this prescriptive and narrow hierarchy, Springman contextualized it, semiotically, with White-centric understandings combined with "trickle down" Reaganomics as the discursive context. Springman's life history and teacher stories presented, paradoxically, a story of recovering and critically reconstructing White privileges while simultaneously recognizing his White racial background. I think this paradox is important in understanding committed White male teachers'

41

identifications, and further, other progressive professional identifications (Giroux, 1998; Kincheloe, 1999; Kincheloe & Steinberg, 1998). Upper-middle and middle class Whites who recognized race and class privileges inherently take up a paradoxical identification of receiving privileges and also attempting to reconstruct them. This paradox provides the focus of Chapter Four on progressive masculinities.

In later high school, through college, and thereafter, Springman sought to broaden this prescriptive and narrow value hierarchy through engagement in "alternative" (Interview 5a, p. 7) music, literature, and film. Below, Springman narrated what "alternative" meant to him:

> To me alternative was not something that everybody did. I mean, everybody in my high school growing up would listen to like Poison or Bon Jovi and sort of the hard rock kind of music, and I was into like Depeche Mode and New Order and Echo and the Bunny Men, those sort of alternative music people. … I think I liked them because they spoke about experiences that I, or feelings that I had had as a teenager, you know, not feeling like part of a big acceptable group. And as a teenager, you know, you have lots of different feelings and you have lots of different experiences and lots of different attitudes and if you're, especially in Southern California and in Orange County, Nixon's place, in the late 80's, if it's not the norm, then somehow you're weird or if you were willing to accept that there were other possibilities, other than the norm popular acceptable attitudes, then you were shunned. …I didn't do the things that people were supposed to do in high school. And that was simply because I didn't have any interest in it. I wanted to spend time with my friends and listen to music and listening to the music that we liked, I didn't really care what everyone else believed. (Interview 5a, p. 14)

Springman narrated, at length, his engagement in alternatives which permeated his life history and appeared in his teacher stories. Springman, in his life history interviews, discussed a profound youth engagement with alternative music, literature, and film that shaped his youthful identifications (Frith, 2003). Springman's identification with alternative media provides an experiential rite-of-passage that expanded "the narrow shell that I thought was just the norm" (Interview 5a, pp. 4–5). Springman, ultimately, credited his engagement with alternative media that led him to a masters in film as "kind of… [making] me who I am today" (Interview 5a, p. 5). Springman's alternative identifications, entrenched in White privilege yet critically reconstructing the White-centric value hierarchy of his youth, tied in directly with his professional identifications.

Springman, through his engagement in alternative music, film, and literature, became intent on recognizing and extending different perspectives in his life and teaching.

> I try to think, and I try to express this to my kids that, you know, there are other viewpoints, the female and then there's people of color's viewpoint that,

you know, people of color have different cultures and in some regard I try to, I guess I try to highlight those, you know, like in the media studies class [his elective] more often than not I try to present perspectives of people of color, you know, try to show that that was made by a woman or made by a non-White man. It's just an all-encompassing effort. I try to be representative of different groups, and then there's also the gay perspective. And especially in middle school, you know, because the kids are developing their outlooks and their sexuality and related attitudes, other aspects. I don't share the same kind of attitudes and perspectives that most White men have, why is that necessarily a bad thing? I try to highlight the perspectives of others. (Interview 5b, pp. 1–2)

Springman, narrating a broadening of students' perspectives in his teaching, sought to reflect and yet reconstruct students' understandings as well, evinced here in representing gay perspectives to predominantly heterosexist Mexican-American and Mexican immigrant middle school students. The theme of recovering and reconstructing his own perspectives during his youth was very much translated into his teaching in which he sought to broaden students' identities in ways he considered important in his life and teacher story interviews.

In relation to teaching, Springman emphasized, in teacher stories, "adaptability" (Interview 5b, p. 3) and students' "personal experience" (Interview 5b, p. 3). Springman narrated:

I can think of one a couple of years ago in one of my regular language arts classes in 8th grade. I had a class that was not working, and they were really not understanding the, you know, they were not understanding the novel we were reading. They were kind of making fun of the book as they were reading it that, you know, *Charlie* [on exceptionality], the main character who is mentally retarded, they, the students were acting like the other characters in the play. And I kind of began to point out, you're behaving like these people who were cruel and unfair to Charlie. You should think about that. And then, you know, I figured out, specifically, but in an important part of the play, I tried to bring in their personal experience. I brought the analysis of the play to the kind of personal experiences where they would write about in their journals, about teachers and adults being un-fair. But instead of focusing directly on racial discrimination, I distanced the question, and I brought up the question of being made to feel ashamed by teachers and adults. Then they would share, you know, some level of discrimination, some experience that they had that they were made or felt ashamed, made to feel or felt ashamed. And this led to discussions of the color of their skin or the location they live in, you know, and experiences they had of discrimination. (Interview 5b, pp. 4–5)

Springman's understanding of adaptability provided a specific example of pedagogical content knowledge (Shulman, 1987) that represents the curriculum wisdom of synthetic teaching and deliberative dialogue discussed in Chapter Two.

Springman articulated his professional identifications that focus on expanding students' perspectives along with synthesizing young adult literature, exceptional identities, students' experiences, and community milieus. Springman, in adapting his teaching as it unfolded, engages in deliberative dialogue in which he listened and deliberated on students' understandings, changed his teaching in-action, and – very much in charge – redirected students' understandings in ways that they could understand textual and teacher-intended meanings.

In member checking, I returned to the theme of alternatives that predominated Springman's teacher story. In making this return, Springman intimated that, for him, teaching inner-city students *was* the alternative life path for him.

> So I decided to follow this path down to its logical conclusion, wherever that leads me. And it led to teaching children, diverse groups of children. And talking about the issue of this job, I really value it because it's a way to sustain a living without being completely beholden to other forces or power, like the corporate conglomerates. I'm not into this job for the money, and it's funny because I always tell people that this job provided me with the most money I've ever earned. They laughed at that, but it's true. I value this career, not for the money, but because it's the right job. It provides a sort of separateness from the norm, and I value that. It's not really so much the money, which isn't a whole lot, but it's living differently, which, to me is of utmost importance. (Interview 5b, p. 14)

For Springman, like Taymes, his professional identifications critically recovered and reconstructed experiences of his youth, broadening narrow identifications understood as "normal" or "acceptable" by his parents and "popular" by his peers. Commitment in Springman's professional identification, as in Taymes', recovered and reconstructed his private concerns in making them public in his teaching. As in Taymes' life history and teacher stories, personal relevance plays an important role in his synthetic teaching.

An Activist Stance

Bennett Ferris, in member checking, emphasized a political voice present throughout his life story and teacher story interviews:

JJ: Are you taking a color-blind position on race?

Bennett Ferris: Well, it's – it's not a colorblind position… I see a certain group of – of children and – and – and those kids are Hispanic and African American and I – and I want to emphasize that they get into the program, so – so in that – in – in that sense I'm – I'm reaching out to – to this segment of – of the population. … I think it's an activist step that I'm taking. So I – I feel a – a need, um, I'd even say, um, I'm taking an activist stance on – on trying to pool kids from the – from the Eastside into the program. (Interview 4a, p. 3)

Ferris's activism, as he understood it in the clip above, ran along lines of race and class.

Ferris, whose father was an itinerant laborer, grew up moving from place to place following his father's work opportunities. Specifically, Ferris recalled moving from place to place as "a double edged sword" (Interview 4a, p. 2):

> Growing up was...both, ah, difficult and, um, at some points very exciting. The difficult part was that...my family moved around often. And so just when I would start to, um, feel settled in one place, the family would – would take off and – and that, as you can imagine, created some difficulties in terms of, I don't know, feelings of stability, ah, feelings of, um, long-term relationships. Ah, the flip side to that was that there was a part of me that really enjoyed the – the moving about. (Interview 4a, p. 2)

Ferris experienced instability and newness as part of his working class childhood, but it was a class sensitivity, from these early experiences, that he recovered as through-line, thematically, in his professional identification.

Ferris recalled his early schooling as enjoyable. He found enormous pleasure in reading, which led to success in a number areas. He recalled reading, avidly, *The Hardy Boys* series, *Tom Sawyer*, and *Huck Finn*. These adventure novels, which paralleled his itinerant experiences of moving, served "as a metaphor for my childhood" (Interview 4a, p. 3). He recalled, during his childhood, playing sports and exploring with his brothers whom he was "pretty solid, [even] into adulthood" (Interview 4a, p. 3). Ferris recalled doing well in all school subjects, especially language arts, history, and geography. While doing well through elementary, middle, and even the beginning of high school, Ferris dropped out in tenth grade. In describing dropping out, Ferris recalled that "I wasn't feeling like I was getting a whole lot from the high school experience" (Interview 4a, p. 4). After having followed his father's work for many years, he found little connection with the high school traditions and routines, and consequently, he found it easy to cut his ties with the high school he was attending. However, even as he was dropping out, he planned to take his love of reading and writing to the community and junior college settings. As Ferris recounted, "What I wanted to do was to...drop out of high school and start taking college classes, and that's exactly what I did" (Interview 4a, p. 4). Like many students from working class families, Ferris's route to higher education followed community and junior college routes.

As Ferris's family continued to move around, he took junior college classes in Oregon, California, and Connecticut. After having maintained a high GPA and transferred hours from one institution to the next, he won a scholarship to Texas Tech in Lubbock, Texas. Regarding Texas Tech, he commented:

> Ah, I saw people around me at Texas Tech ...who had a lot of money, very, very wealthy and that, you ...that didn't bother me ...I was just happy to be there, I was very happy to be going to school on a – on a – on a scholarship but realizing the privilege. (Interview 4a, p. 6)

Ferris, evincing on-going class sensitivities, saw the privileges of Texas Tech and represents himself as just "happy" (Interview 4a, p. 6) to have a foot in the door. During his time at Texas Tech, Ferris studied language, literature, and communications developing a critical perspective regarding power relations. In discussing his education at Texas Tech, he recounted:

> I – I started looking more closely at power structures. Um… The power of the – of the federal government, um, and what the federal government is doing at the Supreme Court level, those – those kinds of – of discussions…We also talked about, um, power of interpersonal relationships… So my sensitivity towards – towards, um, towards these relationships of power certainly, ah, developed and – and increased while I was in that program. (Interview 4a, p. 14)

The university experience at Texas Tech recovered and reconstructed his class identity using critical language that "started looking more closely at power structures" (Interview 4a, p. 14).

Ferris's critical perspective, recovering class sensitivities, flowed into a swirl of critical discourses including corporate structures, green politics, process spirituality, and veganism. Ferris's critical discourses intertwined as he discussed commitments to a vegan life style that developed when he was at Texas Tech:

> I had read a lot of material, ah, about the – about the health component to a vegetarian diet …. And then once I – once I started reading more of the literature and actually started practicing the – vegan, ah, diet, the other constellation of – of arguments started to – started to come into my consciousness, the – arguments for, ah, environment, for example, um, the argument for animal rights, um, those – those arguments started to coalesce for me – then it was for the environment and the animal rights, um, ah, arguments as well. ...Um, politically, um, I was looking at relationships between, um, between food producers and, um, well, I was looking at relationships of – of agribusiness and – and the average consumer and – and what – what happens along that food line and what that – that is about. …A – another argument that I became aware of, too, was the – was the …spirituality argument to – to veganism and I think this argument rests primarily with some of the Buddhist, ah, and – and the Hindu, ah, philosophy, which is to – which is to not harm others, including – including animals. … And – and living in Lubbock…I helped to, um, create …an organization called the Vegetarian Society of Lubbock. That organization still exists today. (Interview 4a, pp. 14–17)

In the narrative following this selection, Ferris elaborated on working with local restaurants on creating vegetarian menus, developing the Society's local activist agenda, and bringing in speakers to support the group's vegan vision. Ferris's critical perspective, developed during his time at Texas Tech, found material expression in activism, a stance that will be echoed in the broad vision of his professional identification.

Regarding his teaching, Ferris's personal identifications came straight into his classroom as professional identifications with magnet and comprehensive school students. In narrating his classroom practice, Ferris's told of curriculum on religious scriptures including Lao Tse's *Tao*, using martial arts exhibitions for instruction when appropriate, discussions of animal rights and vegetarianism in a philosophy elective, and sponsoring a martial arts club to develop relationships with students. Additionally, Ferris talked at length about connecting with students at a "genuine level" (Interview 4b, p. 2). Supporting the notion of relationality described in Chapter Two, Ferris described the importance of teachers' vocation, using students' experiences, and developing relationships with students.

Synthesizing relationships, students' experiences, class sensitivities, and academic study, Ferris embodies synthetic teaching in recounting a unit of study for his sixth grade magnet classes based on selections from Chaucer's *Canterbury Tales* called "Southside Middle Tales." This curriculum unit sought to synthesize students' experiences and social relationships with critical discussions of social class and other identity groups, including race, at the school level. Ferris explained:

> And going back to that, ah, "Southside Middle Tales" lesson, the students brainstorm the different levels of or the different types of, ah, groups at South Middle, um, and – and then they also look at not just the – the levels of – created at Southside Middle by the school system, but they look at the different groups that the students created amongst themselves, so there – they – they often talk about the skater group; they often talk about, um, the punk group; um, they often talk about the schoolboy group; ah, they talk about the rappers; um, and – and sometimes – sometimes their discussion or their – their – their listing, ah, goes along of racial lines, they talk about the – the black group, they talk about the White group, they talk about the Hispanic group, um, so this lesson allows the students to – to – to look at the structures created, um, within the school system, by the school system, but also by the students themselves. And once – once they create, once we – once we put all of this on the board, um, we – we lay out all these different – different types of – of groups and – and structures at South Middle, then the task becomes to – to characterize these groups such as Chaucer did in his *Canterbury Tales* and, um, what – what I like the students to do is to, um, is to pick two or three of these groups specifically and – and to – to create like Chaucer did, ah, ah, rhyming couplets, and characterize these groups in rhyming couplets. (Interview 4b, p. 11)

As in Taymes and Springman's professional identifications, I see synthetic teaching that recovers personal identifications and reconstructs them using students' experiences, academic reading, and critical class interpretations. Additionally, I see socio-political critique in comparing Medieval class structures with hierarchical school relationships that point toward personal school politics for sixth graders. Yet beyond synthetic teaching, Ferris's discussion on authentic relationships and integration of school groups into the curriculum embodies notions of relationality, and his life and teacher stories articulated socio-political critique. Ferris, in having students write in Chaucer's "rhyming couplets" (Interview 4b, p. 11), recovered and reconstructed class identifications of his youth along with students' day-to-day relationships in ways that made school hierarchies visible for comment, understanding, and academic study.

Summarizing and Signalling

I see, in life histories and teacher stories, race-visible professional identifications embodying both critical counternarratives and alternative-progressive masculinity defined in Chapter Two and elaborated on at length in Chapter Four. Professional identifications, as they emerged in the stories, recovered private concerns and reconstructed them for professional identifications as "commitments." This recovering and reconstructing, reflecting process-oriented understandings of professional identifications, exemplify what is meant by race-visible professional identifications in which race-visibility represents one key component of complex private and professional identifications. In Mike Taymes' teacher stories, his identifications with hip hop culture critically reconstruct his family's rural, working class, White supremacy, and this reconstruction enters directly into what he teaches and how he teaches it. Taymes' recovery of his childhood, organized around his father's abandonment, reconstructed his personal narrative of loss and partial recovery as he approached the students he works with. Similarly, Jack Springman's engagement with alternative media and indie music and film critically reconstructed his White-centric family values and youth. As he recounted, his race-visible professional identifications move along the lines of "broadening" his and students' understandings and at the same time creating an alternative-progressive style. Finally, Ferris recovered and reconstructed his experiences of social class that inform his race-visible activist stance. Ferris, in his education, reconstructed his working class past in critical ways that appeared in his teaching stories. In each of the respondents' narratives, professional identifications recovered earlier private "selves", and in ways special to their stories, they reconstructed complex race-visible professional identifications developed over time. These patterns, which include process spirituality, alternative or indie media, and critical politics, are the focus of Chapter Four on contradictory white progressive masculinity.

PATTERNED UNDERSTANDING

Completing Race-Visible Professional Identifications

Further evidence supporting teachers' race-visible professional identifications emerges in patterned understandings from life history and teacher story interviews. Patterned understandings refer to narrative patterns in professional identifications that emerged, to differing degrees, in *all* teachers life story and teacher story interviews. All teachers in this study narrated the patterns below as part of life story and teacher story interviews. These patterns, *race-visibility*, *differences within difference*, and *relational-experiential teaching*, provide further support completing the notion of teachers' race-visible professional identifications. But more importantly, teachers in this study demonstrated the centrality of personal relevance inside synthetic teaching's cultural relevance.

Race-Visibility

I'm know I'm White. My students know I'm White. It's *not* a secret. (Rudy Smith, Interview 2b, p. 1)

It's just, it's just lingering, many, many years worth of repression by White people on minorities and it's all the fault of White Europeans. I don't know, it's pretty obvious. That's the way it is. (Gene Johansen, Interview 3b, p. 2)

It must be said, that all of this [my youth] was happening within a totally White center of gravity. These types of concerns, from my point of view in the US, seem to be classed and raced. Who gets to have these types of dilemmas? (Frank Carmody, Interview 8a, pp. 6–7)

I teach English, so a lot of the stories we'll read will be about young adults and so there'll be young adult black female and a young adult Hispanic male stories kind of stuff. And you can see that people [Editors] are going out of their way to be sure that students don't feel divorced from the curriculum. And I think that's important especially in an English class where a lot of the canon of highbrow literature is dead White men.... (Rudy Smith, Interview 2b, pp. 7–8)

First, in completing the notion of race-visible professional identifications, I return to teachers' race-visibility. Teachers in this study see race in themselves and in their students. Teachers in this study also see race in community and society along with racial representations in curriculum. Teachers in this study speak of race at an experiential level, within discursive contexts of racially charged communities. Teachers in this study understood race and class issues in their schools and communities as intertwined both in themselves and in students' identifications. Five of eight teachers mention race as playing an *obvious* role in day-to-day interactions and relationships with students. All respondents confirm race-visibility in students and themselves, and none of the teachers took a color-blind or race-evasive stance. Teachers' professional identifications, enmeshed with discursive contexts of historical inequality (Kozol, 2005; Spring, 2000; Tyack, 1974), cannot take refuge in typically White "color blind" understandings of race. Race-visibility emerges as a patterned professional identification in teachers' stories forming the over-arching narrative I develop as race-visible professional identifications. In relation to the curriculum wisdom paradigm advanced in Chapter Two, teachers' race-visibility expresses one example of teachers' *social and political awareness* that permeated teaching stories.

Differences Within Difference

Even though we're 90% Latino [and 9% African American], there's the jocks, there's the nerds, there's the burn outs, there's the gangsters. It's interesting all within its own little you know, cliques within a culture .... (Trent Cowens, Interview#7b, p. 6)

...I know a black kid is black and I know a Hispanic kid is Hispanic. But to some kids, the culture, the language, the background means different things to them, you know, and you have to take that into account. (Ron Johnston, Interview 2b, p. 1)

Let kids self-signify regarding their ethnicity. Don't forget about nuance of diversity within diversity. Don't forget about their background and bring their home cultures in whenever possible. Don't confuse home culture with established knowledge like African American literature or Mexican American literatures, though those are important. (Frank Carmody, Interivew#8b, p. 8)

But the particular groups that I'm, that I was referring to, they were majority Mexican-American or Mexican immigrant. I believe there were two, maybe three African-American students from middle SES and more boys than girls in comprehensive classes. I'm sure that the maturity level has something to do with it, girls taking advanced...classes. (Jack Springman, Interview#5, p. 6)

Second, in completing race-visible professional identifications, an understanding of differences within difference emerged as patterned professional identification in the teacher stories. This understanding of difference within difference emphasized working within yet beyond minority difference categories and assume an understanding of difference intersections. Predominant representations of difference in teacher education (e.g., Bennett, 2010; Johnson, Musial, Hall, Gollnick, & Dupius, 2007; Tozer, Senese, & Violas, 2008) work with identity categories that reflect static multicultural identities or social science "types." Differences within difference understand lived, experienced, and self-narrativized identifications (e.g., Bruner, 2002; Butler, 1999; Hall, 2003; Pinar, 2009) that more closely reflect students' lives within boundedness. These subtle difference intersections recognized the importance of students' narrating and shaping their identifications as students inhabit identities in historically and socially specific ways, and none of the teachers in this study provided simple minority types as a means of understanding their students cultures. For example, in discussing his students, David McGrady articulated that "Hispanics," for example, come from different social and historical backgrounds: "[There are] Hispanics who've been here since, say, the Mexican Revolution of 1910 versus the Hispanics that have been here since last summer. They *are* and *aren't* [respondent's emphasis] the same group" (Interview 6b, p. 11).

Teachers cannot assume that minority difference categories represent "cultures" traveling neatly through time and space. As teacher stories articulate, notions of "student cultures" serve as useful heuristic resources for teaching and learning but nonetheless prove themselves to be approximations when entering into specific engagements with students. As teachers' professional identifications articulate, students' experiences did not fit neatly into minority difference categories—students' experiences are more complex than that. Discursive contexts of racially and culturally charged communities, also enmeshed in teachers' day-to-day interactions, enter into teachers' patterned professional identifications perceiving established Mexican American families as different from the many new immigrant families in the community. In relation to curriculum wisdom, teachers' understandings of differences within difference emphasize *relationality* developed in their *deliberative dialogue* with students and community members.

Relational-Experiential Teaching

If students lack experiences to understand my lesson, it's my job to help provide them. (Frank Carmody, Interview 8b, p. 7)

It – it's – it's – it's extremely important to relate to the students, ah, experiences. (Benet Ferris, Interview 4b, p. 10)

If there's not a good relationship between a student and a teacher you can tell when you go into the teacher's classroom ...Some kids will be just out and out disrespectful or disruptive. (Rudy Smith, Interview 2b, p. 9)

It is tough and if you can't – if you can't relate to them [students], they have no reason to relate to you and if – if – if you're unrelated, you're not gonna work well together, they're not gonna work for you. (Jake Baynes, Interview 1b, p. 2)

Well there's, at the beginning of the year I go out of my way to try to let them tell me about themselves. And while they're doing that I will tell them a little bit about myself in order to sort of I guess gain their trust. I, I, let them fill out surveys. They write poems and stories about themselves, and it allows me to, to learn about them...with regard to their, their school, what their plans are, what their hopes are, what their fears are...(Rudy Smith, Interview 2b, p. 9)

Third, a relational-experiential teaching emerged as pattern in teachers' professional identifications. In correspondence with teachers' race-visibility and understandings of differences within difference, all teachers narrated pedagogies emphasizing relational-experiential teaching. Teachers stressed the value of relationships with their students as fundamental in maintaining functioning classrooms. Teachers also focused on adaptability of state standards to students' experiences as necessary in creating lessons that worked in context. This relational-experiential teaching aligned, most closely, with understandings of experience inherent in reflective professionalism (Clandinin & Connelly, 1992, 1995; Dewey, 1902/1990; Schwab, 1978; Henderson & Gornik, 2007) and contextualized pedagogical content knowledge (Shulman, 1987). As a note, this relational-experiential teaching emerged with little or no formal theoretical discussion on teaching and learning, and instead, teachers narrated their insights as personal and practical (Clandinin & Connelly, 1992; Connelly & Clandinin, 1988) resounding with curriculum wisdom traditions.

Through curriculum wisdom traditions, relational-experiential teaching emphasizes *synthetic teaching* described in Mike Taymes, Jack Springman, and Bennett Ferris's teacher stories outlined above.

From teacher stories, personal practical knowledges focusing on relationality and experiences with students emerged rather than theoretical or generalizable knowledge. Teachers in this study talked about personal practical teaching and learning, making relationships, and drawing on students' experiences and backgrounds in ways very similar to Gloria Ladson-Billings's (1995, 2009) *Dreamkeepers*, yet as life histories and teacher stories add, teachers' race-visible professional identifications recovered and critically reconstructed narratives from their childhood, suggesting *personal relevance* as component of culturally relevant teaching that has heretofore received little to no attention. Teachers' life histories and teacher stories, recounted in this research, begin to suggest – adding to curriculum wisdom and cultural relevance – a necessary attention should be lent to preservice and professional teachers' life stories and teacher stories in Deweyan constructivist ways (Lowenstein, 2009). In short, in working with preservice and professional teachers, it becomes clear that, for purposes of committed professional identifications, what is important is constructivist education *for* rather than *about* preservice and professional teachers[5]. Pedagogically, disclosure of life stories might play an important role in articulating what is understood as commitment.

RECAPPING RACE-VISIBLE PROFESSIONAL IDENTIFICATIONS

As articulated in teachers' life histories and teacher stories, race-visible professional identifications developed complexly over time, and "commitment" took various forms special to teachers' life histories and teacher stories. First and most importantly, the race-visible professional identifications recounted here present an important addition to literatures on White teacher identity that heretofore have focused predominantly on White teachers' race-evasive identities (Berlak, 1999; Henze, Lucas, Scott, 1999; Howard, 2006; Hyten & Warren, 2003; Marx, 2004, 2008; Marx & Pennington, 2003; McIntyre, 1997, 2002; Sleeter, 1992, 1993, 1995, 2001). The race-visible identifications, recounted in life histories and teacher stories, initiate *second wave White teacher identity studies* by developing and capacitating professional identifications that see race and culture, articulate and constitute progressive understandings, and emphasize the "importance of antiracist, positive, creative, and affirmational White identity" (Kincheloe & Steinberg, 1999, p. 21; Giroux, 1998; Kincheloe, 1999; Raible & Irizarry, 2007; Perry & Shotwell, 2009).

As I narrate the stories, race-visible professional identifications complicate but further extend existing understanding of White teachers and aggregate narratives of *race-visible curriculum wisdom* to these understandings. Race-visible professional identifications, beyond engaging in complex and intersectional representation of teachers and students' identifications, further develop a discussion on personal practical knowledge relating to teaching, learning, diversity, and culture. Following Xu, Connelly, He, & Phillion (2007) who develop narratives of experience in multicultural contexts, race-visible professional identifications move discussions on practical teaching and learning (Clandinin & Connelly, 1992, 1995; Connelly & Clandinin, 1988; Craig, 2008) squarely into intercultural and intersubjective understandings of teachers and students' identifications. Clearly, from life histories and teacher stories recounted in this chapter, race-visible professional identifications move narrative understandings of practical teaching and learning toward 1) race-visibility that sees race and culture in practical teaching and learning, 2) fine-grained understandings of students' differences within difference inherent in discursive contexts, and 3) a relational-experiential teaching for reaching diverse students. Teachers' life histories and teacher stories, articulating these three components, synthesize practical teaching and learning and culturally relevant traditions – advancing both by articulating race-visible professional identifications and curriculum wisdom. Race visible professional identifications and curriculum wisdom, patterned in life histories and teacher stories, provide – as is my intention – capacitating, constitutive, and generative professional resources and identifications for preservice and professional teachers who might recover and reconstruct their own lives and professional identifications.

NOTES

[1] Chapter Two reworks and further advances: Jupp, J.C. & Slattery, P. (2012). *Becoming* teachers of inner-city students: Identification creativity and curriculum wisdom of committed White male teachers. *Urban Education 47*(1), 280–311. Permission to rewrite this article for this book was obtained in May 2012.

[2] For a detailed discussion of research methodology including purposes and influences of life history along with practical methodological details of this study, see Appendix C.

[3] For a comprehensive reading of the Schwabian tradition along with Clandinin & Connelly's contributions, see Craig (2008). Craig (2008) updates Clandinin & Connelly's (1992) defining article on the practical tradition in P. Jackson's *Handbook of Research on Curriculum.*

[4] Given disparaging images of teachers as public servants in popular media such as *Waiting for Superman* (Chilcot & Guggenheim, 2010), recovering and reconstructing teachers-as-curriculum-makers, seems a key representational politics in the present moment in which public values and support for public teachers are in collapse (Giroux, 2011, 2012; Pinar, 2012).

[5] As part of this discussion, I ask you to consider the present paradox of constructivist teaching models as prescriptive technical-expert "ends" that completely ignore or provide only the smallest consideration of preservice and professional teachers' life histories and teacher stories. Examples of prescriptive technical-expert constructivist teaching models abound in so many educational psychology textbooks as "recommendations" that it is impossible to create a citation list, though I think the readers' experience in teacher education and staff development settings will confirm the paradox I assert. Working with teachers' life histories and teacher stories in approaching a Deweyan sense of professional identifications provides an alternative starting point for teacher educators rather than teaching preservice and professional teachers "how-to-teach."

ON WHITE DOUBLE-CONSIOUSNESS

Structures, Deficits, and a Split-Half View of Teachers'
Professional Identifications

INTRODUCTION

Lead-In Story Clip

Gene Johansen, language arts special education resource teacher at Southside Middle School, provides the contradictory narrative pattern that this Chapter explores. Johansen's statement regarding students' home lives exemplifies the pattern that emerged in life and teacher story interviews with committed White male teachers of diverse students:

JJ: What is the biggest problem you face?

Johansen: Home life.... I think parenting, well, I'm speaking from a White middle class perspective, but, as I told you before about my, the way I grew up, it was very similar to poverty lifestyle. (Interview 4b, p. 7)

Johansen's professional identification, as evinced in this story clip on student differences, begins with an assertion that reinforces deficit understandings of students' families as "problem." Contradictorily, the statement changes direction mid-thought and indicates structural understandings of student differences. Deficit understandings emphasize students' "home life" (Johansen, Interview 4b, p. 7), and structural understandings emphasize "White middle class" (Johansen, Interview 4b, p. 7) perspectives. Structural and deficit understandings provide on-going tensions throughout teachers' life and teacher stories I describe as White double-consciousness, privileged, yet cognizant of "the Other's" gaze.

In Chapter Three, I provide an in-depth reflection on teachers' contradictory narratives on student differences as structures *and* deficits. In providing this in-depth reflection, I return to discursive contexts as a means of understanding teachers' consciousness as complex and contested terrain. In reviewing teachers' structural and deficit understandings along with deficit discursive contexts, I theorize teachers' contradictory split view on student differences through the notion of White double-consciousness, an extension of W.E.B. Du Bois's (1903/1995) Black double-consciousness into present discussions of race in the United States. Finally, I develop the narratives of frustration and exhaustion already visible in teachers' structural and deficit understandings regarding students. Frustrations and exhaustions, intertwined in teachers' professional identifications, serve to remind preservice and professional teachers of the on-going cultural-emotional labor involved in teaching, a tiring, persistent, and little-narrated aspect of teaching absent in teacher education programs along with literatures on culturally relevant teaching and curriculum wisdom but certainly present in teachers' lives.

Emphasized in Chapter Three, teachers' race-visible professional identifications do *not* represent a vulgar "solution" to challenging and unequal historical and social conditions termed variously in deficit language as "underachievement," "failing schools," "achievement gap," "at-risk children," or "ill-prepared teachers." Given tensions and exhaustion intertwined in teachers' professional identifications, race-visible professional identifications discussed in Chapter Two appear, rather, as humanizing meliorist[2] practice in response to continued racial and social class inequalities in public schools (Kozol, 1991, 2005) – schools that more and more are understood as poor schools (Giroux, 2011, 2012). In Chapter Three, I understand teachers' work as I have come to understand my own life history and teacher story, not as facile or feel-good "victory narrative" (Cary, 1999, p. 414), but rather as messy and unfinished yet *not-all-is-lost* "partial" (Lortie, 1975, p. 132) enabling of teachers and students' lives.

Chapter Three Overview

As an Overview, Chapter Three 1) defines and explains deficit and structural understandings of difference to help narrate teachers' tension-filled stories on student differences, 2) recounts the deficit and structural understandings that emerge in teachers' life and teacher stories, 3) contextualizes these tensions within deficitary discursive contexts, 4) theorizes White double-consciousness, an inversion of Du Bois's Black (1903/1995) "double-consciousness" (p. 45), that signals a contradictory yet privileged twilight of Whites' race invisibility, and 5) concludes by narrating the patterns of teachers' on-going frustrations and exhaustion experienced in teaching diverse students in public schools. All of this seeks, through complexly narrating teachers' professional identifications, to inform preservice and professional teachers' understandings of teaching across student differences.

STRUCTURES *AND* DEFICITS

Two Contradictory Understandings

Emerging from committed White male teachers' stories on student differences, teachers in this study narrated student differences along lines of *structures* and *deficits*. Structures and deficits, which appear as contradictions when taken up abstractly, continually appeared in teachers' professional identifications as structural *and* deficit understandings often blended and intermingled in paragraphs, sentences, and clauses in life story and teacher story interview transcripts. Teachers' professional identifications, emphasizing structures and deficits, differ substantially from previous characterizations of White teachers' race-evasive identities discussed in Chapter One.

Structures

When understood as structures, differences exist in relation of historical and social center and margins (Apple, 2000; Gramsci, 2000; Hall, 2004). The hegemonic center emerges from a contested flux of "Western European culture and its institutions" (Julien & Mercer, 1988, p. 2). The margins, as they form in relation to hegemonic centers, represent complex areas of difference that "critical theories are just beginning to reckon with..." (Julien & Mercer, 1988, p. 3, Villenas, 1996, 2000).

Differences, when understood through hegemonic center and margins, emerge as protracted struggle. Critical literatures on US history articulate differences, e.g., differences of race, class, gender, sexuality and other markers, as historically marginalized groups (for US historical overview see Zinn, 1980/2003). Schooling, historically representing expert-technical rationality (Spring, 2001; Tyack, 1974), generally reproduces the relations between the historical and social center and margins (Apple, 2000; Counts, 1932/1978; Spring, 2000; Tyack, 1974). That is, in a general sense, schooling protects, reproduces, and conserves the status quo and its related privileges in ways that advantage students benefitting from the structural status quo and disadvantage students marginalized by it (Anyon, 1995, 1997; Kozol, 2005). Specifically, schooling *does not preclude* social mobility of marginalized students as upward mobility represents a constant (though often unlikely) feature; nonetheless, in its general sense, schooling protects, reproduces, and conserves the structural status quo that over-determines "successes" of those already privileged and celebrates "bootstrap stories" of students who occasionally succeed in a system rigged in favor of the privileged.

Within understandings of structures, schooling never represents a politically neutral activity. Schooling, as progressive educator George S. Counts (1932/1978) correctly noted early in the 20th century, assumes "particular systems of human values" (p. 17). Schooling, institutionally and historically, reproduces the value systems "of the groups or classes that actually rule society" (Counts, 1932/1978, p. 25). Schooling, reflecting the value systems of ruling groups or classes, protects, reproduces, and conserves the ideologies of dominant groups. Currently, schooling, as conserving dominant ideologies, focuses on achievement, accountability, standardized tests, and global economic competition with special valuation of expert-technical rationalism in math, science, and engineering as a mean of economic ascendance among global competitors. Bill Gates' testimony to the US Senate Committee Hearing, embodying what Counts (1932/1978) described as reproduction, exemplifies the ideologies that provide national leadership on education:

The only really proven thing to make an economy work well is to have an educated workforce. We cannot sustain an economy based on innovation unless we have citizens educated in math, science, and engineering. If we fail at this, we won't be able to compete in the global economy. (Gates in Chilcot & Guggenheim, 2010)

Current achievement, accountability, standardized tests, and global economic competition correspond, historically and institutionally, with dominant class ideologies focusing on technical expertise and efficiency in scientific management (Callahan, 1962; Tyack, 1974). Scientific management, reconstituted in the historical present as marketizing education "to compete in the global economy" (Gates in Chilcot & Guggenheim, 2010), takes the form of market efficiency and continuous improvement in state and federal rating systems, pay-for-performance, charter schools, and competitive advanced academies (Giroux, 2011; 2012).

In discussions of structures as they relate to schooling, resistance at the margins takes on importance (Apple, 2000; Gramsci, 2000; Hall, 2004). The marginalized, those representing intersections of race, class, gender, sexuality, and other markers, create spheres of resistance (Foley, 1990; Hebdige, 1979; Willis, 1977). Counter or alternative cultures, subcultures resisting dominant ideologies, take on importance. It is important to note that historical and social centers never dominate completely, and thus, a number of educators argue for critical education (e.g., Apple, 2000; Freire, 1970/2002; hooks, 1994; Shor, 1987, 1992). Schools, as public institutions with a coerced constituency, present possible spaces for cultural resistance. Students coerced into attendance often develop oppositional identifications (Foley, 1990; Ogbu, 1987; Willis, 1977) in relation to schooling's implicit values of diligence, deference, and respect. Paul Willis (1977) explains:

This opposition involves an apparent inversion of the usual values held up by authority. Diligence, deference, and respect - these become things that can be read in quite another way. …This opposition is expressed mainly as a style. It is lived out in countless small ways which are special to the school institution. (Willis, 1977, p. 12)

Critical (e.g., Freire, 1970/2002; hook, 1994; Shor, 1987, 1992) and culturally relevant pedagogies (e.g., Gay, 2000; Howard, 2006; Nieto, 1999; Ladson-Billings, 1995, 2009) directly address cultural resistance, positing the negotiation of differences through interaction or dialogue of students, teachers, community, and academic study. Additionally, literatures on teachers' life histories and teacher stories confirm teachers' complexly intermediary and mediated professional identifications as sites of resistance. Teachers' resistances include oppositions to expert-technical rationalism in education (e.g., Clandinin & Connelly, 1992, 1995; Connelly & Clandinin, 1988) negotiating official curriculum (e.g., Goodson, 1992; Middleton, 1992, 1993), and critical teaching (Goodson & Walker, 1991; Middleton, 1992, 1993). Teachers in this study, whose professional identifications embodied complex negotiations of self, curriculum, and critical teaching, included structural understandings of student differences in their life histories and teacher stories.

Deficits

In contrast to understanding differences as structures, "common sense" representations articulate differences as personal problems or personal "deficits." Discourses representing the hegemonic center actively seek to reduce or discredit structural understandings of difference. Instead, the center emphasizes human "universals" such as "self-interest, competitive individualism, and anti-statism" (Apple, 1993, p. 29) along with other notions supporting free market fundamentalism (Giroux, 2011, 2012; Reynolds & Webber, 2009). Developing alliances of neo-liberal elite with a majority of White upper-, middle-, and working-class groups along with others, the hegemonic center marginalizes difference in terms of *we* who mark the center and *they* who live on the margins. Michael Apple (1993) explains:

> "We" are the "law-abiding, hard-working, decent, virtuous, and homogeneous." The "theys" are very different. They are "lazy, immoral, permissive, heterogeneous (Hunter, 1987, p. 23)." These binary oppositions distance many people of color, women, gays, and others from the community of "worthy" individuals. The subjects of discrimination are now no longer those groups who have been historically oppressed, but are instead the "real Americans" who embody the idealized virtues of a romanticized past. The "theys," unlike the "real Americans," are undeserving of welfare "handouts." (p. 33)

The historical and social center, in the present, recasts structures as personal "deficits" of biology, morality, work ethic, culture, or group and thereby pathologizes lives and experiences of those on the margins. Differences as deficits, blaming the marginalized for challenging conditions, understand complex identification intersections as "lacking the right stuff," "personal problems," "deficiencies of character," "laziness," or "personal failure."

Differences as deficits, redefining historical and social conditions as personal problems, incur the most damage to those living at intersections with poverty. Katz (1989), describing the shift in understanding differences as deficits, recalls how the 1960s War on Poverty became the 1990s War on Welfare prevalent in popular attitudes today:

> By the mid-1980s, a new image dominated poverty discourse. Invoked unreflectively and automatically by commentators on poverty, the concept of the *underclass* captured the mixture of alarm and hostility…What bothered observers most was not their [the marginalized's] suffering; rather, it was their sexuality, expressed in teenage pregnancy; family patterns, represented by female households, alleged reluctance to work for low wages; welfare dependence…propensity for drug use and violent crime…. (p. 185)

Differences understood as deficits, rather than abating since the Welfare Reform Act of 1996, have re-doubled in recent economic crises thereby further exacerbating class divisions (Giroux, 2011, 2012) which in the US intersect with race, culture, language, and other differences. These increased class divisions, instead of being understood as such, take the forms of increased resentments (Reynolds & Webber, 2009), a growing sense of moral-religious righteousness among the "successful," (Giroux, 2012; Reynolds & Webber, 2009), and decreasing tolerance for public programs and expenditures that aid poor and working class people (Giroux, 2012).

In relation to schooling, student differences as deficits represent a continual historical feature (Tyack, 1974; Spring, 2000; Kozol, 2005). Critical literatures in education reveal how differences translate as deficits in the schooling of diverse children (Valencia & Solórzano, 1997; Valenzuela, 1999). Rather than interrogating difference as historical and social structures, "deficit thinking" (Valencia & Solórzano, 1997, p. 160) articulates difference as 1) genetic inferiority, 2) cultural deprivation, or 3) environmental deficiency. Neo-hereditarian views, which focus on measurement and testing of "IQ," articulate the position of difference as genetic inferiority. Hernstein and Murray's The Bell Curve (1994), which compares "intelligence" across different racial groups, articulates deficits as individual's insufficient intelligence to perform complex social roles. Cultural deprivation, which "focuses on attitudinal and behavioral aspects of the underclass that are allegedly at odds with mainstream values and behaviors" (Valencia & Solórzano, 1997, p. 183), articulates difference as deficient cultural background. ED Hirsch's (1988) *Cultural Literacy: What Every American Needs to Know*, which argues for an intervention of Western culture in school curricula, exemplifies differences understood as cultural deprivation. Environmental deficiency, which argues that "low-income parents of color typically do not value education" (Valencia & Solórzano, 1997, p. 190), articulates difference as deficient family structure led by unmarried female heads-of-household. In relation to social work, Communities in Schools (2012) and other federally funded programs, whose purpose is providing "guidance" to parents, articulates the logic of environmental deficiency. Deficit understandings in schools re-articulate students' historical and social differences and inequalities as "problems" or "deficits" of genetics, culture, neighborhood, and family. In re-articulating students' differences as problems, deficit understandings diminish challenging historical and social conditions and amplify hegemonic universals of self-interest, individualism, productivity, and global competition.

Deficits and *Structures?*

Differences understood as structures run counter to differences understood as deficits. With structural understandings, differences represent historical and social structures articulating hegemonic center and margins. In contrast, deficits represent "common sense" understandings that diminish historical and social structures and blame individuals for their problems. Logically, someone who understands differences as social and historical structures should *not* also describe differences as personal deficits. Similarly, someone who understands differences as deficits should *not* also describe differences as structures. Surprisingly, given the seemingly contradictory positions taken, teachers in this study storied structural *and* deficit understandings of differences in on-going, combinatory, and blended ways. In the next sections, I present teachers' contradictory understandings of student differences.

STORIES ON DIFFERENCES: IN TENSION

Structural Understandings

Overwhelmingly, teachers in this study understood differences in terms historical and social structures. Gene Johansen expresses structural thinking regarding differences and how differences play out in school settings. Johansen, in his life and teacher story interviews, narrates structural understandings of race and class in schools that marginalize students.

> The truth is that probably more than 99% of children identified for "special ed" are minorities. ...So racism is constantly happening in school. Teachers are certainly biased against certain children, especially if they don't know them, and often are surprised at the amount of intelligence and cultural awareness of minority children who have been raised in *quote unquote* the right way, you know, the middle class family type of situation instead of the working class family mentality. But it's [racism], it's a daily, it's a daily thing. And as I said, the longer you teach the more experience you have with it, the more, the more visible it becomes. But the fact is that racism, it's very, very common. (Interview 3b, p. 2)

In a follow up conversation, Dave remarked, "race is class in the United States" (Researcher Journal, p. 36). Dave sees structures of difference and how they play out, not only in a broader society, but he also understands how these structures enter into schooling in relation to special education, teachers' perceptions of students, and how "middle class" students represent a dominant reference group as class and race intersect.

David McGrady, in his life and teacher story interviews, also narrated structural understandings of difference as they play out in schools. McGrady narrates:

> White people want to say well, it's all over with, race relations are done, we solved the problem, the laws are changed. People's attitudes are slowly changing, Barack Obama's President. We're done. Well, as in the case of most oppression, if you look at it in history, the person doing the oppressing doesn't get to say when it's done. Okay? ...And like I said before too, if it's almost that esoteric leftist stuff where a lot of people in Austin were worried more about the lake and the runoff into it over whether or not, versus whether or not my students are getting enough to eat. (Interview 6b, p. 9)

McGrady makes specific reference to "re-segregated" (Interview 6b, p. 9) schooling that echoes Kozol's (1991, 2005) on-going concerns. McGrady, who worked at

61

Eastside Middle School during the re-segregating movement to "neighborhood schools" in the early 2000s remembers the period with particular disdain for Whites who think they "solved the problem" (Interview 6b, p. 9). Moreover, McGrady references an "esoteric left" (Interview 6B, p. 9) in Austin seemingly more concerned with Lady Bird Lake than the impoverished condition of Eastside families and children. Overall, McGrady's understanding places him at the intersection between his students who see, live in, and recount an on-going inequality and Whites in the community who felicitously imagine themselves as concerned leftists but do not attend to immediate inequalities in their community.

As Johansen and McGrady's life and teacher stories represent, teachers in this study produced pages and pages of structural understandings on differences. Teachers in this study understood intersections of race, class, culture, and language in lucid ways that invoked Whites' misunderstandings, omissions, and felicitous leftist positions. Further supporting teachers' race-visible professional identifications of Chapter Two, structural thinking moved back-and-forth between structures, students' lives, schools, special education placements, and Whites who seemingly fail to recognize racism.

Deficit Understandings

To a lesser degree yet manifesting a consistent pattern, teachers' contradictory deficit thinking emerged in life and teacher story interviews. Gene Johansen, who elaborated on structural understandings of difference above, also expressed deficit thinking regarding his students.

> Most of them [students in special education resource class] don't have a dad or some of them don't even know their dad. Or some of them, a few of them, don't have a mother, for one reason or another and they live with their grandmother. So it's one parent. Some of them have been abused, especially the emotionally disturbed children that I've worked with have been abused in one way or another. Many of them move from place to place quite a bit, sometimes more than once a year, which is fairly damaging to their learning. Most of them have seen a variety of people, as in mom's boyfriends come through the house, and are able to deal with many difficult situations. They're able to cope with a lot of stuff. Most of them don't apply much, they don't give education much weight in the worthwhile-ness of everything. They know it's important but when it comes right down to it, *so what* if *I* don't get one? [Respondent's emphasis]. They know it's important in theory but not in practicality. And a lot of them don't think they can do it anyway. They're, they've already given up on themselves by eighth grade. (Interview 3b, p. 8)

Gene Johansen, just paragraphs below his structural understandings, narratively switches to deficit understandings. Johansen's deficit understandings emphasize home life, single parent families, "mom's boyfriends" (Interview 3b, p. 8), lack of motivation, and failure to identify education's importance "in the worthwhile-ness of everything" (Interview 3b, p. 8). Making a reversal from his structural thinking, Johansen, who speaks at length on structural understandings a few breaths prior, reorganizes structural understandings under a deficit rubric of parents, students, and families' reproducing most categories of deficits (Katz, 1989; Valencia & Solórzano, 1997). Also, within his reversal, Johansen takes a tone of frustration as evinced in the rhetorical question he poses to students and their families: "They know it's [education is] important but when it comes right down to it, *so what* if *I* don't get one?" (Interview 3b, p. 8). Johansen, within his reversal, seems to reference the intractability of challenging social and historical conditions in a personal face-to-face way with students and their families' oppositional identifications (Foley, 1990; Ogbu, 1987; Willis, 1977) following "motivation problems" in deficit discourses. In the textual clip, Johansen's frustrations emerge that later came out with more clarity in the Focus Group meeting.

Additionally, David McGrady, who also elaborated at length on structural understandings above, narrates deficit understandings of difference.

JJ: Yeah, I was, I found very disturbing inequities at schools, and I would talk about it to people not in the schools. They would want to blame the parents. And that was a bit beyond me.

David McGrady: I mean parents do need to take a lot of blame. Uh. I've never in my experience I've never seen so many parents try to be friends with their kids. Instead of a parent. Well the deal about that is, or whatever is the criticism. They don't seriously take up their role. Many of them are in jail, many other of the kids are living with, with their grandparents. The grandparents don't have it in them to do what is needed, and the kids just get to do whatever they want. That often means getting knocked up, or getting into gangs or doing drugs. What do I have to say? All this is completely common, and the people who are directly there, well – they are the parents, aren't they? So what would I say to you or anyone who let their kids get involved in gangs and drugs? (pp. 6–7)

McGrady, like Johansen, narrates structural understandings of difference as evinced above, and making a reversal, he goes on to narrate deficit thinking on parents, family, morality, and single parent families (Katz, 1989; Valencia & Solórzano, 1997). McGrady, after discussing structural understandings of difference like segregation, White people's misunderstandings, continued contexts of oppression, and esoteric leftists, narratively switches to parents' deficits. McGrady, in taking up this topic as common sense "facts," describes the school contexts of single parent families, jailed family members, gangs and drugs as "completely common" (Interview 6b, p. 7), and he recognizes, echoing deficit thinking (Katz, 1989; Valencia & Solórzano, 1997), the parents as ultimately "the people who are directly there" (Interview 6b, p. 7).

McGrady, imploringly in the interview, seems to say "These are the hard facts: Someone at home needs to in charge of my students, and who else if not the parents?"

McGrady also remarked several times in other conversations answering his own question: "I wish we could keep the kids here at school all the time, feed them, see to them, make sure they ate well, and slept enough, but in Texas they call that socialism, Stalinism even..." (Researcher Journal, p. 52). McGrady, in his off-hand remarks, imagines the drastic structural changes required but ironically understands that would be "socialism, Stalinism" (Researcher Journal, p. 52). Bound up in McGrady's deficit thinking, paradoxically it seems, was concern about basic rights to a childhood that parents and grandparents in their structural oppression could not rightly attend to because of reasons McGrady mentions.

Blendings

Not only did teachers' life and teacher story interviews evince structural *and* deficit understandings of difference, the two understandings often emerged in combinatory fashion. Here is an example, taken from Bennett Ferris, who mixes structural and deficit thinking:

> One of the things that I wanted to, um, to do as a – as – as a teacher at this Magnet School was to make sure that we pulled in a lot of the kids who would not get the opportunity, ah, to – to go this type of school and – and so – so for me it was important to tap into the, um, to the – to the kids on the East Side, the Hispanic and the – and the African American kids on the East Side. Um, I see – I see that population as a – as a, um, as a forgotten population of – population, um, who would not otherwise have the opportunity to go in an advanced, ah, ah, program like this, ah, like this. (Interview#4b, p. 1)

Ferris evinces structural understandings of difference along the lines of geopolitical race and class in Austin as they relate to his work, but he also reifies the deficit understandings in his comment on "forgotten population" (Interview 4b, p. 1). The notion of "forgotten population" (Interview 4b, p. 1) crosses from structural back to deficit understandings in implying indirectly the same parental negligence referred to by Johansen and McGrady above. While blending structural and deficit thinking, Ferris clearly signals the hegemonic center as those who are remembered and the margins as "forgotten population" (Interview 4b, p. 1).

Additionally, Mike Taymes provides an example of blending structural and deficit thinking.

> So again there's a disproportionate number of African American students in our [special education] class as opposed to the outside population. We have – we have some students who – who have been orphaned, living with aunt and uncles where a lot of them are in situations where the adults and the role models in the their life have been kind of forced into that position or thrust into that position, and they don't really have a good handle on it, and so they're, you know, so there's a lot – there's a lack of structure and consistency and those – those

expectations lead to them [students] being able to make inappropriate choices often without feeling the same kinds of consequences that a student in a – in a more traditional environment would – would feel. ...They display oppositional defiant characteristics, they disagree just because they wanna disagree, they are all very interested in fairness and are very quick to point out faults in others and very rarely do they take issue with anything that they do wrong or – and they're quick to point out inconsistencies in the teachers' behavior but not their own, which again is, you know, pretty common in, I think, in the world. ...But more so there – there's – it's a – it's a power structure and people are vying, they're vying for power, and they're vying for perceived limited resources, you know... (Interview#1b, p. 5)

Taymes is the teacher of the "emotionally disturbed" unit who mentioned class and race over-representation in his classroom. Nonetheless, deficit understandings follow structural understandings of "parents who lack structure and consistency" (Interview 1b, p. 5), "oppositional defiant characteristics" (Interview 1b, p. 5), and "inappropriate choices," (Interview 1b, p. 5) as deficit understandings. Contrastingly, Taymes clearly marks the hegemonic center with the mention of a "more traditional environment" (Interview 1b, p. 5).

Finally, Frank Carmody also blends structural and deficit understandings of difference in narrating his students and their families. In discussing students' backgrounds, Carmody narrates the paradoxes of integrating students' backgrounds into schools, especially when these backgrounds are influenced by gangs.

How do we, as teachers, make sure that students get at dominant White standards and retain important aspects of their backgrounds? We get caught up in how to make sure kids are doing grade level work. Generally speaking, many of our students are *not* [respondent's emphasis] in the mainstream. In fact, as one teacher pointed out to me, "some of the kids don't really conceive of a world in which gang cultures are completely irrelevant." And in conclusion of this statement, because it's hard to be relativistic about a kid getting involved in gang culture as part of his or her "home culture" – I mean, who would want a twelve year old girl to get gang-banged in? – how ridiculous this position of insisting on the universality of gang culture appears to those Whites on the outside. West Austinites, the rich and beautiful Whites, scorn, or alternately are amused, or alternately are indifferent to this problem. Gang cultures, for the concerned academic, might appear as legitimate or in need of offering a viable school alternative, but for Whites, including myself sometimes, appear as the cruelest ruse perpetrated by the mass media. Thanks Nike for the Red Air Jordans [Bloods' signifier]! Yet, many of the most difficult students to reach take gang culture as "true" learning and experience that contrast to official messages of any teacher. My position is that gang culture is also co-opted by mass media and clothing companies. (Interview 6b, p. 8)

Carmody's narrative on students' backgrounds presses against distinctions between structural and deficit understandings. Carmody recognizes hegemonic whiteness in curriculum and teachers' professional identifications, and he represents the teachers as the bearer of White identity, yet his discussion of gangs and their activities – twelve year old girls' getting "gang-banged in" (Interview 6b, p. 8) – reference common sense disdain for behaviors he considers pathological. Carmody, clearly referencing students' oppositional identifications (Foley, 1990; Ogbu, 1987; Willis, 1977), suggests that students' oppositional identifications are commoditized before students take them up. Despite blending structural and deficit understandings and even pushing their distinctions, reversing Carmody's lead tenet reveals the hegemonic center. A reversal of Carmody's position would read like this: *In fact, as one student pointed out to me, "some of the teachers don't really conceive of a world in which academic learning is completely irrelevant."* Structurally, as Carmody explained, teachers "are in the obverse position of negotiating White standards to their students" (Interview 8b, p. 3).

Teachers in this study, as shown above, demonstrated structural *and* deficit understandings of students' differences. Paradoxically, teachers understood students' and their families as oppressed by historical and social structures. Nonetheless, teachers' structural understandings did not cancel out deficit understandings of student differences. Despite structural understandings of race, class, culture, language, and other differences, teachers elaborated on students and their families' deficits of morality, character, family structure, and motivation (Katz, 1989; Valencia & Solórzano, 1997) with the exception of biology. Structural and deficit understandings came one right after the other and blended in-and-out-of each other. In these discussions on difference, the hegemonic center revealed itself as academics, standards, traditional families, and "appropriate" choices.

Teachers, in their discussions on difference, appeared as negotiators of hegemonic structures such as academic study and standards who found the absence of "traditional" family and household features as factors that worked against their negotiating role, and having demonstrated aspects of culturally relevant teaching (e.g., Gay, 2000; Nieto, 1999; Ladson-Billings, 2009), teachers' professional identifications as negotiators bring into relief this little-discussed intermediary aspect of culturally relevant teaching. Despite the education for critical consciousness inherent in culturally relevant teaching, teachers provide and constitute an intermediary role with the hegemonic center *as they critique it* in their thinking and teaching. Moreover, combining teachers' race-visible professional identifications with structural and deficit understandings, an over-arching story appears in which culturally relevant teaching (e.g., Gay, 2000; Nieto, 1999; Ladson-Billings, 2009) does not *always* provide a victory narrative (Cary, 1999) nor does it provide a "pure" structural consciousness regarding student differences. Teachers, even though they variously discussed students and their families structural oppression, their professional identification seemingly required the negotiation of identifications between hegemonic center and margins. This negotiation, as life and teacher stories on differences indicated, emerged as conditioned by common sense dilemmas (Delpit, 1986, 1988) about power structures *and* deficits.

Teachers' in this study, in their deficit thinking, drove at immediate concerns. Gene Johansen was concerned about students' academic study. David McGrady was concerned with students' well-being and safety. Blendings of structural and deficit understandings saw the two as hard to separate but always pointing back to the hegemonic center. A study of discursive contexts serves to contextualize thinking and go beyond paradoxes in teachers' heads.

A RETURN TO DISCURSIVE CONTEXTS

Deficit Discursive Contexts

After revealing structural and deficit understandings of differences along with blendings of the two, life history research requires the emplotment (Polkinghorne, 1995) of these narratives within broader contexts (e.g., Cole & Knowles, 2001; Goodson, 1992, 1995; Goodson & Sikes, 2001; Plummer, 2001). Discursive contexts, here examined for deficit understandings, provide broader historical and social narratives for contextualizing teachers' paradoxical professional identifications in this chapter. Deficit discursive contexts emerged in faculty meetings, national reports, community newspaper stories, and campus governance meetings, among other contexts.

First, curriculum meetings provide a deficit discursive context. Before this study, I worked with two of the teachers side-by-side as a teacher at Southside Middle School in Austin ISD. During this time, I worked on a critical literacy and curriculum project and collected field notes and other data. At a curriculum meeting, the Assistant Principal, a Mexican-American man, provided the following text I copied into my field notes:

> We basically have a situation that we can't hope for much from the parents. We have parents that have completely lost control of their situation. I know that if my kid acted the way many of our kids up here acted, she'd be *dead* [respondent's emphasis]. But we need to own that, we need to accept that our parents aren't doing enough, will never do enough, have lost control. They are on drugs, partying, disregarding the law. ...If we can't expect anything from the parents, then what are we going to expect from the kids? But that's what we're dealing with. We're dealing with parents who just aren't doing what they are supposed to, they aren't taking care of their children. Many of them are in jail, or on the streets – and they aren't looking after or working with their children or making sure that they are doing their homework. (Field notes 2003, p. 96)

The Assistant Principal, like teachers in this study, describes every category of deficit understanding (Katz, 1989; Valencia & Solórzano, 1997) with the exception of biology. Again, the hegemonic center is defined by the middle class oriented household in which parents "work...with their children and make...sure that they are doing their homework" (p. Field notes, 2003, p. 96). In this clipping, it becomes painfully obvious that deficit thinking is *not* exclusive to White teachers, and teachers, from this deficit discursive context, receive leadership and direction. Nonetheless, viewing the teachers' deficit thinking as a reflection of the Assistant Principal's represents an over-simplification, and on different occasions, the Assistant Principal spoke about structural oppression of students and community in ways similar to the teachers (Field notes, 2003). More important to note, deficit discursive contexts not only describe the school setting, they also constitute it through White flight and district zoning practices that ghettoize some neighborhood schools and "protect" others.

Second, national accountability discourses provide a deficit discursive context. The Fordham Foundation's (2006) *How are the States Educating our Neediest Children?* provides a key discursive context on the "educational crisis" regarding the neediest students:

> The achievement results are bleak. The average state grade is D; three states flunked, and none earned better than D+. But these low marks were not the result of an impossible grading scheme. Were the same scale applied to White students, the national average would be a B. ...Still some states do better by their disadvantaged students than others. Of course, these are still desperately low numbers, hardly worth celebrating. (p. 13)

The context above represents race, class, culture, language, and other differences without structural references. Instead, student differences are understood as "disadvantaged" (Fordham Report, 2006, p. 13) presenting a "problem" to be fixed by the states in schools. In this case, the phrase *neediest students* in the title of the report refers to culturally "disadvantaged" deficit understandings (Valencia & Solórzano, 1997). States, for not fixing the problem through school achievement, receive failing or low grades according to the Fordham Foundation indices. In this national policy discourse, difference appears as culturally disadvantaged (Valencia & Solórzano, 1997).

Central office staff in Austin ISD borrowed positionings from national discourses like the Fordham Foundation Report (2006) and postured themselves as "concerned progressive leaders" yet attended very little to schools and had even less presence in the community. Instead of meaningful community relationships, involvement, interactions, Austin ISD's Central Office staff collected data, disseminated it, and judged the results declaring failures of those schools, teachers, and by extension, students, who did not meet standards or who met them with little margin.[3] Clearly, in these accountability discourses, the hegemonic center diminishes structural understandings (Apple, 1993; Katz, 1989) of race, class, culture, language, or other differences and emphasizes student achievement as solution to challenging historical and social conditions. What matters in these discussions is only a free market language emphasizing the "bottom line" or even worse "get'er done" or perish business ethics (Apple, 1993; Giroux, 2011, 2012). Teachers in this study discussed accountability discourses that frame and increasingly dominate their work place as on-going sources of frustration, incomprehension, cause for teacher turn-over, mindless reforms and change, and ultimately, burnout among administration and staff.

Third, a local newspaper article on Eastside High School in Austin ISD provides another discursive context. I copied the following fragments of this newspaper article into the researcher journal. In this article, the reporter interviews Eastside High's Reading Coach:

> Later, in an office piled with a new shipment of *Hop on Pop* and other Dr. Seuss books, reading coach Melanie Marley pulls out a test that required 11th graders to read aloud words like "how" and "may-be = maybe." Half the answers are marked wrong. "It's almost like we need to be judged by different standards," she says. (Researcher Journal, p. 36)

And later in the same article, the reporter takes on a "factual" tone:

> Many schools earn their failing label because of a single problem: low math scores among 10th grade Hispanics, for example. But for schools like Eastside High School, the issue is where to start...African-American students falling behind in math? Here, seven students in 10 can't pass the state test. The national dropout epidemic? Students leave Southeast High at almost five times the state's goal. (Researcher Journal, p. 37)

Every Austin community member who reads this article knows that this school serves poor, black, brown, and immigrant students, so race and class are both text and subtext. This discursive context, articulating a local newspaper's deficit understandings, contextualizes participants' deficit understanding using a language of crisis pathology (Katz, 1989). Since I know many teachers and students that worked and studied at Eastside High School, what is missing is any representation of teachers' hard work and students' achievement.

Fourth, another deficit discursive context comes from Austin ISD's school attendance zones. In a campus governance meeting, a school district representative came to explain Eastside Middle's new zoning lines. Affixing the map to an easel prior to the meeting, all of the middle school attendance zones were visible to committee members. After viewing the map, the committee members became outraged at the gerrymandered lines that thinly snaked outlining a bridge across Lady Bird Lake to encircle two housing projects on the Southside. The committee, composed of Mexican- and African-American parents along with the Principal and predominantly teachers of color, became outraged at the gerrymandered "zones," and as a group, the committee questioned Eastside Middle's ability to maintain an "Acceptable" status in the state rating system given the influx of over one hundred new Title I students combined from the two housing projects. The meeting, as it wound down, turned farcical as members sardonically free-formed on school attendance zones across the district. I took notes on this meeting in the researcher journal:

> In these discussions, the political-racial inclinations of the Board were quite clear. I remember, as we [campus governance committee] all focused on our gerrymandered zones and the odd-ball other zones on the map that this nine-lives-bureaucrat had brought with him. Then David McGrady, just as our remonstrating was winding down, flipped the analytical frame very adeptly. He pointed out one very perfect and logical line: West Central Middle School's line. It was brilliant really, as a counter to all these gerrymandering lines and zones for Eastside schools. McGrady said, "Look at the story told by *West Central's line*. ...Doesn't *that* speak volumes? Lily-white, rich..." (Researcher Journal, p. 46)

The deficit discursive context of school attendance zones constituted, through gerrymandering practices, segregated "neighborhood schools." What was clear, and very much evident in McGrady's comment, is that the Board reproduced the *de facto* segregationist interests "of the groups or classes that actually rule society" (Counts, 1932/1978, p. 25). The overall impression I had, after working for Austin ISD for eight years, was that with Eastside schools – their attendance lines, programs, curriculum – anything was on the table for manipulation, experimentation, or even (now) closure.[4] Contrasting with wealthy and predominantly White Westside schools, these comprehensive schools remain in place with little if any suggestion of change. The Eastside gerrymandered school attendance zones, contrasting with the Westside clean and unencumbered zones, provide but one example of manipulations.

Returning to teachers' professional identifications, deficit discursive contexts reveal and emphasize that deficit thinking exists *not* only in teachers' "heads" but also intertwines into the material conditions that surround them in their work. Deficit discursive contexts, describing teachers and students' particular historical and social boundedness, provide a continuous barrage of "common sense" deficit understandings that constitute teachers' deficit understandings but also structure their teaching in material ways. From deficit discursive contexts, teachers' professional identifications, represented complex and contested terrains. Important for understanding teachers' professional identifications, deficit discursive contexts provide an important view into day-to-day work and material conditions of schools ignored in research on White teacher identity (e.g., McIntyre, 1998; McIntyre, 2002; Sleeter, 1992; Sleeter, 1993; Sleeter, 1995; Sleeter, 2002) yet visible in critical work on this topic (e.g., Anyon, 1995, 1997; Kozol, 2005). From deficit discursive contexts, a more subtle understanding of teachers' race-visible professional identifications emerge that describe pervasive common sense deficits intertwined with structural critiques of deficit understandings. Teachers in this study, it seems, are trapped by a dilemma of understanding structural oppression yet simultaneously imploring students and their families to "overcome" oppression through education's obvious yet uneasy relationship to the hegemonic center. Like teachers' contradictory structural and deficit understandings of difference, discursive contexts provide for the emergence of and discussion of a White-double-consciousness.

WHITE DOUBLE-CONSCIOUSNESS

In Working Across Student Differences

Teachers' contradictory structural and deficit understandings, bounded by deficit discursive contexts, tell quite a different and more complex story from existing research on White teachers' race-evasive identities (Berlak, 1999; Henze, Lucas, & Scott, 1998; Hyten & Warren, 2003, Marx, 2004, 2008; Marx & Pennington, 2003; McIntyre, 1998; McIntyre, 2002; Sleeter, 1992; Sleeter, 1993; Sleeter, 1995; Sleeter, 2002). Rather than understanding White teachers as "wrong-headed" depositories of race-evasive identities, teachers' life histories and teacher stories articulate race-visible professional identifications that narrate on-going tensions between structural and deficit understandings, even blending the categorical distinctions in fluid ways. Teachers, representing deficit understandings and experiencing deficit discursive contexts, also represented critical structural understandings that push back against deficit understandings yet did not cancel out those understandings. These contradictory tensions in teachers' understandings of student differences require the introduction of a new concept into the literatures on White teacher identity: *White double-consciousness*.

White double-consciousness, a complementary concept to W.E.B Du Bois's Black double-consciousness, provides an important extension of critical White studies currently omitted in the present. In Du Bois's (1903/1995) famous essay "On our Spiritual Strivings," Du Bois theorizes Black double-consciousness as a split-view into American life. Blacks, using Du Bois's language, find themselves in a dilemma of seeing themselves, always, through the dominant gaze of Whites and White culture. In knowing themselves through this White gaze, African Americans develop a split-view of themselves both as Americans and as Black Americans. Du Bois (1903/1995) explains:

> Negro is a sort of seventh son, born with a veil, and gifted with second-sight in this American world,—a world which yields him no true self-consciousness, but only lets him see himself through the revelation of the other world. It is a peculiar sensation, this double-consciousness, this sense of always looking at one's self through the eyes of others, of measuring one's soul by the tape of a world that looks on in amused contempt and pity. One ever feels his two-ness,—an American, a Negro; two souls, two thoughts, two unreconciled strivings; two warring ideals in one dark body...(p. 6)

Whiteness and White privilege, discussed in Chapter One along with White teachers' race-evasive identities, by-and-large affirm Du Bois's ground-breaking understandings on African-American and White identities. In understandings of

71

whiteness and White privilege, the identities of people of color are racialized, and White identities occupy the hegemonic center as universal "individuals" who see others' race but do not experience race themselves. Contrastingly, and supported also in Chapter Two's discussion on race-visible professional identifications, teachers in this study have a split-half view of structural and deficit understandings of difference. This race-visible split-half view, consistently demonstrated in Chapters Two and Three, seemingly question this understanding of Whites as non-racialized individuals and begin to suggest an understanding of White double consciousness seemingly overlooked in existing understandings of White identity.

Contrasting with the understanding of Whites as non-racialized universal "individuals," teachers in this study evinced both racial-structural understandings, and to a lesser degree, deficit understandings as clear patterns in life and teacher story interviews. Committed White teachers of inner-city students, while manifesting White privilege, expressed an acute split-view regarding students differences. In teachers' contradictory structural and deficit understandings of students' differences, a split-view and tension-filled White double-consciousness becomes visible. Privileged, contradictory, and un-resolved, this White double-consciousness emerges as confluence with race-visible professional identifications in which Whites are also racialized (Giroux, 1998; Kincheloe, 1999; Kincheloe & Steinberg, 1999) in the historical present. Teachers in this study, racialized in their contact with students and communities, did not *belong* on the margins yet seemingly perceived the "Other's" gaze and internalized it as counter-narrative ever-present in their stories. Teachers in this study did not see themselves as universal individuals but as Whites who implored in remonstrative ways as intermediaries and negotiators of a split-view that understood racialized historical and social oppression on the margins. Yet simultaneously, teachers in this study urged students and their families to heroically understand education as a means of overcoming structural oppressions. They did this despite an ever-encroaching feeling of being overwhelmed and frustrated, as the conclusion below will re-iterate.

This internalization of the "Other's" gaze, a reverse and privileged echo of Du Bois (1903/1995) Black double-consciousness, provides a life-history-and-teacher-story basis for beginning to theorize White double-consciousness in which White identities emerge, not as universal individuals, but as historically and socially White racialized beings understood through the gaze of people of color. White double-consciousness, for understanding teachers' White identities and White identities writ large, seems important in a future in which the number of Whites diminishes and numbers on the margins rise. It also seems important for understanding professional identifications in service professions such as teaching, nursing, and social work with predominantly White practitioners serving historically marginalized groups, and I think it provides and important pedagogical opening for teaching preservice and professional teachers on topics of race-visible professional identifications. This White double-consciousness, manifest in structural and deficit understandings, provides a new lead for understanding and teaching White teachers' and other professions' identifications.

CONCLUSION

A Narrative Vacuum: Stories of Frustration and Exhaustion

In Chapter Three, I attempt to further theorize committed White teachers' race-visible professional identifications. Teachers' race-visible professional identifications, intertwining structural and deficit understandings and discursive contexts, required an additional concept – *White double-consciousness* – to explain complicated and contested representations in split-half structural *and* deficit understandings of student differences. In articulating White double-consciousness, I have driven toward the excruciating center of contradictions, my own contradictions as well as those of teachers in this study.

After driving at the center of contradictions, the insights provided by the concept of White double-consciousness emerge as a narrative vacuum. White teachers' race-visible professional identifications, although promising in their race-visibility, structural understandings of difference, and relevance for teaching across difference, nonetheless appear to come up short, disappoint, go half-way in their deficit understandings of student differences. Unlike other understandings of culturally relevant teaching (e.g., Gay, 2000; Nieto, 1999; Ladson-Billings, 1995, 2009), teachers' race-visible professional identifications do *not* necessarily suggest that all will be well because of education, nor do they recount that typically American tale that education provides solutions to challenging historical, social, and even global conditions. The narrative vacuum, emphasized in the present chapter, represents the teachers' possible impotency to recreate the "victory narrative" (Cary, 1999, p. 414) with its feel-good ending assumed by many of culturally relevant teaching's interlocutors (e.g., Gay, 2000; Howard, 2006; Nieto, 1999; Ladson-Billings, 2009) and advocates of education for global economy.

Important in this narrative vacuum is an understanding that pedagogical solutions like those represented in race-visible professional identifications, serve meliorist ends. Race-visible professional identifications enable particular teachers and many of their students, yet structural inequalities, seemingly and continually reversed in "common sense" deficit understandings and discursive contexts, provide implacable historical and social material conditions that require structural transformation for real and lasting change in the United States. Cornel West (2001), in discussing structural and deficit understandings, describes the left-right double binds that these understandings create. West, in describing this left-right, structural-deficit double-bind, argues that only through ameliorating poverty and elevating material conditions is it possible to create dignity and lasting change:

> First, we must acknowledge that structures and [deficit] behaviors are inseparable, that institutions and values go hand in hand. How people act and live are shaped – though in no way dictated or determined – by the larger circumstances in which they find themselves. These circumstances can be changed, their limits attenuated, by positive actions to elevate living conditions. (p. 19)

David Tyack (1974), in commenting on John Dewey and his colleagues meliorist pedagogy, expressed that pedagogical solutions like the one expressed in teachers' race-visible professional identifications help students but also recreate inequalities in partially-kept and -fulfilled promises. After eighteen years in public schools and after having studied and narrated teachers' life histories and teacher stories, I agree with Tyack's somber assessment. Teachers' race-visible professional identifications, messy in their contradictions and partial promises, *provide for understanding and up-from-below descriptions of committed practices rather than neat programmed solutions to be administrated.*

In emphasizing historical and social understandings, I finish this chapter, emphasizing the narrative vacuum by narrating committed White male teachers' frustrations and exhaustion – evident in narratives above – leading with my own comments on my purpose as researcher in this chapter:

> We have to ask the hard questions and provide the difficult conditions because the work is hard. So, when I take up thinking, I make the thinking difficult, because you can't just say "I have the solution now," like too many multicultural education and critical theorists do. As a teacher, I never had "the solution" to teaching across differences. I had to continually think hard, drive at my own contradictions, become better, reinvent my practices. That's the point of this research. To engage preservice and professional teachers in complicated thinking they might extend into their reflective practices. (Researcher Journal, p. 39)

And onto the teachers' frustrations and exhaustion:

> Okay, you're [to student] right, you may need to be in a gang to survive out there or you may need to, you know, fight or may need to do this or that, but to be successful in business or to be successful in academia, to be successful in – in, you know, the way society is, you need to have – and it's unfortunate, but you need to have two sets of rules, two different ways that you act, and so often the students that I work with are right there on the fence and there's people tugging at them from either side, the street side and the school side, and you need to have to have a support system in – in – in place to push you one way or the other. Are you gonna be in the, you know, out there or are you gonna be in here? Well, then this is how you need to act in here. And having administration that'll back you up with discipline, when they bring in those street type behaviors, the drugs and the fighting and the weapons, and – and having a – a system set up with some real consequences is important because otherwise students don't choose. Or, I should say, by not choosing, they choose the street. (Mike Taymes, Interview 1b, p. 9)

***

You have a roomful of challenging kids and you know what they can do and you know what they can't do and you try very hard to get them to be able to do what you need them to do in order to pass this test, in order to be more literate. To be successful. Downtown, you know the teacher on the ground's perception of downtown is that there's whole lot of people down there and we're not entirely sure what they're all doing except you know, making more work for us in order to sort of, to make themselves feel like their, their you know, jobs are worth doing I guess. (Rudy Smith, Interview 2b, p. 14–15)

***

And there are a lot of things that I, I envision, and all of them have to do with teaching, teaching children. So I think teaching is who I'm supposed to be, but I'm not sure teaching remedial reading class is who I'm supposed to be. Know what I mean? I wish I could teach art, but I don't have a certificate for that. I mean I know teaching the resource class is doing a service that many in this school can't do, but it's not, it's not the, it's not the meaning that I'm gonna achieve. ... In fact, it almost feels like I'm overstaying my welcome in this profession right now. (Gene Johansen, Interview 3a, p. 20)

***

I think a lot of the lessons that don't work out well, um, fail because there's a lack of – of planning across the board, not just personal planning, but planning across the curriculum and planning – planning with colleagues. Um... It – it's – it's very difficult to – to – to plan with colleagues, um... Part of the difficulty comes from – from the fact that we're – we're often, um, pressed for time and in so many meetings that – that we don't really have time to sit down and do the – the – the planning that's – that's required, so I think a lot of the failure comes from the fact that things aren't planned, um, correctly the first time. (Bennett Ferris, Interview 4b, pp. 14–15)

***

I mean, really for the last 4 years just, at least 3 years, I was developing curriculum as I went. It wasn't so much okay, here's what I'm going to teach. It was simply okay, I'm going to try this out, and if it works great! I know what I'm doing. If not, then I'll realign and, you know, some of the meetings I would go to were okay, sometimes the meetings were useful to a degree. But all along, I'm trying to develop curriculum. I'm developing the curriculum because I'm in the classroom doing it. Or you have to have some kind of training and all you really needed, and you really wanted was some down time to simply think about what was successful and how to build on that, in the sense of curriculum development. Instead, I'm spending all this time at meetings and trainings. (Jack Springman, Interview 5b, pp. 14–15)

***

Most things that come from downtown are useless and that's central administration. They're reacting under pressure from the state, which is reacting under pressure from the feds, which is reacting under some sort of political pressure. Or even locally there's a political pressure and so therefore there's a, an adjunct that downtown to address that issue. AISD, God love 'em, they like to do 100 things half-assed instead of 10 really well. (David McGrady, 6b, pp. 14–15)

***

Not feeling supported by both your co-workers and uh, administratively… we have a one-size-fits-all accountability program from downtown. They continually ask: Why are you not looking the same exact way as the schools on other sides of the city. I want to say look at our schools, we do an excellent job given our circumstances, you know, it's frustrating. I accepted it, it's a necessary evil. We are an institution. (Trent Cowens, Interview 7b, p. 13)

***

I was generally more academic when teaching Pre-AP or other advanced sections. I was generally more experiential when teaching "regular" sections. There are no formulas, you've got to try stuff, in a very pragmatic sense, and see how it works. All delivery strategies are acceptable, but value the ones that make for independent learning and higher order thinking. At each turn, you've got to ask yourself, is this going to work? And, for example, if it's hard and necessary for kids to learn, like writing a multi-paragraph essay, then you have to ask yourself, even if it's not working so well because it's difficult, do students' have to know this? If so, I have to stand my ground, expend my authority, and make them learn it. It's very exhausting, so I continually ask myself: Is this piece of curriculum worth expending all of my authority on getting done? In the case of academic and personal essays, the answer to that question is "yes." So I slog through it, battling it out. (Frank Carmody, Interview 8b, p. 11).

***

NOTES

[1] Chapter Three reworks and further advances: Jupp, J.C. & Slattery, P. (2010). White male teachers on difference: Narratives of contact and tensions. *International Journal of Qualitative Studies in Education 23*(2), 199–215. Permission to rewrite this article for this book was obtained in May 2012.

[2] My understanding of the word "meliorist" in this description does not assume a facile belief in an ever-improving world. Rather, I take up the word meliorist, as does Kliebard (1995), in describing a complex progressive tradition in education and elsewhere. West (2004), as contemporary expositor of this tradition, understands that the meliorist tradition is *against-the-grain* and *against-the-odds*, perhaps tragic. West, it follows, argues we take up traditions of self-creation that I have called identifications: "The democratic fervour is found in the beacon calls for imaginative self-creating in Ralph Waldo Emerson, in the dark warnings of imminent self-destruction in Herman Melville, in the impassioned odes to democratic possibility of Walt Whitman…" (West, 2004, p. 22). West, critically engaged in the pragmatic actions, argues that we develop a moral compass and commitment

to continually do the right thing staring directly into the face of evil like that found in unequal schools. In critically engaged pragmatic actions, West finds the possibility and potential spark of democratic hope and change. Teachers' life and teacher stories, *against-the-grain* and *against-the-odds*, provide an example of West's "no guarantees" meliorist stance.

[3] In the spring of 2008, when Eastside Middle School eked out an acceptable classification after having slipped into an unacceptable one in the spring of 2007, administrators and teachers celebrated en masse. Unfortunately, Austin ISD's office staff reflected, greatly, the attitude of the Fordham Foundation report (2006). We had earned a D. Right after we had brought the campus back to "acceptable," one highly-ranked district official visited the campus and did not even mention it. Understandings like the one represented in the Fordham Foundation report (2006) constitute and reflect administrative understandings.

[4] Despite predominantly acceptable ratings at Eastside Middle, Austin ISD Central Office administration is replacing comprehensive schools with charters and academies, and one Elementary school has recently been closed and re-opened as a charter. Eastside Middle, once a comprehensive school, now requires an application as current district officials seemingly make plans to close it down despite having earned, predominantly, acceptable school ratings in state accountability systems. Westside and Northside schools serving rich, White constituencies, also earning predominantly acceptable ratings, continue their operations without any interruption. It seems that "school reform" and "charter schools" are both really about race, class, culture, and language *not* academic status.

WHITE PROGRESSIVE *MASCULINITIES?*

Counternarratives, Contradictions, and A Second Split-Half View

INTRODUCTION

A Lead-In Story Clip

The over-arching narrative of committed White male teachers' life stories recounted a self-distantiation from the Conservative Restoration and its received privileges. This over-arching narrative emphasized teachers' counternarrative identifications to White male privileges re-established in the Conservative Restoration of the 1970s and 1980s (Apple, 1993; Apple, 2000) that continues through the present (Reynolds & Webber, 2009). During this conservative era, teachers in this study attempted to live alternatively by developing lived counternarratives. Returning to Chapter One's definition, *counternarratives* refer to *small narratives that counter* " 'official' *and* 'hegemonic' *narratives of everyday life"* (Peters and Lankshear, 1996, p. 2; Bamberg, 2004; Bamberg & Andrews, 2004).

In the focus group meeting, teachers' counternarratives provided the centerpiece of the four-hour session. As teachers engaged each other on the emergent findings, a heated discussion on the meaning of their youthful illegal drug use developed. This discussion on youthful illegal drug use became emblematic of the counternarratives recounted in this chapter. In the discussion, Frank Carmody (Focus Group Meeting) provided the following counternarrative I use as a lead-in for Chapter Four:

> I remember voting for Ferraro and Mondale and I just remember thinking everything, I mean Reagan, was just totally fucked up. I mean I must have been 20–21 when all that was happening and thinking all of that was total bullshit. I couldn't stand it. I was aware politically and totally against every aspect of it. I remember Nancy Reagan coming on TV and saying *Just say no to drugs*, and we lit up a huge spleef and smoked it. [Laughter] (pp. 1–2)

Because all teachers in this study used (and later quit) illegal drugs during their youths, this clip provided a key story for understanding teachers' counternarrativized identifications. First, the clip countered a key semiotic of the Conservative Restoration: *The Reagan Presidency*. The Conservative Restoration, with the Reagan Presidency as pivotal sign, provided *the boundedness* against which teachers elaborated counternarrative identifications. Second, the clipping provided a vehement gut-level repudiation of the Reagan Presidency that emerged *not* as a logical political argument *but rather* as counternarrative *style*. Third, the clipping signaled a progressive masculinity, counternarrativizing hegemonic masculinity yet laden with contradictory privileges of self-distantiation on the margins. Overall, this clipping provides a lead-in story that begins to narratively frame teachers' *counternarratives* and *contradictions* taken up in this chapter.

Chapter Four Overview

In Chapter Four, I narrate complex progressive masculinities to inform male teachers' identities. Working with life story and teacher story interviews of White male teachers in inner-city schools, I contextualize this chapter with a story on my lived masculinity inside and outside the classroom that integrates a review of the literatures on male teachers. After contextualizing this chapter, I define and elaborate life history concepts including *identifications, counternarratives*, and *progressive masculinities* briefly defined and discussed in Chapter One. Further developed here, identifications, counternarratives, and progressive masculinities serve as concepts that help me narrate teachers' life stories. Key to teachers' progressive masculinities that emerge in this chapter are four counternarratives: 1) *illegal drug use*, 2) *process spirituality*, 3) *alternative or indie media*, and 4) *critical politics*. Through these counternarratives, teachers' progressive masculinities emerge from the stories as contradictory phenomena that simultaneously self-distance *yet* reify White male privileges. Like double-consciousness discussed in Chapter Three, teachers' progressive masculinities provide a second split-half view of White and male privileges that move precariously between political alliances and self-referential nihilism, potentials and impotencies.

LIFE HISTORY REVIEW OF LITERATURES

Second Option/Creativity

Like many male teachers, I got into teaching as a "second option" as literatures on male teachers confirm (Benton DeCorse & Vogtle, 1997; Cushman, 2005; Lortie, 1975). Teaching as "second option," not yet fully narrated in the literatures (Benton DeCorse & Vogtle, 1997; Cushman, 2005; Lortie, 1975), appeared to me as a lesser of evils. Coming from middle class and conservative West Houston, I took up teaching after having played in garage bands in the Austin music scene in the late 1980s during and several years after I attended the University of Texas as an undergrad student. Eventually becoming disenchanted with the scene's scope, I left the US disgusted with globalized neocon America, especially its social class divisions and vulgar careerist "success" stories of the late 80s and early 90s. I moved to Mexico as an expatriate and stayed there for ten years first in Mérida, Yucatán, while teaching in language schools for five years, and later, in Matamoros, Tamaulipas for another five while teaching in South Texas.

Good Role Model/Fucking Faggot

As I mentioned in Chapter One, over my eighteen years as a classroom teacher I taught in three separate Title I Schools. All of these schools served predominantly Mexican-American and Mexican immigrant along with African-American populations. These schools struggled, for the most part, with discipline issues and test scores, and having an orderly classroom and passing scores at the end of the year were most certainly considered "successful." Throughout the mid to late 1990s, I crossed the international border every day from Mexico to the United States teaching while earning my professional certificate and later my masters degree at the University of Texas at Brownsville. The Post-Baccalaureate Program in Texas provided me and other male teachers in this chapter with a privileged "glass escalator" (Williams, 1992, p. 263) that quickly elevated us into teaching without credentials. We could basically earn credentials *on the job*, which provided advantages for us but clear disadvantages for students.

My first public school position was in Los Fresnos, after being hired mid-year to replace a teacher whom the students had, as the Principal recounted, "run off because of classroom management issues." This pattern repeated itself six years later when I took an inner-city job in Austin, Texas when I was hired to take over classes of another teacher, as my Principal told me then, who "was going to quit because of her seventh period class." As gender issues literatures on male teachers indicate, principals often hire "male role models" to handle discipline for children "lacking" those models at home (Allan, 1993; Benton DeCorse and Vogtle, 1997; Cushman, 2008; Sargent, 2000) and thus assume and understand male teachers' masculinities along traditional lines (Francis & Skelton, 2001; Cushman, 2008). As a bilingual male who taught predominantly Mexican immigrant and Mexican-American students, I felt good when the Principal and other administrators started to write "good role model" in my walk-throughs and yearly evaluations, as I understood the complement in privileged and uncomplicated ways. Nonetheless, even though I became good at discipline and better at culturally relevant teaching (e.g., Jupp, 2004; Ladson-Billing, 1995; 2009), several male students over the years, when in a disciplinary pinch with me, would hiss behind clinched teeth: *You fucking faggot.* As it turned out, male teachers' masculinity, privileged with a "glass escalator" (Williams, 1992, p. 263) into the profession, turned out to be an easily disparaged double bind (Allan, 1993; Cushman, 2005; Sargent, 2000, 2004).

Way to Be

Despite this well-documented double bind in literatures on male teachers, teaching and being an educator turned out, nonetheless, to be a negotiated solution, recognizing male and White privileges (Hartman, 2002; McIntosh, 1988) yet providing a counternarrative identification I could live with. In teaching and being an educator of Mexican immigrant, Mexican American, and Latino students, I came across, through an encounter, a negotiated masculinity that provided alternative lived experiences I conceptualize in detail below as contradictory progressive masculinities.

LIFE HISTORY CONCEPTS

More on Capacitating Concepts

Life history research avoids understandings of essentialized group identities *and* essentialized "individuals" prefabricated in the left-right political spectrum. With this non-essentializing purpose in mind, I go more in depth on capacitating concepts presented in Chapter One and highlighted here. The concepts include *identifications, boundedness, counternarratives*, and *progressive masculinities*.

Identifications and Boundedness

Identifications, drawing on understandings of identity as self-narrativized (Bruner, 2002; Butler, 1999; Hall, 2003), understand identities as on-going private-and-public, personal-and-social activity and engagement with cultural, social, historical, and autobiographical resources. Macedo (2011), in discussing identifications, explains the individual's "self-determination – his or her relationship to structures – happens by identification processes" (p. 8). Identifications, in emphasizing processes, understand "lives" not as essentializing states of *being* but rather as social and historical processes of narrativized *becoming* which the individual engages in, elaborates on, and completes. Identifications, as they relate to teachers' life and teacher story interviews in Chapter Four, emphasize teachers' counternarrative identifications highlighting self-narrativized decisions within structured contexts I call boundedness.

Boundedness refers to structured contexts that, by degrees, structure and call identities into being through interactive processes. As teachers in this study came of age in the 80s and 90s, the Conservative Restoration provided the boundedness, broadly speaking, against which teachers' identifications emerged, though each respondent elaborated this boundedness in ways special to his own life story. Notably mapped by William Reynolds and Julie Webber (2009), the Conservative Restoration, began with the Nixon Presidency but clearly flourished by the early 1980s with Ronald Reagan as Christian patriarchal figure. The Conservative Restoration, as it co-constructed successful "identities," consolidated an ascendant agenda of hegemonic practices emphasizing essentialized and right-appropriated "individuals," Christian fundamentalist identities, and "competitor" identities for a global economy. Essentialized individuals, drawing on crude interpretations of the Jeffersonian tradition, legitimized resurgent White male authority in national politics, finance, international business, and correspondingly, the domestic sphere. Whiteness resurged as an epicenter for productive and patriotic individuals in which 50s and 60s Civil Rights struggles and US racialized history were diminished in importance or forgotten. Masculinities also received a makeover during the Reagan Presidency emphasizing and authorizing instrumental-technical meritocratic "success" over masculinities inherent in service themes of JFK's first inaugural address or 1960s protests and demonstrations. Christian conservative and fundamentalist values, "Biblical" though conspicuously absent in the Synoptic Gospels, organized political resentment against feminists, gays, poor people, and racialized "others." At the same time, fundamentalist values narrowed and castigated ecumenical process spirituality embraced, ostensibly, in 1960s pop stars' gurus. *Just say no* anti-drug campaigns, specifically Nancy Reagan's project, became public policy while, paradoxically, youth drug use rose into the early nineties. Visible in semiotic raced, classed, and gendered shorthand of the 80s and early 90s (MBA, CEO, BMW, CPA, IPO, takeover, power tie), the Conservative Restoration, emanated from the US and articulated an international historic bloc that privileged individualism, international corporations, free markets, and privatization as tough-minded, competitive, realist "common sense" for diminishing or dismantling "liberal" Great Society programs. Though this chapter focuses on lived masculinities, teachers' identifications, narrated below, emerge within boundedness in which politics, race, religion, pop media, and other discourses emerge as central to their progressive masculinities and counternarrative identifications.

Progressive Masculinities and Counternarrative Identifications

Working understandings of bounded identifications, progressive masculinities extend work in gender studies that understand gender as socially constructed. Rejecting reductions of gender to biological sex (Butler, 1999), masculinities writ large draw on gender as relational gestalt (Francis & Skelton, 2001) defining masculinity as active, logical, aggressive, and dominating and positioning femininity as quiescent, emotional, passive, and submissive. While recognizing and counternarrativizing hegemonic masculinities of the Conservative Restoration that bounded their lives, teachers' progressive masculinities attended to the production-consumption of masculinities that sought to reconfigure hegemonic masculinity *against-the-grain.*

Progressive masculinities, with the Conservative Restoration as boundedness, pushed against-the-grain of hegemonic instrumental, technical, and goal-oriented masculinities. Counter to masculinities of the Conservative Restoration, teachers' progressive masculinities actively sought to reconfigure notions of meritocratic success. In reconfiguring meritocratic success, teachers' progressive masculinities *did not* seek reversals that feminize men *nor did* progressive masculinities seek to "deconstruct" gender – both which appear as exhausted strategies in the present. Instead, teachers' progressive masculinities and counternarratived identifications attempted what Raewyn Connell (1987) describes as "the reconfiguring, by the dynamic of social relations, of the points of tension in personality development and the politics of personal life" (p. 224). Especially visible in Connell's (1995) life history research on progressive eco feminist men, this reconfiguration of the politics of personality, when

83

viable as progressive politics, emphasizes the centrality of an embodied "alliance politics" (Connell, 1995, p. 238) with "others." Connell explains (1995):

> What is involved here, rather than a men's movement, is *alliance politics*. Here the project of social justice depends on the overlapping of interests between interest groups (rather than the mobilization of one group around its common interest). (p. 238)

At this point, I reiterate that this chapter studies progressive masculinities of *White* teachers and should be understood as outlining an answer to the question: *What Are White Progressive Masculinities?*[1]

Important in teachers' progressive masculinities are counternarrative identifications. Counternarrative identifications, building on notions of counternarratives defined in the lead-in (Peters & Lankshear, 1996), highlighted identifications as sites of cultural consumption-and-production. Further, counternarrative identifications recognized the political potential in these narratives that offer complex representations *against-the-grain* of the Conservative Restoration. Specifically, teachers' progressive masculinities emerged along four counternarratives to the Conservative Restoration narrated in detail below: *illegal drug use, process spirituality, alternative or indie media,* and *critical politics*. Each of these counternarratives pointedly critiqued drug-free, White, Christian, meritocratic identities of the Conservative Restoration. Recognizing teachers' counternarrative identifications yet expanding foundational theorizing (Peters and Lankshear, 1996; Giroux, 1996; McLaren, 1996), counternarrative identifications, as articulated here, drive at counternarratives' contradictions (Bamberg, 2004; Bamberg & Andrews, 2004).

Teachers in this study developed counternarrative identifications that focused on "*doing* being critical" (Bamberg, 2004, p. 361). That is, *doing* being critical, as it relates to teachers here, laudably meant moving beyond discussing "the issues" and instead moved toward trying to *live differently, alternatively, against-the-grain in counternarrative style*. Nonetheless, counternarrative identifications, in articulating *doing* being critical, partially and paradoxically reify hegemonic and official messages they seek to critically *un-do*. Following Michael Bamberg's (2004) understandings of counternarratives, counternarrative identifications recognize and develop counternarratives' complexities, incongruencies, and contradictions inherent in ostensible "counternarratives." Bamberg explains (2004) the analytical position developed in counternarrative identifications discussed here:

> there are always certain aspects of dominant stories that are left intact, while others are reshaped and reconfigured. Speakers never totally step out of the dominating framework of the master narrative but always remain somewhat complicit and work with components and parts of the existent frame "from within." (p. 363)

Specifically, teachers in this study developed counternarrative identifications that distanced themselves from hegemonic or official messages of the Conservative

Restoration's emphasis on drug-free, White, Christian, meritocratic "individuals." Nonetheless, in developing counternarrative identifications, these teachers quite unconsciously reconstituted *subject strong identities* that also reify privileges.

Important to note, these counternarrative identifications, in developing progressive masculinities, re-constituted relevant historical identity resources. Specifically, counternarrative identifications and progressive masculinities clearly recreated inconformity and insurgent style of Beat (Burroughs, 1953/2003 Ginsberg, 1956/1973; Kerouac, 1965/1995) masculinities. Beat masculinities, in turn, worked with resources of Emersonian inconformity and anti-materialism in Thoreau and Whitman. Since all teachers in this study assumed heterosexual identities, perhaps Beat writer Jack Kerouac best recognized the contradictions inherent in teachers' progressive masculinities. Kerouac (1965/1995), in his penultimate novel, emphasizes contradictions in counternarrativizing his life against-the-grain:

> And also don't think of me as a simple character— a lecher, a ship-jumper, a loafer, a conner of older women… In fact, I don't even know what I was— Some kind of fevered being different as a snowflake. …In any case, a wondrous mess of contradictions (good enough, said Whitman) but more fit for Holy Russia of the 19th century than for this modern America of crew cuts and sullen faces in Pontiacs. (p. 257)

Kerouac's understanding of contradictions appeared at the center of teachers' counternarrative progressive masculinities. Contradictions, represented particularly in teachers' nihilisms that contrasted with critical politics, suggested progressive masculinities as a project "courting annihilation" (Connell, 1995; p. 136) yet driving at a "self-destructive utopia" (Tolson, 1977, p. 144).

COUNTERNARRATIVE IDENTIFICATIONS

Four Patterns

In this section, I articulate counternarrative identifications that begin to outline the contours of progressive masculinities. Although teachers' identifications in life story transcripts *all* articulated broad narrative patterns of *illegal drug use, experiential or process spirituality, alternative or indie media,* and *critical politics,* each life history below renders one counternarrative identification.

Dropping into Drugs

Rudy Smith dropped out of business school and into drugs. From San Antonio, Smith, whose childhood was thrust into poverty after his parents' divorce, recalled that his mom "kind of survived…was deeply, deeply in debt, but determined to get us through school and get us into college" (Interview 2a, p. 2). Rudy narrated having enjoyed school and that, in middle school, he "played in orchestra, that kind of,

I think, saved me" (Interview 2a, p. 2). Smith, by high school, was deeply involved in music, constant practice, and auditions, and when he was a senior he got fourth chair in all state orchestra and ended up with "music scholarships from different schools, from Baylor, I know, Rice, and I accepted the one from UT" (Interview 2a, p. 21). As it turned out, Smith had planned to use his scholarship, not to advance his love of studying music but rather for access to the UT business school. Smith accepted the scholarship to UT, as he reported, because it "didn't require me to be a music major" (Interview 2a, p. 21). Following a through-line of scholarship, meritocratic success, and a bootstraps narrative favorably recreated in the Conservative Restoration, Smith started studying business at UT's prestigious Red Combs Business School— but that did not last long.

After despising business classes for a few semesters, Smith "just stopped going to class and wasn't very surprised to get a round of Fs in the mail" (Interview 2a, p. 2). Having dropped out of business school and lost his scholarship, he quit playing in orchestras and left the viola behind. At this time, Smith entered a period of experimentation he described as "spiritual in that I was learning things about myself, I guess, and, you know, it was a period of – of growth" (Interview 2a, p. 11). Smith, having severed ties with music and the university, took up restaurant work at the Magic Mushroom for several years, which turned out, as was common in Austin, to be a drug scene. Smith, especially animated in recounting this life story segment, narrated:

> I was living with a friend and we moved in with two other friends and I can't remember how it all shook out, but we were both working at the Magic Mushroom, that restaurant, and we were offered an opportunity to move into a house with three fellows…much bigger than the little two-bed – room apartment that we were sharing with two other guys, so we decided to go ahead and do it, and we moved into this place and it was five of us, and it immediately turned into, like, the scene house for the – the restaurant. We met a fellow who was a chemistry major at UT and he had a – this is his story, but he was a very smart guy and I tend to trust him, but he had researched and found out certain narcotics that JFK was taking at the – in the White House [laughs], he said, "This is the X that JFK took." Anyway, I don't know what he made, but he made this huge bag of – of X and that summer he made a great deal of money, and we had a great many parties, and I made a lot of friends, and eventually stopped going to school. I did a lot of acid, did a lot of X, did as much coke as we could find, speed, as much pot as we could smoke, liquor, just to sort – liquor and beer, just to sort of even things out. (Interview 2a, pp. 8–9)

In reflecting on this part of this narrative, Smith continued

> For me personally it was – it was experimenting not just with drugs, but with the whole lifestyle; up unto that point in my life I had been very cautious and careful, and this was the first time in my life that I went out of my way to not

be cautious and to not be careful. I took – threw caution to the wind and, you know, it wasn't – the drugs were sort of a part of it, they weren't necessarily the – the – the point of it, they were just part of it. It was – yeah, it was very spiritual in that I was learning things about myself, I guess, and, you know, it was a period of – of growth and it was the first time, you know, in my life that I was out on my own and having to – to depend on myself to get by, and I made a lot of mistakes, you know, and I messed up some things, but I can't really say I regret having done it. (Interview 2a, p. 11)

Difficult to locate on a left-right political spectrum, nonetheless, Smith's dropping out of UT business school after having spent countless hours in practice rooms getting into it, provided a pointed counternarrative identification in relation to the Reagan Presidency's mantra of *Just Say No* to drugs. After all, UT's Red Combs school of business, one of many nationally recognized centers of conservative intellectual production for supply-side economics, privatization, trickledown theories, and rugged entrepreneurial individualism (Giroux, 2011), promoted and authorized the Conservative Restoration's meritocratic "success stories."

Smith's dropping out business school into a drug scene and following a path of "spiritual growth" (Interview 2a, p. 11), echoed Beatnik counternarratived identifications and masculinity (Kerouac, 1958/1976) found also in Connell's (1995) eco-feminists. Rudy, an upwardly mobile member of the working class, counternarrativized masculine privileges, not with logical political arguments, but with masculine alternatives that, as this chapter argues, tied tightly into progressive masculinities. Following Connell's eco-feminist men (1995), *all* teachers engaged in (and later quit) illegal drugs in counternarratives that Smith's life story emphasized.

In closing, Smith mentioned that the social learning he did during this time, especially at the restaurant, was important to becoming a teacher. Smith recalled that, working in this scene, he had to developed confidence, eye contact, an ability to project a persona, and ultimately a "shtick that as a teacher came back to me" (Interview 2a, p. 8).

Spiritual Connections

After a period of spiritual questioning, Gene Johansen found his connection working with children in the Arizona juvenile offenders system. From a family reflecting New Orleans working class "poverty values" (Interview 3a, p. 2), Johansen recalled being "the first generation in my family to go to college...or with any significant education, really" (Interview 3a, p. 2). Within a conservative Southern working class background, Johansen emphasized his family's very traditional roles:

Women were treated as the ones who always had to do the cooking and cleaning. Men were traditionally the bread winners. Although the women sometimes took jobs, they were not important jobs." (Interview 3a, p. 2)

In recounting his Southern working class identifications, Johansen recalled "coming from an extremely racist place, and my, my parents, especially from one side of my family, were extremely racist, just refusing to have anything to do with Blacks or Mexicans" (Interview 3a, p. 3).

Having disliked schooling, Johansen recounted that he had "just barely passed" (Interview 3a, p. 8), though he reported having learned a lot and especially having enjoyed liberal arts and humanities with a special knack for art. Upon graduating from high school, Johansen studied at the University of New Orleans, which, he described, "basically as a business college" (Interview 3a, p. 8), where he earned a degree in graphic design, and thereafter, he worked as a bar tender and freelance artist. Three years into freelance work, he moved to LA and continued freelancing while studying graphic design at Cal Arts where he became involved in alternative art and music scenes. Eventually tiring of freelance work's continual feast-or-famine economy, he returned to New Orleans, where he initiated a period of spiritual searching in his late 20s and early 30s, which led him into teaching inner-city children in the corrections system.

As he narrated in his life story interview, Johansen "started looking for meaning in my life and the world in general…I wanted to still be part of some sort of spiritual philosophy" (Interview 3a, p. 17). As Johansen (Interview 3a) elaborated,

> So I, I got into for a long time reading the Bible, reading the Bibles and different in all of its different incarnations and then reading Native American shamanism stuff and then got into Buddhism and Zen Buddhism, and even looked at Islam for a while. I just explored all these different religions trying to find something that sort of clicked for me. And got into meditation and yoga. And I don't know how to, I guess I've never really resolved anything. I haven't really decided on one, but I sort of came to an understanding that that made as much sense as could be made out of all of it, with absolutely no proof anywhere, ever. (p. 17)

It was during this same period that Johansen started subbing in schools, and then the first summer after subbing, he took his first real step, as he recalled it, to becoming a teacher by working with kids in the juvenile offender system as part of an Arizona wagon train:

> …And then, as a substitute teacher you don't work in the summer, so during that summer I took a job in Arizona working on a wagon train. This is where a lot of these thoughts finally came together, because I was able to lay out under the stars every night and just think…. The job was working with incarcerated kids, and this was like a last chance, before prison, and I was pretty well-suited for it having worked on a ranch with horses and stuff, and we had to hook these horses up to a, an actual wagon train, horses and mules, and take them down the back roads from Utah down to the southern Arizona and back and forth. And I did that for about five months. And decided if there was a job harder

than this, that, there was no job harder than this in the entire universe. It was the hardest job ever. But it was all at-risk kids from California and Arizona and most of them were in gangs and most of them, all of them were in jail for dealing drugs...And I really got close to some of the kids and decided that I wanted to do this kind of work. (Interview 3a, p. 18)

Johansen, whose narrative took up process spirituality as a resource for connecting to "incarcerated kids" (p. 18), counternarrativized his identification, again, like Smith above, in very pointed oppositional ways to the Conservative Restoration's emphasis on fundamentalist Christianity, meritocratic "success," and rugged individualism.

Like Connell's (1995) eco-feminist men, *all* teachers recounted self-effacing spiritual counternarrative identifications tied to progressive masculinities. This reworking of spirituality, which directly took up "Buddhism and Zen Buddhism" (Gene Johansen, Interview 3a, p. 17) among other spiritual resources also echoed Beat (Kerouac, 1958/1976) and 1960s (Watts, 1966/1989) spiritual pluralism as a counter-narrative for American materialism and meritocracy.

In closing, it is important to emphasize the direct relationship of Johansen's search for spiritual connection with teaching. As Johansen narrated, his search for spiritual connections that made him decide "I wanted to do this kind of work" (Interview 3a, p. 18).

Good Enough for Garage Bands

Trent Cowen found "success" in a bad business. Cowens' interest in and love of music, specifically alternative music, drowned out any other topic that emerged in his life story interview. Cowens, who recounted privileged boundedness, recalled growing up "in Maryland, a suburban of Washington DC" (p. 1), being "fairly religious," (p. 1), and attending "Catholic Schools" (Interview 7a, p. 1) up until high school. Cowens narrated a childhood focused on a living in a tight family, getting in trouble at school, doing Catholic community service, and being involved in sports and music, but "mostly music" (Interview 7a, p. 3). As Cowens recounted in his life story interview, he excelled at music "so music became a big part of my life" (Interview 7a, p. 2).

Cowens, who moved to Austin in 1995 to play in "garage bands and the type of thing" (Interview 7a, p. 3), narrated the importance of music in middle and high school:

I loved being in band, the bass tuba, the bass guitar in jazz band and that became a pretty big focal point in my life through middle and up into high school. ... Jr. High, in the 8th grade, the band director gave me the bass guitar and said you're the bass player in the jazz band because I was the only one who could read bass clefts that wasn't already playing in the jazz band so I had to learn on my own, never took a lesson ...Uh. I also got into bands with some friends in high school and again, uh, ended up playing sort of that classic rock type of music. (Interview 7a, p. 3)

89

Disinterested in "hair metal" like Bon Jovi, Poison, and other pop acts, Cowens reported having listened to "Black Sabbath, which was what the grunge guys had been listening to" (Interview 7a, p. 4), and this discussion of grunge bands, like Nirvana and Pearl Jam, led into a discussion of his engagement in alternative music.

Later, while earning a degree in history at Fordham University, Cowens' activity in music linked directly to alternative music in New York City.

> Uh, in college in New York City I met a lot of people who were into alternative which was breaking out a lot in the early '80s and punk rock and I went to some pretty intense hard core shows in Greenwich village at some little clubs which really turned me on...Something I always felt that I was never good enough to be a professional musician but good enough to play in garage bands and that type of thing. Moving to Austin was, one of the reasons I moved here was to continue doing that.... (Interview 7a, p. 3)

In discussing alternative music of the 90s, Cowens recounted:

> ...because from junior high up until high school what was going on was hair metal and pop bullshit and if you weren't in to this thing, you didn't have a lot of options, at least as, again, as a kid who wasn't so in to it... so as alternative became more uh, visible as a music and it was just different, it was not as macho, slightly androgynous with things like and the Smiths and less ego than a lot of the metal stuff were. That's what really, alternative was to me you know... (Interview 7a, p. 4)

Explicitly, as Cowens and other teachers indicated (Interview 5a; Interview 8a), alternative music involved a different masculinity that "was not as macho, slightly androgynous ... less ego" (Interview 7a, p. 4) than the hyper-masculinity of hair metal bands or other "classic" rock bands like the Rolling Stones, Led Zeppelin, or Aerosmith. Cowens and other teachers (Interview 5a, Interview 8a) directly referenced masculinity in alternative music mirrored by Kurt Cobain's contradictory statements like "I wanted to have the worship of John Lennon but have the anonymity of Ringo Starr."

Cowens, whose suburban boundedness sharpened his perceptions of privilege, also directed comments toward the contradictory character of alternative music:

> In high school, it was REM, and the Smiths and the Cure and if you were more radical it was the Dead Kennedys and uh, oh, Government Issue or GI and what was that band in DC that was so big, Fugazzi. ...Kids then entered the college, it was very, it was the college music scene at that point it was CMJ was the magazine, *College Music Journal* that you would get to find out what was going on in the college music scene. And pretty soon it became pretty funny as grunge blew up in 91 or 92, the alternative became the mainstream. (Interview 7a, p. 4)

Cowens, finishing his narrative on alternative music, drove at its contradictions describing it as "the college music scene" (Interview 7a, p. 4), and, in the end, referencing how "alternative became mainstream" (Interview 7a, p. 4). In discussing his present band, Cowens distanced himself from the 90s alternative scene by saying "instead of jumping on the grunge bandwagon, we seemed to be going back to our early alternative…they are 70s influences, Iggy Pop and stuff" (Interview 7a p. 5). Cowens, as he continued his work in bands, understood it within a broader garage band tradition that included "Punk's holy trinity – the Velvet Underground, Iggy and the Stooges, and the MC5" (Kaye, 1987, p. viii).

Similar to Smith's dropping out of business school and into a drug scene or Johansen's embrace of self-effacing spirituality, Cowens' engagement in garage bands as "musical tradition" also contests the Conservative Restoration's meritocratic "success," yet unlike Kurt Cobain's grand suicide as comment, Cowens recognized and lived with the contradictions of such a move. "Bad Business," the name of Cowens' band, specifically alluded to anti-careerist identifications, turning "success" in business on its head in postmodern counternarrative identification.

In closing, Cowens specifically related this counternarrative identification to teaching as his way in the world and as critical ethics for his students. Regarding teaching, Cowens (Interview 7b) commented that teaching represented an alternative "way to craft a living" (p. 17), and as he taught students, he recognized that they come from a different background but narrated a critical approach that emphasized "after knowing how the system works they [students] might say 'fuck you, I get your system and I'm going to work out my own way of success'" (p. 17).

The Political is Personal

David McGrady provided predominantly a political voice, though he privately insisted his teaching not be reduced to politics. Though all teachers in this study developed counternarrative identifications through critical or left progressive politics, McGrady's life story interview emphasized a political voice that carried over into his teaching.

McGrady, in his teacher story interview, discussed *de facto* segregated schools of the present "as not that much different than oh, I don't know, 59, 60 in Austin" (Interview 6b, p. 8) of *de jure* segregation. Echoing Kozol's (2005) concerns for inequality, McGrady commented on unequal physical facilities, dank restrooms, and shabby equipment for his students in comparison to students in White and middleclass schools on the Westside:

> To me it kind of boils down to looking at a guerilla video I talked about where you go into and you take a picture of just the exact physical facility and compare it to the exact physical facility of Eastside Middle School and say well… Is this equal? And what, and I would like to have people either tell what they felt or thought about that question or fill out a questionnaire. 'Cause it's not equal… and uh, I think the district re-segregated. (Interview 6b, p. 7)

And McGrady's political voice carried into his teaching:

> Well, when we talk about culture, I mean, what we start with is, is race [because it] is very important to them, they're highly sensitized to it. Uh. So every year at the beginning, I try to get them to think about that, and what does it mean? How would it be different if you were White? I mean, that's one of my warm ups. Uh. At the beginning of the year I ask how would it be if you were White? Also with students' culture, I mean, uh, I try to use it challenge them in discussions. We talk about *la migra*, we talk about immigration laws, we talk about voting, we talk about not voting, we talk about paying taxes and what taxes do, we, we talk about the economy and jobs what work is and what's work like in your family, and we talk about work and class. (Interview 6b, pp. 12–13)

McGrady's teacher stories, concerned with conscientizing students, narrated political topics relevant to community and students' lives such as segregation, race, White identity, *la migra*, immigration laws, voting, taxes, work, economics, and social class in order to "challenge them [students] in discussions" (Interview 6b, p. 13). Given that McGrady came from a political family, his connection of teaching and politics made sense.

McGrady, the oldest teacher in this study, grew up in the 1970s and came of age in the early 80s, though his memories of the 1960s were vivid. In recalling his childhood, McGrady recalled his father as a "big shot who worked with Governors Price Daniels and John Connelly" (Interview 6a, p. 2). McGrady's father later moved to Washington DC to work for the Johnson Administration, and in the Johnson Administration, McGrady recounted his father's work for "the Federal Water Pollution Control Administration which was the forerunner of the EPA" (Interview 6a, p. 8). When McGrady started attending school, he recounted:

> My parents wouldn't let me go to the local school because it was completely segregated, and instead I went to Woodridge 'cause it had Black students in it and this would have been in 1963. (Interview 6a, p. 1)

McGrady, narrating his early years, referenced "Martin Luther King's I Have A Dream speech" (Interview 6a, p. 2), the assassinations of JFK and RFK, the King assassination, Nixon's 1968 victory, the Vietnam War, race riots, his big sister's hippy identification, and her influence on his counter-narrativized identification that spanned the 1970s. McGrady also recalled that, due to his dad's ascendance in politics followed by other career opportunities, the family had moved constantly living in Austin, Washington DC, New Jersey, Houston, and Dallas, always following his dad's career by uprooting the family over-and-over again.

By the mid-1970s, McGrady's involvement in post-hippie counter-culture surged:

> I was a freak by then. …You didn't do what everybody expected you to do. You were turned on. Uh. You loved rock and roll music. Uh, you liked being thought

of as different and weird. Or not even different. Uh. I used it [freak identity] like a weapon a lot of times with authority figures and stuff. And later on I was President of my class again and I had hair down to my shoulders and beyond when I was elected that way …I mean it was like things were gonna change, man. This was change and things were changing. You weren't gonna just work for nothin' all your life with nothin to show for it except some pension and a gold watch. Uh, but if you wanted to do something weird it was entirely acceptable as long as you didn't hurt yourself or anybody else. (Interview 6a, p. 28)

Very explicitly, David understood, as other teachers in this study emphasized, alternative stylistics as political: "I mean it was like things were gonna change, man. *This was change* and things were changing" (Interview 6a, p. 28) [emphasis added]. David, in culminating this period in his life story, reported on dropping out of the university, moving to Ireland (the family's ethnic homeland), and taking on an expatriate identification through the mid-1980s, all of which extended his self-education through study of history and literature.

By his return to the US during Reagan's second term, David's counternarrative identification had suffered a complete collapse of meaning. By 1990, David found himself a thirty-two year old drug addict and alcoholic without strong family connections and with only a few over-extended friendships based on "using." During this period, David slipped into several periods of deep depression while working off-and-on in construction, and he was still drinking and using drugs. After two suicide attempts, David joined alcoholics anonymous, got straight using the steps, paid his way through college, earned an education degree, and re-created himself from top-to-bottom as a teacher of inner-city students where he worked until his retirement in 2011.

Over the years in professional interactions and friendships, McGrady and I would discuss national, state, community, and school politics, and in our discussions, there was always a point – after much debate and discussion – that he would turn his political identity toward the personal:

I got into teaching because I wanted to help people. I wanted to teach middle school because that was the time in my life where everything went off track. That was the time that – because my father was always working – working even in a different cities from Austin and I never saw him. I started getting into trouble, trouble with alcohol and you know, drugs. I got into teaching because I wanted to help kids *not do what I did*. [McGrady's emphasis]. I wanted to guide them so that they wouldn't have to be in the same circumstance that I was at thirty-two, with two suicide attempts, hopeless, and a drug addict. (Researcher Journal, p. 47)

In reviewing the transcripts, focus group meeting, and researcher journal on David, I think he made this point in a didactic way for me, to remind me that teaching cannot be reduced to politics.

ADDITIONAL PATTERNED SUPPORT

Analysis of Narratives

Each counternarrative pattern – *illegal drugs, process spirituality, alternative or indie media,* and *critical politics* – cut across all teachers' life stories, as these counternarrative identifications emerged in the "paradigmatic analysis of narratives" (Polkinghorne, 1995, p. 13). This section, supporting the life histories above, provides further patterned support for teachers' counternarrative identifications represented above. The following table (see pp. 95–96) provides an overview of the counternarratives that appeared in each teachers' life and teacher stories. I interpret each counternarrative pattern in the corresponding subsections that follow.

Illegal Drug Use

All teachers in this study reported on using (and later quitting) illegal drugs. Narrated above in Rudy Smith's life story, teachers' life story interviews narrated, predominantly, an understanding of life style, male camaraderie, drug scenes, and counternarrativized opposition. Of all teachers in this study, only David McGrady referred to the meaning of the drug experience following 1960s representations (Leary, 1983/1990), as "cosmic" (Interview 6a, p. 19). Other teachers, rather than narrating cosmic insights, instead narrated a counternarrative or oppositional style (Willis, 1975/1993) that focused on abilities such as handling "the street," being able to "score" drugs, having "snap" around police, or hanging out in music or drug "scenes." Frank Carmody's commentary, serving as introduction to this chapter, exemplified the counternarrative style in narrating Nancy Reagan's Just Say No speech during which he and his friends "lit up a huge spleef and smoked it" (Focus Group Meeting, p. 2). Supporting the understanding of illegal drug use as counternarrative style, teachers in this study emphasized drug use in terms of "Southern Cal time" (Gene Johansen, Interview 1a, p. 12), contradicting "what you are hearing from the government" (Mike Taymes, Focus group meeting, p. 20), escaping "the insanity of middle class life" (Jack Springman, Focus Group Meeting, p.19), and engaging in intellectual "counter-cultural activities" (Bennett Ferris, Interview 4a, p. 11). It is important to note, and clearly represented in Rudy Smith's (Interview 2a) life story above, "the drugs were sort of a part of it, they weren't necessarily the – the – the point of it" (p. 11). With the exceptions of David McGrady's "cosmic" (Interview 6a, p. 19) references regarding illegal drug use, teachers in this study narrated youthful engagement not for lived insights that drugs provided but rather as an expression of counternarrative style (Willis, 1977; Willis, 1975/1993). This finding clearly extends Willis' (1975/1993) work on illegal drug use conducted at the Centre for Cultural Studies at the University of Birmingham in which drug use is identified as counter-hegemonic youth culture. This counternarrative style, particular to each teacher's life story, provided a masculine bravado that countered

	Illegal drugs	Alternative media or life style	Experiential or process spirituality	Critical politics
Mike	I think illegal drug use definitely reinforced the mind set of this government is corrupt, and the more positive experiences with drugs contradicts what you are hearing from the government or the media. (Focus group meeting, p. 20)	I was really into hip hop, I had always been. … and that was my first exposure to some really underground rap, and stuff back then (Interview 1a, p. 5)	My Buddhist practice allows me to be the best educator I can be because I do not pawn off responsibility to students, parents or administrators. Instead I rack my brain for a way to touch the lives of my students based first on my prayer for a positive impact. (Interview 1c, p.1)	And – and instead of looking, you know, about unfair things like poverty, instead of really attacking those, too often I feel like people in the community are just being criminalized, you know, locked up.… (Interview 1b, 13)
Rudy	I made a lot of friends, and eventually stopped going to school. I did a lot of acid, did a lot of X, did as much coke as we could find, speed, as much pot as we could smoke… (Interview 1a, p. 9)	Rudy and I [Researcher] brought our guitars and played a few songs. We talked about having gone to shows at Liberty Lunch, and we realized that we had both seen the Butthole Surfers and other bands play at Liberty Lunch. (Researcher Journal, p. 42)	… the drugs were sort of a part of it, they weren't necessarily the – the – the point of it, the were just part of it. It was – yeah, it was very spiritual in that I was learning things about myself, I guess, and, you know, it was a period of – of growth (Interview 2a, p. 11)	And I think diversity in literature – that's important especially in an English class where a lot of the canon of high-brow literature is dead White men. (Interview 2b, p. 6)
Gene	And it was, you know smoking some ganja in the back yard underneath the, underneath the orange tree and pulling one or two off whenever you got a little thirsty or hungry and eating an orange, spitting out the seeds and laying out in the sun, for days. (Interview 1a, p. 12)	I was going to see a lot of alternative music, hanging out with musicians and artists and seeing lots of plays and experimental art shows. (Interview 3a, p. 14).	So I, I got …reading the "Bibles" in all of their different incarnations and then reading Native American shamanism stuff and then got into Buddhism and Zen Buddhism.… (Interview 4a, pp. 17)	It's just, it's just lingering, many, many years' worth of repression by White people. I don't know, it's pretty obvious; I don't need to go into that, do I? (Interview 4b, p. 2)
Bennett	Well, the times we spent, um, in these counter-culture activities, ah, to me were – were some very important intellectual, ah, experiences combined with smoking marijuana. (Interview 4a, p. 11)	Also another counter-culture element, um, was, like my commitment to, ah, to a vegan lifestyle, which happened in about 1989 and that – especially living in the – in East, Texas, that put me pretty – pretty far out there. … (Interview 4a, p. 14)	I kind of leaned towards the – the, ah, the Hindi and the Buddhist, ah, interpretation of spirituality in understanding veganism. (Interview 4a, pp. 17–18)	I see primarily Hispanics, ah, Hispanic population income also relatively low. Um, that's contrasted with the, um, the – the schools on the west side and on the north where I see the students as primarily – um, White middle class (Interview 2b, p.3)

(Continued)

(Continued)

	Illegal drugs	Alternative media or life style	Experiential or process spirituality	Critical politics
Jack	I used drugs because it was completely useful to me – a medication for the insanity of middle class life in Orange County. (Focus Group Meeting, p. 19)	Let's see, the alternative music thing was, I would say really significant and, you know, the music also kind of ties into the film also and the literature at the same time. Although music was definitely the leader of the three. (Interview 5a, p. 7)	So I decided to follow this alternative path…And it led to teaching children, diverse groups of children. It provides a sort of separateness from the norm, and I value that. … it's living differently. (Interview 4b, p. 15)	Ah, "white-centric" is almost like a superiority thing it's almost like, not so much overt racism, but the kind of position that, well the White man is the top and everything trickles down from him. (Interview 5b, p. 1)
David	I was well to at that point and I just mean I was a daily user. I mean I wasn't shooting drugs or snorting them yet, daily or anything. I loved psychedelics. We used to pick mushrooms by the grocery paper bag full. (Interview 6a, p. 29)	Being a freak? Well, uh, you didn't do what everybody expected you to do. You were turned on. You loved rock and roll music. Uh, you liked being thought of as different and weird.… I used it as like a weapon a lot of times with authority figures and stuff. (Interview 6a, p. 29)	And there was the coastline of Ireland outside of Dublin [expat "homeland"]. I was like "Fuck, I have found it!" (Interview 6a, p. 36)	Uh. 'Cause it's not equal and it's not, and uh, I think we re-segregated…I'll bet it's not that much different than oh, I don't know, 59, 60 [legal segregation] in Austin… (Interview 6b, p. 8)
Trent	Um, yeah as soon as you get into music, marijuana, pot was there and it was like awesome. This is what I have been waiting for all my life. (Interview 7a, p. 8)	Uh, in college in New York City I met a lot of people who were into alternative which was breaking out a lot in the early '80s and punk rock and I went to some pretty intense hard core shows (Interview7a, p. 3)	Fuck you, I get your system and I'm going to work out my own success." … I chose teaching. Teaching does not have money or status attached but it does have cred. (Interview 7b, p. 17)	The West side of Austin, the wealthier side of Austin, regardless of race, blames the individual…I think ultimately if you keep looking back it's the society has failed. (Interview 7b, p. 5)
Frank	But by my senior year in high school, I was smoking dope constantly. (Interview 8a, p. 6)	I remember my first time at the Beach [alternative music club]. The True Believers were playing the Velvet Underground's "Foggy Notion" which they used to segue into the Ramones' Beat on the Brat. 'Motherfucker… my cup runneth over,' I smiled inwardly. (Interview 8a, p. 9)	But my serious study and concern for the truth value of the Bible led me on a dilemma way of thinking until Chris quoted the Buddhist monks: "Reason makes a good slave but a terrible master." (Interview 8a, p. 5)	It must be said, that all of this was happening (respondent's youth) within a totally White center of gravity. These types of concerns, from my point of view in the US, seem to be classed and raced. (Frank Carmody, Interview 8a, pp. 6–7)

official messages, especially, of the Conservative Restoration's drug-free, White, male linked ostensibly to careerism, consumerism, and upwardly mobile White identities of that period. Nonetheless, the subject strong identity noted in the term *bravado* begins to point toward this counternarrative identifications' contradictions.

Alternative or Indie Media

Besides engaging in illegal drug use, all teachers in this study reported on immersing themselves in alternative or indie media. Exemplified in Trent Cowen's life story above, alternative or indie media took distinct counternarrative forms that included film, literature, internet sites, revisionist history, visual media but especially music (Frith, 2003). Alternative or indie media, "alternative" even in its descriptor, articulated teachers' desires to live differently and supported communities of like-minded individuals with similar aims. Like Jack Springman recounted, teachers in this study articulated that "music was definitely the leader" (Interview 5a, p. 7) in relation to other media. Teachers in this study emphasized, for example, "hip hop" (Mike Taymes, Interview 1a, p. 5), "punk" (Frank Carmody, Interview 8a, p. 4, Trent Cowens, Interview 7a, p. 3), "rock and roll" (David McGrady, Interview 6a, p. 28), "alternative music" and art shows (Gene Johansen, Interview 3a, p. 14; Jack Springman, Interview 4a). Regarding the focus on alternative or indie music, Frank Carmody's (Interview 8a) passion for this unofficial knowledge is emblematic:

> I took it [music] extremely seriously. I listened to all of it, especially punk rock, with a lot of passion for its unofficial message about drugs and experience. It pointed in a lot of different directions. I ended up listening to P-funk, Muddy Waters, Howlin' Wolf, Mingus, Miles, Bird, —and I mean studying it, musically. Let me add to this list—Sex Pistols, Ramones, Doors, Richard Hell, Lou Reed, Velvets. I learned to play, and I dug it. (p. 4)

Teachers' engagement in alternative media with an emphasis on music paralleled, very closely, cultural critic Giroux's (1996) understanding of 1990s "slacker culture." In commenting on slacker culture, Giroux emphasized that "youth are increasingly faced with the task of finding their way through a decentered cultural landscape..." (p. 74). All teachers' engagement in alternative and indie media provided narrative empirical data supporting the decentered task adroitly theorized by Giroux (1996), and five of the eight teachers reported on using alternative media as part of their regular teaching. These same five teachers, according to their life story interviews, understood teaching in inner-city settings as a logical extension of alternative identifications developed during their youths. Emblematic of these five teachers' direction, Jack Springman (Interview 5b) explained his position during member checking sessions:

> I decided to follow this alternative path down to its logical conclusion, wherever that leads me. And it led to teaching children, diverse groups of children. (p. 15)

97

Tied up in self-distantiation from the Conservative Restoration, teachers in this study counternarrativized dominant representations through sincere, albeit, contradictory and at times simplistic engagement in "alternatives" from hegemonic norms.

Experiential or Process Spirituality

Besides engaging illegal drug use and alternative media, all teachers in this study articulated an anti-materialist experiential or process spirituality. Four of the teachers' narratives focused on an anti-materialist experiential spirituality. Representative of anti-materialist spirituality, these teachers emphasized "living differently" (Jack Springman, Interview 4b, p. 15), having "found it!" in expatriate life style (David McGrady, Interview 6a, p 36), valuing "cred" over money (Trent Cowens, Interview#7b, p. 17), or reporting on drug use as "spiritual" growth (Rudy Smith, Interview 2a, p. 11). Important in these four teachers' narratives was an anti-materialist ethical content that echoed, very much, the anti-materialist positions developed in Beat poet and writers' emphases on living differently, experience, and independent thought over material rewards (Ginsberg, 1956/1973; Kerouac, 1965/1995; Burroughs, 1953/2003). For these four teachers, "doing being critical" (Bamberg, 2004, p. 361) required a lived anti-materialist stance that emphasized a rejection of hegemonic masculinity's economic instrumentalism (Beynon, 2002; Connell, 1987, 1995).

The other four teachers in this study talked about process spirituality making direct references to spiritual traditions and resources. With the group of teachers who directly referenced spiritual traditions and resources, process spirituality required rupture with "received" Christian traditions that, rather than embracing atheism, found counternarrativized spiritual identifications in Eastern traditions. Four teachers in this study developed counternarrative identifications that referenced "Buddhist practice" (Mike Taymes, Interview 1c, p.1), "'Bibles" in all of their incarnations" (Gene Johansen, Interview 4a, pp. 17), "the Hindi and the Buddhist, ah, interpretation of spirituality" (Bennett Ferris, Interview 4a, pp. 17–18), or meeting a "Bodhisattva on my path" (Frank Carmody, Interview 8a, p. 5). These findings extend Connell's (1995) initial insights into eco feminist men's spirituality and practice of yoga. Importantly, as this study relates to the US context, teachers' rupture with Christianity echoes Beat (e.g., Ginsberg, 1956/1973; Kerouac, 1965/1995) and (prior to that) Transcendentalist (e.g., Emerson, 1844/2000; Thoreau, 1854/1983) writers and poets' religious inconformity and transgressive rejections of received Christianity.

Critical Politics

All teachers in this study emphasized critical politics in personal and professional identifications. Working in inner-city settings with diverse students, all teachers' critical politics provided race-visible professional identifications that understood race and class dimensions in their work as outlined in Chapter Two and further elaborated on in Chapter Three. This subsection on critical politics briefly fortifies positions already developed.

Teachers in this study understood raced and classed structural inequalities including unfair "criminalized" communities (Mike Taymes, Interview 1b, p. 13), traditional curriculum about "dead White men" (David Smith, Interview 2b, p. 6), historic social arrangements based on racial "repression" (Gene Johansen, Interview 4a, p. 2), white-centrism placing White people on "the top" (Jack Springman, Interview 5b, p. 1), "re-segregated" neighborhoods (David McGrady, Interview 6b, p. 8), unequal racial societies that "blame the individual" (p. Trent Cowens, Interview 7b, p. 5), and their own identities as "classed and raced" (Frank Carmody, Interview 8a, p. 7). Briefly reviewed here, teachers' personal and professional identifications, mixing, of course, in the recounting of their life and teacher stories provided critical knowledges and understandings that informed their life and work as teachers of diverse inner-city students.

DISCUSSION: *A SECOND SPLIT-HALF VIEW*

Narrative Analysis

This section takes up "narrative analysis" (Polkinghorne, 1995, p. 15) that, rather than seeking to find patterns in teachers' life stories, uses narrative emplotment to narrate and analyse the story of the stories. Taking up narrative analysis (Polkinghorne, 1995) in the emplotment of patterns above, this section drives at contradictions in teachers' counternarrative identifications (Bamberg, 2004; Bamberg & Andrews, 2004) that reveal a second split-half view that moves between impotencies and potentials.

Split-Half

Teachers' contradictory counternarrative identifications, when taken together, provided a beginning outline for White progressive masculinities. Teachers' patterned counternarrative identifications marked at every contour a striking self-distantiation from bounded and received White male privileges of the Conservative Restoration. Countering drug-free, White, Christian, meritocratic identities of the Conservative Restoration, teachers in this study developed counternarrative identifications. Teachers' illegal drug use countered official drug free messages from the Reagan Presidency. Teachers' experiential and process spirituality rejected the economic instrumentalism of hegemonic masculinity (Connell, 1987, 1995) and provided a lived-critique of Christian fundamentalism. Teachers' engagement in alternative and indie media represented a counter-hegemonic practice (Giroux, 1996) of self-identification (Frith, 2003) emphasizing thinking and living differently. Teachers' critical politics suggested an important self-distantiation from the hegemonic center and identification on the margins with oppressed "others." As Connell (1995) remarked regarding eco feminist men: "These men are not day-trippers playing at being Sensitive New Men. They are committed to a real and far-reaching politics of personality" (p. 136), and their counternarrative identifications contrasted greatly with friends, family members, and other White identities who unproblematically "took back America" and "joined the Regan Revolution" felicitously enriching themselves and their families.

Nonetheless, teachers' counternarrative identifications, performed in self-distantiation, paradoxically recreated White and male privileges by taking up ostensibly "alternative," "oppositional" or "counternarrative" identifications. Counternarrative identifications, when seen through the emplotment of narrative analysis (Polkinghorne, 1995) recounted a privileged overarching story: White male progressives experienced inconformity with White middle class norms, searched for lived alternatives, encountered identification resources (like drugs, media, and spirituality), and narrated "formed-alliances" with students, community, and children – those who are oppressed. Important to note and residual in this counternarrative identification was a very typically "American" subject-strong identity that seemingly reconstituted Beat (Burroughs, 1953/2003; Ginsberg, 1956/1973; Kerouac, 1965/1995) masculinities or, even preceding those, U.S. Transcendental masculinities' inconformity, religious transgression, independent thinking, and in a phrase, "self-reliance" (Emerson, 1844/2000, p. 132; Thoreau, 1854/1983). It becomes apparent, then, that teachers' doing being critical (Bamberg, 2004) – so central to counternarrative identifications' insurgent position – reworks, in its narrative emplotment (Polkinghorne, 1995), very conservative identity resources, especially in relation to subject-strong identity.

Pushing forward along the lines of subject-strong identity, a further reworking of Connell's (1995) eco feminist men's commitment "to a politics of personality" (p. 136) emerges as a second split-half view. Reading teachers' life story interviews closely and analytically, progressive masculinities' counternarrative identifications bifurcated, split in two, presented two sides of a single phenomenon that did not quite fit together – but potentially could, in a subjunctive-passive conjugation. In recognition of teachers' subject-strong identities (seemingly obligatory for doing being critical), one side of progressive masculinities' emplotted narrative, in the basest and most privileged sense, drove at self-annihilation, using drugs, alternative media, and process spirituality as thinking and living independently from White middle class norms. Paradoxically, and seemingly inextricable from thinking and living independently, the other side of progressive masculinities' counternarrative identifications potentially served to reconfigure masculinity flipping the privileged consumption of subject-strong identity, contradictorily, toward the production of potentially passive political alliances. In this contradiction, spiritual connectedness (Emerson, 1844/2000; Ginsberg, 1956/1973; Kerouac, 1965/1995; West, 2004) presents a central counternarrative identification for progressive masculinities' potential alliance politics.

Impotencies or Potentials

Zeroing in on these contradictions in teachers' counternarrative identifications revealed a precarious possible nihilistic impotent identity that White men could not direct or serve as masculine "leading protagonists" in alliances and instead must passively receive conferred legitimacy or cred as allies, relationally, taking the role of feminine object to be loved by masculinized activists in alliances. Contradictorily, progressive masculinities' subject-strong identity moves toward a difficult, personally challenging, relationally feminine role. Driving at this contradiction between subject-strong progressive masculinities taking on a relationally feminine role, it becomes possible to understand how progressive male teachers could simultaneously be conservative "good role models" in schools and fucking faggots to hetero-masculine students, an unusual artefact from my life story. Herein lies the contradictions and difficulties of White progressive masculinities that are simultaneously subject-strong yet relationally feminine in political alliances. Progressive masculinities conjugate political alliances in a subjunctive passive voice and depend on generous interpretations and understandings (West, 2004) by "others" in realizing their potentials or providing honorary cred. In short, the alliance politics suggested in Connell's (1995) work requires a careful balancing of subject-strong identities in ostensibly progressive or critical politics combined with dialogic feminine relationality.

CONCLUSIONS

This final chapter attempts to add further perspective on progressive masculinities through reading committed White male teachers' life and teacher stories. It is important to note that life history research does not seek, representationally, a discussion on *what, essentially, White male teachers' experiences really are,* or *how they really behave.* That representational task, seemingly underpinning previous research on male teachers (e.g., Allan, 1993; Benton DeCorse & Vogle, 1997; Cushman, 2005, 2008; Sumsion, 1999; Sargent, 2000, 2004), seems exhausted in discussions of shortages, male teachers' double-binds, a debate about male tokens in a female profession, or monolithic male complicity with hegemonic masculinity in schools. What I have presented in this chapter, following lived masculinities (Beynon, 2002; Connell, 1987, 1995; Tolson, 1977) in life story interviews, drives at a different set of questions that might re-invigorate the study and understanding of male teachers. Clearly moving beyond shortages, double binds, tokens, or male hegemony, a different set of questions emerges from reading committed White male teachers' life stories.

Here are a few of the new questions that emerge: What does it mean when men take up "women's work" (Williams, 1993) *in the first place?* What is the critical, moral, and ethical content of men *"choosing" teaching as a second option?* What, beyond double binds, is the *relational negotiation* that men undergo in working with women and teaching diverse students? What practical *relational wisdom of "becoming"* might men who develop commitments impart? How might this relational wisdom of becoming *be adapted in teacher education programs* for developing male teachers' commitments to teaching and learning with diverse students? How might *critical counternarrative identifications*, problematic subject- strong identities, be developed with relational understandings? And, how might these knowledges laid out above – *counternarrative identifications, split half-views, impotencies and potentials* – be used to seriously engage male teachers in reflection about what they are trying to accomplish as teachers? How might these new knowledges in this chapter *inform male teachers' reflective engagement in teaching and learning* – their own and their students? Certainly teachers in this study give teachers and teacher educators a lot to think about regarding teachers' professional development as teacher education schools and the accrediting bodies proceed along technical and "gender-neutral" positions.

NOTE

[1] Masculinity of, say, African-American or Latino men (or teachers) are not discussed in this Chapter and would require a separate study. Of interest to the teaching profession, it is difficult to speculate on African-American or Latino masculinities within discussions of this research as all teacher-respondents are White males who grew up in the US context.

CHAPTER 5

SECOND WAVE WHITE TEACHER
IDENTITY STUDIES

Reflecting on Professional Identifications

OVERVIEW

This chapter draws together, discusses, and advances the thematic patterns developed in previous chapters. First, I focus on professional identifications storied in this book that recover and reconstruct *personal relevance* inherent in race-visible professional identifications' cultural relevance. Second, I revisit *race-visible curriculum wisdom* highlighting deliberative dialogue, relationality, synthetic teaching, and socio-political critique visible in teachers' professional identifications. Third, I drive at *unresolved split-half identifications* inherent in White double-consciousness and White male progressive masculinities reviewing potentials and contradictions in these identifications. Finally, I return to existing understandings of White teachers' race-evasive identities in arguing that research on White teachers move toward *second wave White teacher identity studies*. In closing *Becoming Teachers of Inner-city Students*, I return to my life and teacher stories in articulating a final message of encouragement for preservice and professional teachers in forging race-visible professional identifications for inner-city students and other diverse populations.

PRESERVICE AND PROFESSIONAL TEACHERS' *BECOMING*

Personal Relevance in Cultural Relevance

In reconstructing life and teacher stories, I understand *personal relevance* lies at the heart of professional identifications and what is called "commitment to the profession." In the case of committed White male teachers of inner-city students, *personal relevance* provided the key narrative pattern in teachers' choosing the teaching profession as "second option" (Benton DeCorse & Vogtle, 1997; Cushman, 2005, 2008; Lortie, 1975). In their life histories and teacher stories, teachers recovered childhood and youth thematic content and reconstructed that content in developing race-visible professional identifications.

Briefly, I review this clear, striking, overarching pattern that provides direction for preservice and professional teachers' understanding of professional commitment. Mike Taymes, whose father abandoned him and his mom on the side of the road in

San Antonio, Texas, recovered and reconstructed his father's childhood abandonment as *a gift* for teaching inner-city children. Jack Springman, whose alternative media identifications of his youth expanded his family's white-centric worldview, recovered and reconstructed teaching as an alternative *separateness* from the norm and sought in teaching to expand students' perspectives. Bennett Ferris, whose itinerant family moved across the United States throughout his youth, recovered and reconstructed his working class identity in taking *an activist stance* in his teaching. Rudy Smith, who dropped out of Red Combs' business school, recovered avenues of spiritual and personal growth in *dropping into drugs* in reconstructing a style, attitude, and shtick for teaching inner-city students. Gene Johansen, who tired of commercial art and sought spirituality, recovered and reconstructed *spiritual connections* in teaching inner-city students. Trent Cowens, who narrated his youth identifications with alternative music as a *bad business*, recovered and reconstructed an alternative ethic for himself and his students in suggesting alternative paths for "success." David McGrady, who suffered a collapse of meaning during the Conservative Restoration, came to find *the political is personal* in recovering and reconstructing his family's Great Society values. Varied and special to boundedness, teachers' life histories and teacher stories recounted *personal relevance* in describing their commitment to teaching inner-city students.

Personal relevance, as it emerged in teachers' life histories and teacher stories, came to signify that – inside technical standards' "commitment to the profession" – resided private concerns with much *autobiographical truth at stake* (Pinar, 2012, Slattery, 2006) in teachers' professional identifications. As it emerged in the life histories and teacher stories, personal relevance narratively drove the commitments inherent in teachers' race-visible professional identifications. Driving commitments behind race-visible professional identifications evinced throughout the chapters, personal relevance came in the form of an "inciting incident" in all life and teacher story interviews' narrative arch. Additionally, personal relevance also provided a reflective "dénouement" in five teachers' member checking sessions. As teachers' race-visible professional identifications paralleled cultural relevance of Ladson-Billings' *Dreamkeepers* (2009), *I suggest that private personal relevance drives cultural relevance inherent in race-visible professional identifications.*

As these findings relate to preservice and professional teachers' identifications, finding personal relevance in their life and teacher stories as they confront challenges of becoming teachers appears as key. Preservice and professional teachers' work followed an inner-route in recovering crucial life story themes and reconstructing them in professional identifications as part of personal and professional development. As these findings relate to teacher education, an increased emphasis on humanistic, personal, cultural, and professional resources for developing personal relevance in professional contexts requires equal time with technical discussions of teaching. Milam *et al.* (In press), in a practical discussion on teaching diversity in teacher education, provides an excellent pedagogical space to get started in thinking along the lines of preparing teachers' self-disclosure for autobiographical commitment to teaching. For teacher education, this requires recovering and reconstructing notions of professional development as personal-professional-life story work (Butt, Raymond, McCue, & Yamigishi, 1992; Cole & Knowles, 2000; Knowles, 1992) in forging committed professional identifications.

Race-Visible Curriculum Wisdom's Capacitating Concepts

Besides identifying personal relevance inherent in cultural relevance, this research provided *life-history-and-teacher-story-based* concepts for teaching and learning I called *race-visible curriculum wisdom*. In narrating teachers' race-visible professional identifications in-action, I studied literatures on teaching and learning across difference moving back-and-forth conceptually between literatures and teachers' stories until I reached conceptual *saturation* both as reader-narrator of the stories and as researcher on teaching and learning across differences. In this dialectic back-and-forth between teachers' stories and literatures on teaching and learning, I saw over-arching themes that over-lapped both in teachers' race-visible professional identifications *and* in literatures on teaching and learning with diverse students. In these over-arching and overlapping themes, the following *thick narrative patterns* emerged as capacitating concepts I call race-visible curriculum wisdom: deliberative dialogue, relationality, synthetic teaching, and socio-political critique:

1. *Deliberative dialogue* narrated and represented teachers who work with students' experiences, interests, identities, and cultures as part of the curriculum with the intention not merely of reflecting them but of recovering, reconstructing, and critically evaluating them for advancement of students' understandings.
2. *Relationality* narrated and presented teachers' need for direct relationships with students, families, communities, and social agencies that reflected feminist dictum that *the personal is the political.*
3. *Synthetic teaching* narrated and presented fluid representations of professional identifications in action that understood teaching and learning as actively synthesizing subject area knowledge, curriculum, social milieus, community contexts, and students and teachers' identifications in producing workable lessons that engaged students.
4. *Socio-political critique* began with understandings that education is political and that enabling students to perform academically represented a type of political praxis that included critique as part of teaching subject area lessons.

As this life history and teacher story research articulated in the essays, notions of deliberative dialogue, relationality, synthetic teaching and socio-political critique provided central capacitating concepts for *race-visible curriculum wisdom.*

105

Spit-Half Views

In addition to personal relevance and race-visible curriculum wisdom, Chapters Three and Four, drove at existing contradictions in teachers' professional identifications. In Chapter Three "On White Double-Consciousness," existing contradictions took the form of structural *and* deficit understandings of student differences. Life and teacher story interviews provided pages upon pages that discussed structural understandings of student differences, yet in a contradictory turn, teachers retained deficit understandings of students as well. Though they appeared to a much lesser degree in teachers' life and teacher stories, deficit understandings of student differences represented a clear story pattern that required my attention as narrator. In further contemplation, I began to understand *White double-consciousness* as a privileged yet mirrored reflection of students' ambivalences and resistances toward learning (Ogbu, 1987; Foley, 1990; Valenzuela, 1999; Willis, 1977). That is, researchers have documented students and families' ambivalence toward the hegemonic world of learning, college, achievement, and success (Ogbu, 1987; Foley, 1990; Valenzuela, 1999; Willis, 1977), and teachers in this study also displayed ambivalences in their *White double-consciousness*. In these shared ambivalences, teachers' relationality and ability to conceive of education in relevant ways is prized, yet implicit in teachers' relationality lies the students' radical, heroic, and existential good faith as well. Teachers in this study exhibited *White double-consciousness* yet also told stories that understood and supported relationality in their teaching, so it becomes important for preservice and professional teachers along with education professors and researcher to understand that "consciousness" is not a zero-sum winner-take-all-game. *White double-consciousness* and student ambivalences and resistances, both appear as *de-capacitating* historical blockages to academic learning, real-material obstacles, and yet *preservice and professional teachers are the ones who* must *attend to this labor, despite frustrations recounted in Chapter Three.*

In Chapter Four, existing contradictions focused more broadly on teachers' identifications in life and teacher story interviews that recounted White progressive masculinities. Teachers opposed hegemonic representations of the Conservative Restoration ascendant in the Reagan Presidency, and they resisted these representations through counternarrative identifications that included *illegal drug use, process spirituality, alternative or indie media,* and *critical politics.* Committed White male teachers in this study purposefully counter-narrativized lives that distanced *themselves* from the hegemonic center, yet in doing so, paradoxically, recreated White and male privileges in counternarrative identifications. Progressive White masculinities, narrated in life and teacher stories, suggested promise as potential alliances with "others," yet such a suggestion appeared as a passive voice feminine relation in which cred might be conferred. Again, this contradiction prized relationality and connectedness that appeared in teachers' life and teacher stories. Even so, as so much depends on relationality, both tensions in White double-consciousness and White progressive masculinities seem to be made possible only in their *relational performance,* and these tensions, resolved only in temporal action, appeared in highlighted ways in my life history in Chapter One yet were suggested in other teachers' life and teacher stories as well. *Becoming* teachers of inner-city students depended on relational performances with students in very specific context-situated ways.

Toward Second-Wave White Teacher Identity Studies

In seeing the personal relevance in cultural relevance, describing race-visible professional identifications, and driving at split-half views, this life history and teacher story research expands previous research on White teacher identity and drives at *second wave White teacher identity studies*.

As mentioned in Chapter One, existing understandings of White teacher identity narrate race-evasive identities. Christine Sleeter (1992, 1993, 1995, 2001), in consciousness raising interventions on White teachers in staff development, reported and sustained that White teachers demonstrated little understanding of students' racial backgrounds. Sleeter's interventionist research (1992, 1993, 1995, 2001) on White teachers, foundational in any discussion of White teacher identity, drove at the conclusion that White teachers "did not have a convincing framework for thinking about racial inequality" (1992, p. 22). Alice McIntyre's work (1997, 2002), working with preservice teachers in interventionist action research, affirmed Sleeter's (1992, 1993) findings on White teachers' race-evasive identities. McIntyre (1997) reported partial successes in critical consciousness-raising interventions on White preservice teachers. In her research, McIntyre (1997) emphasized respondents' persistent race-evasive "White talk" (p. 45) as obstacle to consciousness raising efforts with her respondents. McIntyre defined White talk as "talk that serves to insulate White people from examining their/our individual and collective roles in the perpetuation of racism" (p. 45). White teachers, reported McIntyre (1997, 2002), in discussing race presented and represented race-evasive identities that systematically avoided understanding their own and students' ethnic, cultural, linguistic, and racial backgrounds. Other interventionist-oriented research on White preservice teachers (Berlak, 1999; Marx, 2004; Marx & Pennington, 2003) and White teachers (Henze, Lucas, & Scott, 1998; Hyten & Warren, 2003, Marx, 2008) overlapped with, developed, or further articulated notions of White teachers' race-evasive identities by expanding particular patterns within interventionist studies. Gary Howard (1999/2006), early multicultural education activist and President of *Respecting Ethnic and Cultural Heritage* (REACH), codified this well-worn pathway in *We Can't Teach What We Don't Know*. In summary, existing understandings of White teacher identity have intervened on White teachers' consciousness articulating White teachers' often-reticent race-evasive identities with varying degrees of success in elevating their consciousness.

Recently, several studies on White teacher identity have begun to suggest that this research on White teacher identity was too simplified. Only recently has new research emerged on White teacher identity that suggests that critical consciousness-raising interventions on White teacher identity might provide over-simplified understandings of White teacher identity (Asher, 2007; Jupp & Slattery, 2010, 2012; Lensmire, 2011; Lowenstein, 2009; McCarthy, 2003; Miele, 2011a, 2011b; Raible & Irizarry, 2007). I wrote this book, following this new direction, to press forward toward understandings of White teachers' professional identifications in ways that moved beyond race-evasive identities toward more complex representations and pedagogies. *Second-wave White teacher identity studies* presented and represented narrative and process-oriented professional identifications that developed over time. I press toward second wave White teacher identity studies *not* as an attempt to dismiss existing understandings on White teacher identity *but rather* in order to provide a more holistic view of previous studies of White teacher identity. As I reported in Chapter One, I understand White teachers' race-evasive identities because I performed them during my masters' degree program after reading McIntosh's (1988) famous article. Despite recognizing myself in White teachers' race-evasive identities, in this study I recounted teachers' life and teacher stories that, through personal relevance and commitment, developed *race-visible professional identifications* and *curriculum wisdom*. Even so, I've attempted to pull no punches in that I drove at contradictory split-half views in describing White teachers' *White double-consciousness* and *progressive masculinities*.

Important in driving at race-visible professional identifications and curriculum wisdom along with split-half contradictions is an *expansive and more complicated view of White teachers' work in teaching across differences*. My purpose as an ex-teacher and now researcher of White teachers' life and teacher stories was to provide *enabling, encouraging, capacitating* second wave understandings that, nonetheless, avoided facile victory narratives or over-simplified "conclusions." White teachers, still a staggering 88.6% majority of combined elementary and secondary teachers (NCES, 2004), continue to work with a growing population of 44.2% (NCES, 2010) students of color. Increasingly, White teachers and students of color meet in schools that, as statistical research demonstrates (NCES, 2009), are increasingly re-segregated. Second wave White teacher identity studies strive to recount, through life and teacher stories, White teachers' intercultural and intersubjective processes of becoming within boundedness and discursive contexts. Although life histories and teacher stories certainly do not provide a "solution" to the "problem of race" in education, my intention was to provide preservice and professional teachers with professional identifications as generative cultural resources for teaching across race, class, culture, language, and other differences. Nonetheless, a second wave of White teacher identity studies is not something that one can undertake alone, and so I am glad to have found others to share the work, especially Anthony Miele of the University of San Francisco and Tim Lensmire of the University of Minnesota along with others. This group of scholars and I have begun to move toward careful readings and understandings of White identifications in education as constructivist-and-affirmational yet problematic resources for White teachers and educators who wish to work – in careful and relational ways – toward social justice for students in schools yet tell no lies and make no felicitous assumptions in doing so.

A FINAL RETURN

In a final note to readers who accompanied me through life histories and teacher stories here, I wanted to tie all of this back to the important work with preservice and professional teachers' identifications. Since I left public education in 2008, I have worked as a writer and professor of curriculum and pedagogy in two departments of teaching and learning in the South. In my classes, I have taught many of the concepts that appear in this book, and I have also accompanied many White preservice and professional teachers out into schools as they earn their credentials. Despite the low prestige of working in Departments of teaching and learning, I am drawn back to classrooms and the field with teachers who are practicing – teaching across differences of race, class, culture, and language – in attempting to engage students, narrating their own personal changes as they *become* teachers of diverse students, some in inner-city settings.

In closing, I emphasize instability and delicacy of constituting professional identifications as preservice and professional teachers enter and develop in the profession. I also emphasize the importance of expecting challenges and change in the development of preservice and professional teachers' race-visible professional identifications. I provide a composite sketch of recent interactions with my students serving in schools. Here is the composite sketch:

> Teaching is what I always thought that I wanted to do, but now that I'm doing it, I'm finding it much harder than I thought I would. I guess I just never imagined myself working in class with *almost all* African American students – there's like one White kid in each class, but I got into teaching with the idea that I could help, could make a difference. I admired teachers that helped me, and I wanted to make a difference in students' lives. I see how I can do that, but it's hard. I had no idea how hard teaching, in fact, really was when I sat there as a student in classes. *But this is the person I want to become*, and I'm becoming that person. I'm changing. I finally understand what you meant by teaching to use students' cultural resources along with my own, and I finally see – in fits and starts – what works in my classroom, though I'm still figuring that out. I've adapted several of the lessons and reading strategies that you shared in the curriculum and pedagogy class. The neighborhood maps project and study of students' statistics units worked well because they included what the students knew. It wasn't perfect, but students responded better to me in those lessons.

I realized in writing this book that teacher education is the work that my advanced degree prepared me for, and my purpose in writing about committed White male teachers' life history and teacher stories is to inform preservice and professional teachers in *developing* impactful professional identifications, *becoming* teachers that can negotiate race, class, culture, language and other differences in real classrooms. Even though the work is against the grain, teachers need to *keep on pushing* as they change themselves and become teachers.

CAPACITATING CONCEPTS

Research essay on evidence-based concepts[1]

INTRODUCTION

For researchers and interested students, Appendix A defines, explains, and narrates capacitating concepts supporting the life histories and teacher stories found in this book. Capacitating concepts have two purposes. First, as emerging from and reflected in life histories and teacher stories, capacitating concepts help me narrate the stories. Second, in helping me narrate the stories, capacitating concepts inform preservice and professional teachers' identifications. Capacitating concepts, with dual purposes of narrating and informing, provide a set of life-history-and-teacher-story-based concepts that help me narrate committed White male teachers' life histories and teacher stories, and simultaneously, capacitating concepts provide evidence-based resources for preservice and professional teachers' on-going development and becoming. *Capacitating concepts*, reviewing the definition from Chapter One, refer to *concepts that inform and capacitate teachers' professional identifications as teachers work across borders of race, class, culture, language, and other differences.*

In the first half of Appendix A, I provide capacitating concepts directed at preservice and professional teachers' identity. Specifically, I review existing understandings of White teacher identity with the purpose of conceptualizing what I call capacitating *second wave White teacher identity studies*. Second wave white teacher identity studies emphasize professional identifications and other related concepts. Professional identifications and related concepts, differing from existing understandings of White teachers' identity, emphasize narrative and process-oriented race-visible professional identifications. Professional identifications help narrate life histories and teacher stories *and* serve to conceptualize preservice and professional teacher identity in complex and progressive ways.

In the second half of this chapter, I provide capacitating concepts in relation to practical teaching and learning in classrooms with diverse inner-city students students. Specifically, I define and explain capacitating concepts from the practical progressive tradition (e.g., Clandinin & Connelly, 1992, 1995; Connelly & Clandinin, 1988; Craig, 2008; Dewey, 1902/1990; Schwab, 1978, 1983) that develop understandings of curriculum wisdom (e.g., Davis, 1997; Henderson & Gornik, 2007; Shulman, 1987). In this discussion, I synthesize the practical progressive tradition with more recent anthropological and cultural studies traditions (e.g. Ladson Billings, 1995, 2009; Gonzales, Moll, & Amanti, 2005; Gay, 2000) emphasizing students' cultures and identifications. Importantly, I synthesize the practical progressive and culturally relevant traditions to help recount committed White male teachers' life histories and teacher stories as resources for other preservice and professional teachers as they teach across differences in classrooms. It is crucial to note, as well, that these concepts very much emerged in *my own teaching, research on teaching and learning*, and *in teachers' stories*. In this way, the capacitating concepts emerged as I reached *analytical saturation* from simultaneously discovering the concepts and telling the teachers' and my stories.

CAPACITATING WHITE TEACHER IDENTITY

Toward a Second-Wave of White Teacher Identity Studies

In approaching second wave white teacher identity studies' capacitating concepts, I begin by reviewing existing understandings of White teacher identity. Existing understandings of White teacher identity are tightly tied to the introduction of critical White studies into teacher education.

Existing understandings of White teacher identity came from the introduction of critical White studies into teacher education curriculum and professional development programs. Critical White studies, a sub-category of critical race theory, developed in cultural studies (Dyer, 1988; Hall, 1981), feminist theory (hooks, 1992; Frankenberg, 1993; McIntosh, 1988), critical legal studies (Delgado & Stefancic, 1997), and labor history (Ignatiev, 1995; Roediger, 1994). Critical White studies, a burgeoning field of cultural criticism in the 1990s and early 2000s, made several contributions to teacher education curriculum and professional development programs. First, critical White studies, among its contributions, emphasized that White racism existed not just in individuals' consciousnesses but also in assumptions about values, knowledge, and social-historical reality. Second, critical White studies, in emphasizing White racism in assumptions, posited an inherent Whiteness in social-historical reality providing White people with privileges. This emphasis on White racism in values, knowledge, and reality influenced the way education professors and staff development consultants taught preservice and professional teachers, and these new knowledges revealed educational institutions as inherently racialized in ways that disadvantage people of color. *Becoming Teachers of Inner-city Students* is committed to the insurgent knowledge of whiteness.

Critical White studies, in influencing professors and consultants, provided significant contributions in understanding how race works in education. Race in education, from the purview of critical White studies, works not only in the minds of racist individuals but operates through whiteness and White privilege in structured contexts such as national and state policy, curriculum and instruction practices, and institutional operations like the tracking of students. Seeing whiteness and White privilege where previously invisible provided preservice and professional teachers with racialized ways of understanding, for example, dropout rates of rural poor and urban students as reflecting national and state policy, curriculum practices, or teachers' instruction.

Contributions of critical White studies, revealing whiteness and White privilege, take on increasing importance as professional and preservice teachers are predominantly White and students are increasingly diverse[2]. Existing efforts to educate teachers on the contributions of critical White studies typically enact critical consciousness-raising interventions on White preservice and professional teachers. These critical consciousness-raising interventions, designed by university professors and educational consultants, have insisted that preservice and professional teachers recognize whiteness and White privilege as a result of exposure to professors or consultants' consciousness-raising lessons and activities and suggest a conversion to critical consciousness as outcome. Existing understandings on White teacher identity, within the context of consciousness-raising interventions, have narrated *by-and-large* White teachers' rejections, resistances, or evasions of critical White studies' contributions to education. These evasions of critical White studies' contributions articulate what the research calls White teachers' *race-evasive identities. Race-evasive identities*, as definition, refer to *White teachers' rejections, resistances, or evasions of racialized identity or race as structuring context in education or elsewhere.*

My purpose here is to develop support for critical White studies' contributions to teacher education curriculum and professional development programs, but in developing this support, I take a *very different tack* from critical consciousness-raising interventions. Rather than reporting on the outcomes of critical consciousness raising interventions as previous professors and consultants have, this life history and teacher story research narrates progressive *race-visible professional identifications* and *curriculum wisdom* developed over time in the practice of teaching inner-city students. In developing life histories and teacher story research, *Becoming Teachers of Inner-city Students* drives – as its central purpose – at narrating race-visible professional identifications as resources for others' professional identifications.

Existing Understandings of White Teacher Identity

Existing understandings of White teacher identity, according to research on the topic, describes White preservice and professional teachers' race-evasive identities. Christine Sleeter's (1992, 1993, 1995, 2001) research is foundational in existing understandings of White teacher identity. Sleeter (1993, 1992), who used ethnography to implement critical-consciousness raising interventions in the early 1990s, reported that White teachers demonstrated little understanding of diverse students' racial backgrounds, and White teachers, instead of acknowledging their own or students' backgrounds, purposefully evaded understandings that might inform their teaching and ways of interacting with racially, ethnically, and culturally different students. Sleeter (1993) summarizes White teachers' race-evasive identities:

> Faced with the paradox of liking and helping students of color while explaining away the subordination of people of color and adhering to social structures that benefit themselves and their own children, the White teachers I studied responded in patterned ways. Many simply refused to "see" color. Others searched for "positive" associations with race by drawing on their European ethnic experience.... Discussing race or multiculturalism meant discussing "them," not the social structure. (p. 168)

Sleeter's research (1992, 1993, 1995, 2001) drives toward the conclusion that White teachers "did not have a convincing framework for thinking about racial inequality" (1992, p. 22).

Alice McIntyre's (1997, 2002) research affirms Sleeter's (1992, 1993) findings on White teachers' race-evasive identities. McIntyre (1997), who conducted critical interventionist action research on White preservice teachers, reports partial successes in critical consciousness-raising interventions. Nonetheless, McIntyre (1997) emphasizes respondents' persistent race-evasive "White talk" (p. 45) as obstacle to her consciousness raising efforts with her respondents. McIntyre (1997) summarizes what is meant by White talk:

> One of the most compelling and disturbing aspects of the group talk was the way in which the participants controlled the discourse of whiteness so that they didn't have to shoulder the responsibility for the racism that exists in our society *today*. Just as I slipped into uncritical talk that reified myths about children of color, so it was with the participants who, many times, found themselves embroiled in what I refer to as "White talk" —talk that serves to insulate White people from examining their/our individual and collective roles in the perpetuation of racism. (p. 45)

McIntyre (1997), in reporting on action research with White preservice teachers, recaps Sleeter's understanding of White teachers' race-evasive identities. White teachers, says McIntyre (1997, 2002), develop race-evasive identities that evade understanding their own and students' ethnic, cultural, linguistic, and racial backgrounds. Importantly, beyond affirming Sleeter's research (1992, 1993, 1995, 2001), is the over-arching narrative that McIntyre's (1997, 2002) work provides for other interventions on White preservice and professional teachers. McIntyre's (1997, 2002) research provides an over-arching narrative identifying 1) preservice and professional teachers' naïve or "false" consciousnesses, 2) professors and consultants' consciousness raising interventions, 3) preservice and professional teachers' race-evasive identities, and finally 4) preservice and professional teachers partial critical conversions or adherences to the interventions.

Other interventionist researches on White preservice teachers (Berlak, 1999; Marx, 2004; Marx & Pennington, 2003) and White teachers (Henze, Lucas, & Scott, 1998; Hyten & Warren, 2003, Marx, 2008) overlap with, develop, or articulate part of McIntyre's (1998, 2002) over-arching critical consciousness-raising pattern. Ruth Marx and Julie Pennington (2003) and Ruth Marx (2004, 2008) provide similar accounts in which preservice teachers evade and yet partially adhere to racialized understandings. Ann Berlak (1999), developing a pedagogy of bearing and becoming witness to oppressions, narrates problematic evasions of preservice teachers of color who collude with White preservice teachers to obstruct critical consciousness-raising interventions. Rosemary Henze, Tamara Lucas, and Beverly Scott (1999), emphasizing the importance of creating a context for critical dialogue, reported on race-evasive discussions in a staff development setting with elementary school teachers. Hyten and Warren (2003), articulating the pervasive ways that professional teachers evade White studies critical consciousness-raising, provide a typology of these evasions including appeals to self, progress, authenticity, and extremes. Marx (2008), continuing a focus on race-evasive identities, reveals that popular teachers of Latino students connect on the basis of personal experience but evade critical content of race with their students. What emerges from research on White teacher identity, as unifying overarching pattern, now represents a well-worn pathway articulating naïve or "false" consciousness, professors or consultants' critical consciousness-raising interventions, preservice and professional teachers' race-evasive identities, and instructors' partial successes in consciousness-raising interventions. Studies following McIntyre (1997) further articulate, delve into, or represent singular aspects of this pathway.

Gary Howard (2006), early multicultural education activist and President of *Respecting Ethnic and Cultural Heritage* (REACH)[3], codifies this well-worn pathway through reflection and anecdote in his recent work. Howard (2006) summarizes REACH's interventions and urges teachers, administrators, and corporate staff to take the journey from race-evasive to "White ally" identities outlining different stages of identity change and conscientization. Howard (2006), discussing his critical consciousness-raising interventions over the last several decades, represents the state of the well-worn pathway on White teacher identity:

> For the past thirty years I have been blessed to be part of a close multicultural network of colleagues and friends, the REACH national trainer network.... We work together in diverse teams of trainers at a time, attempting to bring a transformative multicultural vision to teachers, administrators, students, and community leaders in a wide variety of settings, often working within the context of highly charged and resistant environments. (p. 141)

Howard (2006), referencing three decades of critical consciousness-raising interventions and evasions in "highly charged and resistant environments" (p. 141), testifies to having stayed-the-course over thirty (now over forty) years.

In summary, existing understandings of White teacher identity from critical consciousness raising interventions have a long and stable trajectory of reflecting, representing, and constituting race-evasive White identities. Recent educational foundations textbooks[4], articulating the well-worn pathway, provide similar discussions on White teacher identity in support of standards-based teacher education (e.g., Darling-Hammond & Bransford, 2005; National Council for the Accreditation of Teacher Education, 2008). White preservice and professional teachers, in the standards-based and "best practices" teacher education, are expected to change worldviews from race-evasive to "White ally" identities as a result of professors' interventions. White ally identities, felicitous as "outcome" of an intervention, suggest preservice and professional teachers' attainment of the standard in the present moment.

Only recently has new research emerged on White teacher identity that suggests that critical consciousness-raising might provide an over-simplified model that constitutes either-or race-evasive or White ally identity outcomes (Asher, 2007; Eichstedt, 2002; Jupp & Slattery, 2010, 2012; Lensmire, 2011; Lowenstein, 2009; 2012; McCarthy, 2003; Miele, 2011a, 2011b; Raible & Irizarry, 2007). This new research, initiating second wave White teacher identity studies, critically conditions existing understandings of White teacher identity – not to discredit these understandings – but rather second wave research seeks to rekindle critical discussions on complex and authentic progressive professional identifications. Second wave White teacher identity studies, critiquing consciousness-raising as over-simplified model, sustains that developing competent race-visible professional identifications might represent a life-long professional endeavor. Second wave White teacher identity studies, contrasting with existing understandings of White teacher identity, suggest the life-changing experience *might be working with students over time* instead of an outcome of an intervention. Following Lowenstein (2009) and others, second wave White teacher identity studies, skeptical of either-or outcomes, begin to suggest a constructivist, narrative, and Deweyan pedagogy for teaching and learning about race-visible professional identification central to *becoming* teachers or for *further developing* professional teachers' identities.

Second Wave White Teacher Identity Studies

Patrick Slattery and I (2010, 2012) have referred to this new research – research that acknowledges existing understandings of White teacher identity yet moves toward complex progressive discussions – as second wave White teacher identity studies. *Second wave White teacher identity studies*, contrasting with existing race-evasive White teacher identities, seek to *reflect, represent, and proliferate complex and progressive conversations on White teachers' race-visible professional identifications*. Characterized as second wave yet paradoxically drawing on and suggesting complex, historicized, and progressive representations of race in education (e.g., Douglas, 1845/1986; Du Bois, 1903/1995; Hinojosa, 1973/1994, 1977; McCarthy & Crichlow,

1993; Paley, 1978/2000; West, 1993, 2001; Vasconcelos, 1925/1997), second wave White teacher identity studies emphasize White progressive (Giroux, 1998; Kincheloe, 1999; Kincheloe & Steinberg; Perry & Shotwell, 2009) and scholars' of color (McCarthy, 2003; West, 1993; Yúdice, 1995) recommendations for broad progressive identities that include White teachers' complex identifications. Given the textbook, standardized, and institutionalized status of critical consciousness-raising interventions, I argue for second wave White teacher identity studies that rekindle critical and progressive discussions through constructivist and experiential Deweyan pedagogy of professional growth and becoming.

Emblematic of reaching back historically to initiate a second wave, I emphasize Vivian Paley's (1979/2000) sensitive and humanistic professional identifications in *White Teacher*. Paley, narrating professional identifications over time, takes up questions of race in education after the racialized tensions of the 1968 race riots. Paley, contrasting with professors and consultants' critical conscious-raising interventions, performs complex race-visible professional identifications as on-going narrative of professional growth. Paley, performing her professional identifications, encounters circumstances, students, and parents that *out* whiteness and require continual personal and professional growth about students, milieus, and curriculum. Paley, experientially narrating her insights as Jewish child in a Christian-centered world, insists that "color blind" identities whiten students just as "secular" identities Christianized her Jewish childhood. Paley, developing narrative professional identifications, works with complexities that public school teachers face that go beyond affirming or evading a critical consciousness-raising intervention. Paley's narrative understandings include: how to create the conditions for students to discuss backgrounds, the difficulties of disciplining Whites and children of color for inappropriate behavior, the complexity of leveraging parents' of color support in schools, difficult-to-discern moral judgments about what is right and wrong when teaching diverse students, and critical lessons on race, class, and culture. Of note with Paley and contrasting with critical consciousness-raising interventions are her complex, narrative, professional identifications representing a process of *coming-to-know*, a process of *becoming*. Paley's professional identifications – always processing, developing, *becoming* – provide an important predecessor for what I drive at in *Becoming Teachers of Inner-city Students* as this research moves away from the model of interventions inherent in existing understandings of White teachers. *Becoming Teachers of Inner-city Students*, moving beyond interventions, furthers second wave White teacher identity studies that seek constructivist, narrative, and Deweyan understandings as on-going process along with a professional repertoire or race-visible professional identifications.

Second Wave Capacitating Identity Concepts

Second wave White teacher identity studies, returning to Paley's (1979/2000) work, require second wave identity concepts for capacitating preservice and professional teacher identity. Second wave identity concepts, contrasting with existing understandings of White teacher identity, emphasize narrative processes called identifications (Bruner, 2002; Butler, 1999; Hall, 2003) for articulating life history and teacher story research. Stuart Hall (2003) explains the notion of identifications I use here:

> Though identities seem to invoke an historical past with which they continue to correspond, actually identities are about questions of using the resources of history, language, and culture in the process of becoming rather than being: not "who we are" or "where we came from", so much as what we might become, how we have been represented and how that bears on how we might represent ourselves. They arise from *narrativizations of the self.* (p. 4)

Professional identifications, beginning with understandings of narrative identifications, suggest a focus not on *who-we-are* but rather *who-we-might-become* within historical and social boundedness. It is with this understanding of identifications that I define and present the following terms that help describe and narrate committed White male teachers' life and teacher stories: *identifications, boundedness, professional identifications, discursive contexts*, and *progressive masculinities*. Each of these concepts represent *capacitating concepts* defined above because they follow Paley (1979/2000) in suggesting process-oriented, narrativized, intercultural, and intersubjective identifications required for working across differences in classrooms.

1. *Identifications*, as definition, refer to *narrative process identities within historical and social boundedness*. Identifications, contrasting with assigned and static race-evasive or White ally identities in existing understanding of White teachers, hasten a second wave of White teacher identity studies by describing and narrating how identities emerge over time. Identifications, in describing and narrating identities as emergent, recognize that historical and social boundedness structure what in common sense ways are understood as "lives." Nonetheless, identifications, in recognizing boundedness, attend to narratives of day-to-day experiences, especially experiences of race, class, culture, language and other differences.[5] In relation to teachers' life histories and teacher stories, identifications emphasize narrative processes of *becoming*.

2. *Boundedness*, as definition, refers to *structured contexts that, by degrees, shape and call identities into being*. Boundedness, contrasting with assigned race-evasive or White ally identities, affirms specific historical and social contexts yet recognizes counternarratives that can challenge, resist, or recode boundedness. Boundedness, contrasting with static assigned identities and historical "structures," suggests greater identification malleability and recognizes individuals' creativity as inner self-narrativization in relation to outer historical and social boundedness. As a consequence, counternarrativizing boundedness for committed White male teachers here is understood as on-going narrative process rather than as result of a single critical consciousness-raising intervention.

3. *Professional identifications*, as discussed previously in Chapter One, refer to *narrative process identities within discursive contexts that understand and enact curriculum wisdom in classrooms.* Professional identifications, contrasting with assigned race-evasive or White ally identities, synthesize understandings of practical curriculum wisdom outlined in the second half of this chapter with understandings of identifications above. Professional identifications, in synthesizing practical understandings of professionalism and identifications, seek to articulate practical professional identity as it relates to the day-to-day practice of teaching and learning with students across borders of difference.

4. *Race-visible professional identifications, as definition, refer to professional identifications developed over time that recognize race and other identities in ways that inform teaching and learning across borders of difference.* Race-visible professional identifications, as understood in life histories and teacher stories here, emerged in the practice of teaching students in inner-city schools. Like professional identifications, they narrate practical day-to-day teaching practices that emerge from teachers who are cognizant of race among other identity intersections. Race-visible professional identifications, it follows, focus not only on narrating teachers' changed identifications and understandings from immersion in inner-city schools but also on *race-visible curriculum wisdom* that teachers developed.

5. *Discursive contexts*, as definition, refer to *historical and social boundedness in schooling of particular teachers and students.* Discursive contexts, in referring to schooling of students in this study, describe and articulate institutional boundedness in which students and teachers labor. Discursive contexts, as institutional boundedness of students and teachers' shared labor, are very much like the words "contexts" or "structures," but the word "discursive" suggests a greater sensitivity to languages or discourses that very much shape, influence, and order these day-to-day practices. Discursive contexts imply structuring discourses that shape day-to-day practices and experiences of students and teachers inside institutions yet also imply malleability about them understanding that discursive contexts are social and historical, can be influenced, and in fact change. As key examples of discursive contexts, discourses on "school failure" and "student deficits" pervaded students and teachers' shared labor.

6. *Progressive masculinities*, as definition, refer to *contradictory and, at times, utopian distantiation from hegemonic instrumental, technical, and goal-oriented masculinity.* Progressive masculinities relate specifically to and help narrate committed White male teachers' identifications in this study. Progressive masculinities are tied to teachers' counternarrative identifications. Explained at length in Chapter Four, *counternarrative identifications*, working along personal-political lived stylistics, refer to *small narratives that counter "'official' and 'hegemonic' narratives of everyday life"* (Peters and Lankshear, 1996, p. 2).

Second wave White teacher identity studies, as I undertake them in *Becoming Teachers of Inner-city Students*, require second wave identity concepts among which I outlined identifications, boundedness, professional identifications, discursive contexts, and progressive masculinities.

CAPACITATING PRACTICAL TEACHING AND LEARNING

Life Histories and Teaching Stories; Practical Teaching and Learning

Second wave White teacher identity studies, emerging from and reflected in life histories and teaching stories, acknowledge yet critique dichotomous either/or race evasive or White ally identities in existing understandings of White teacher identity. Second wave White teacher studies, in acknowledging and critiquing existing understandings, move beyond critical consciousness-raising interventions to suggest that the changes sought after in prescriptive interventions might be better taught, less-defensively understood, and more thoroughly learned through life histories, teaching stories, and other constructivist understandings. Second wave White teacher studies, rather than enacting and narrating critical consciousness-raising interventions, begin with an understanding that practical teaching and learning (Clandinin & Connelly, 1992, 1995; Cole & Knowles, 2000; Connelly & Clandinin, 1988; Davis, 1997; Schwab, 1978, 1983) represent a type of life-long research activity often under-represented and misunderstood by the public, policy makers, and (at times) university-level researchers. Cole and Knowles (2000), who emphasize the connection between life history and teaching, summarize the understanding of research on practical teaching and learning taken up in second wave White teacher identity studies:

> Thus the assertion that teaching *is* inquiry. Engaging in research on one's own practice and being reflexive about one's professional practice are one and the same when the inquiry begins and returns to the teaching self. In other words..., ongoing professional development is essentially a career-long autobiographical project [and] understanding teaching *must* be framed by one's own experiences, perspectives, values, and beliefs. (p. 94)

Second wave White teacher identity studies, drawing on understandings from teacher research, seek to tell, recount, and narrate not only capacitating concepts for White teachers discussed in the previous section but also practical teaching and learning that accompanies race-visible professional identifications. Valuing race-visible professional identifications and practical teaching and learning with diverse inner-city students, I approach capacitating concepts for practical teaching and learning emerging from and reflected in this life history and teaching story research. Capacitating concepts for practical teaching and learning draw on and reflect assumptions of philosophical pragmatism. Capacitating concepts for practical teaching and learning reflect and embody understandings of philosophical pragmatism as they relate to Dewey's reflective wheel, practical inquiry, reflective professionalism, and culturally relevant teaching.

Pragmatism

Philosophical Pragmatism

Philosophical pragmatism provides the broad tradition for discussing capacitating concepts for practical teaching and learning. Pragmatism, cosmopolitan in its orientations, draws on Immanuel Kant's notions of moral and critical intelligence, Fredrick Douglas's determination and personal heroics, John Stuart Mill's practical utilitarianism, and Elizabeth Cady Stanton's egalitarianism. Pragmatism, as it developed in the United States, follows a complex path through Ralph Waldo Emerson, Charles Peirce, William James, W.E.B Du Bois, John Dewey, C. Wright Mills, James Baldwin, Martin Luther King, and others. Pragmatism, rejecting strictly empirical "scientistic" understandings implied in scientific "best practices," emphasizes human beings' understandings and actions as simultaneously co-creating, making, representing, constituting, and producing history and society. Pragmatism, optimistically understanding human beings as makers-of-history-and-society, rejects fixed orthodoxies and static understandings, and instead pragmatism develops process-oriented, experiential, constructivist, and contingent understandings of the world. Pragmatism, as process-oriented, experiential, contingent, and constructivist, couples these understandings with a moral conviction that exercises critical intelligence in improving our communities, institutions, and world. West (1993), contemporary expositor of pragmatism, explains pragmatism's moral convictions:

> Pragmatism has to do with trying to conceive of knowledge, reality, and truth in such a way that it promotes the flowering and flourishing of individuality under the conditions of democracy. ...These foundations consist roughly of, first, the irreducibility of individuality within participatory communities. ...Second, is the heroic action of ordinary people in a world of radical contingency. And third, is a deep sense of evil that fuels the struggle for social justice. (p. 32)

Teachers in this research, echoing West's (1993) insights on pragmatism, draw on and reflect pragmatic understandings because of their process approach to professional identifications, commitments to teaching and learning, and moral conviction that their work makes a difference, however modest, for the children and communities in which they work.

Dewey's Reflective Wheel

In continuation, pragmatism exercised great influence in understanding and thinking about many US institutions including educational ones. In education, John Dewey (1902/1990, 1910/1997, 1916/1997, 1938/1997) became the foremost expositor of pragmatism providing progressive-constructivist understandings of teaching and learning, schooling practices, and reflective thought among other topics, and Dewey's influence is very much relevant today in contemporary discussions on practical teaching and learning (Clandinin & Connelly, 1992, 1995; Cole & Knowles, 2000; Connelly & Clandinin, 1988; Davis, 1997; Schwab, 1978, 1983; Shulman, 1987). Regarding teaching and learning, Dewey argues for the teachers' careful and intricate

121

connections between students' experiences and subject area knowledges. Regarding schooling practices, Dewey understands the school as a microcosm of democracy that, in order to produce democratic citizens, needs to work in democratic ways including voices from teachers, students, and other institutions. Regarding reflective thought, perhaps his most important contribution, Dewey articulated what I call in my teaching *Dewey's reflective wheel*.

As continual concern in his work, Dewey's reflective wheel proposes an on-going process of reflection that includes *original understanding, experience, reflection,* and *new understanding*. In the wheel, original understanding represents the starting point. From this, new experiences, including professional knowledges and classroom experiences, inform on-going reflection. From reflection on these experiences, new understandings emerge that provide professionals with continual personal growth and improvement in professional practices. Dewey (1916), through the on-going reflective wheel, proposes a process in which teachers – as students of their own teaching practices with children – can continually rework their practice in context specific ways. Inherent in the reflective wheel is a constructivist type of teaching and learning that allows for on-going personal growth as it relates to the professional activity of teaching. Teachers in this research, in life and teacher stories, live out this reflective wheel as they engage in process-oriented and developmental personal and professional identifications. Professional identifications informed by personal identifications (and vice versa) were on-going, developmental, and process-oriented as they related personal life to public professional commitments.

Practical Inquiry

Further elaborating on Dewey's reflective wheel, practical inquiry (Connelly & Clandinin, 1988; Clandinin & Connelly, 1992, 1995; Schwab, 1978, 1983) provides a capacitating concept for teaching and learning. Practical inquiry, further developing and extending Dewey's reflective wheel, argues that practical teaching and learning present a highly contextualized professional activity (Connelly & Clandinin, 1988; Clandinin & Connelly, 1992, 1995). Practical teaching and learning, as highly contextualized, require professional thinking and problem solving informed by the context where teaching and learning take place. Practical inquiry, taking contexts into account, holds that teaching must be understood within four common places of teaching and learning: 1) students' lives and interests, 2) subject area curriculum, 3) teachers' personal lives and expertise, and 4) social milieus and structures (Schwab, 1978, 1983). The four common places, by way of explanation, emphasize that at times teachers will focus on students, subject areas, teacher expertise, or social milieus and structures for effectively teaching a group of students. That is, there is not a single set of scientific "best practices" for teaching and learning, and effective teaching, as it relates to the common places, does not come from static, prescriptive, or one-size-fits-all "expert" science. Rather, practical inquiry alternately takes up the four common places within specific contexts contingently and *as-needed* (Connelly & Clandinin, 1988, Clandinin & Connelly, 1992, 1995). Practical inquiry, subordinating expert science, emphasizes the teachers' contextualized professional deliberations and argues that the teacher develop his or her teaching as on-going deliberative and eclectic art. Teachers in this research, represented in narrative teaching stories, talked about the struggles and challenges to engage diverse inner-city students in their classrooms in ways that reflect and constitute practical inquiry. As teaching stories show, there was a constant adjustment and adaptation regarding the emphasis of the four common places of student, subjects, teacher, and milieus that came into play. Practical inquiry, as reflected in the teaching stories, suggested that only through capacitating teachers for deliberative judgments can any authentic educational reform take place. Practical inquiry suggests that the required direction for any improvements in education come from reconstructing the idea of the teacher as curriculum maker (Clandinin & Connelly, 1992; Connelly & Clandinin, 1988; Craig, 2008).

Reflective Professionalism (... More on Dewey's Wheel)

Expanding on Dewey's reflective wheel and practical inquiry, reflective professionalism (Shulman, 1987; Schön, 1983) further elaborates these capacitating concepts. Reflective professionalism, as developed by Donald Schön (1983), elaborates on Dewey's reflective wheel as it relates to the professions including engineering, social work, nursing, law, public administration, and teaching. Schön's (1983) reflective professionalism, very much related to teachers in this research, discusses the crisis in professions that face intractable social conditions like poverty, lack of health insurance, reduced budgets, and negative public perceptions. Schön (1983), following pragmatism's rejection of scientistic understandings of the social world, rejects "technical" explanations and "expert" knowledge associated with scientific "best practices." Scientific best practices, Schön (1983) insists, lack contemporary understandings of human dynamism or collaboration and instead insist on traditional-hierarchical relationships in which university-level technical experts assume they can successfully direct field-level practitioners from the ivory tower. Schön (1983), emphasizing the impossibility of technical-experts' "direction" of field practitioners, elaborates a complex and dynamic model of collaborative professionalism that describes practitioner-centered *reflection-in-action*. Schön's (1983) reflective professionalism, contrasting with traditional-hierarchical relationships, develops this notion of *reflection-in-action*, defined as, *localized, context-bound, and problem-based understandings of professional knowledge in-action*. Reflective professionalism, seeking to capacitate professionals, recognizes that even though professionals use the same professional knowledges they adapt such resources specifically according to local needs, contexts, and problems they face at hand.

Reflective professionalism, valuing experiential, practitioner-based, reflection-in-action, seeks to enable professionals through providing portraits – many times life and professional stories like the ones recounted in this book – of committed and skilled professionals and the knowledges they develop in real-world contexts. Related and central to my purposes, I seek to capacitate preservice and professional teachers' understanding of reflection-in-action through developing life histories and teaching stories. These life histories and teacher stories recounted here sought to provide experience-based understandings of race-visible professional identifications and examples of reflection-in-action for teaching across differences in inner-city settings.

Reflective Professionalism (...More on Practical Inquiry)

Taking Schön's (1983) understandings of professionalism directly into teaching, Lee Shulman (1987) further elaborates on practical inquiry (Connelly & Clandinin, 1988, Clandinin & Connelly, 1995, 1992; Schwab, 1978, 1983) in teaching. Shulman (1987), in elaborating on practical inquiry, uses narrative descriptions of teachers' practices and knowledges similar to the stories I developed here. Shulman (1987), narrating teachers' practices and knowledges, extends understandings of practical inquiry by carefully describing the knowledges that effective teachers have, and more importantly, Shulman describes teachers' use of these knowledges to develop *pedagogical content knowledge*. I'll quote Shulman (1987) at length on his description of teacher knowledges inherent in teachers' practical inquiry:

1. Content knowledge;
2. General pedagogical knowledge, with special reference to those broad principles and strategies of classroom management and organization that appear to transcend subject matter;
3. Curriculum knowledge, with particular grasp of the materials and programs that serve as "tools of the trade" for teachers;
4. Pedagogical content knowledge, that special amalgam of content and pedagogy that is uniquely the province of teachers, their own special form of professional understanding;
5. Knowledge of learners and their characteristics;
6. Knowledge of contexts, ranging from the workings of the group or classroom, the governance and financing of school districts, to the character of communities and cultures; and,
7. Knowledge of educational ends, purposes, and values, and their philosophical and historical grounds. (p. 8)

Shulman's (1987) enumerated resources, extending on practical inquiry's focus on students, subject matter, teacher knowledge, and social milieus (Connelly & Clandinin, 1988; Clandinin & Connelly, 1992, 1995; Schwab, 1978, 1983), further articulates the knowledges that effective teachers possess and the complicated relationships between these knowledges that make effective teachers "good" at what they do. Effective teaching, in Shulman's (1987) description, includes understandings of content knowledge, knowledge of teaching and learning, understanding of established curriculum, knowledge of the students, knowledge of contexts (cultures, communities, and identities), and philosophical-moral understandings of social foundations of education. All of these knowledges, as Shulman (1987) understands it through his case studies of effective teachers, come together in teachers' pedagogical content knowledge. *Pedagogical content knowledge*, as definition, refers to *the special amalgam of content and pedagogy that effectively communicates subject area content to specific groups of students.* Particularly, as it relates to this life history and teacher story research, I elaborate teachers' and my own race-visible professional identifications and teaching stories, and in doing so, specific examples of pedagogical content knowledge emerged for working with diverse students in inner-city contexts that I call race-visible curriculum wisdom. These examples of race-visible curriculum wisdom provided examples and ideas that other preservice and professional teachers might elaborate on and make their own through processes of *transferability* and *adaptation*.

Culturally Relevant Teaching and Learning

Further articulating capacitating concepts' pragmatic understandings in Dewey's reflective wheel, practical inquiry, and reflective professionalism of previous sections, culturally relevant teaching and learning (Ladson-Billings, 1995, 2009) completes the capacitating concepts necessary to recount life history and teacher stories in this book. Culturally relevant teaching, in completing capacitating concepts, moves from pragmatic understandings of students' experiences in contexts toward recognizing that students' experiences take place within the complexity of cultural and collective identities. Culturally relevant teaching, recognizing students' cultural and collective identities, embraces the influence of anthropology and cultural studies on educational practices. Increasingly, anthropology and cultural studies demonstrate that teaching and learning represent culturally negotiated practices that intersect with both teachers and students' identities. Anthropology and cultural studies, supporting pragmatic understandings of experience in context in practical inquiry, articulate the centrality of students and teachers' identities, school and learning cultures, and community and social relationships important in educational success (Cummins, 1986, 1996; Gonzales, Moll, Amanti, 2005; Ladson-Billings, 2009), or conversely, failure (Valenzuela, 1999; Willis, 1977). Jerome Bruner (1986, 1990, 1995), developing a notion of cultural psychology in education, summarizes this very simple yet important point that ties cultural identity to questions of teaching and learning:

> Although meanings are "in the mind," they have their origins and their sign and their significance in the culture in which they are created. ...On this view,

learning and thinking are always situated in a cultural setting and dependent upon the utilization of *cultural resources*. (1995, p. 3–4)

Although important for all students, culturally relevant teaching and learning represents a priority in teaching poor students of color whose culture is typically subtracted in the education process (Valenzuela, 1999; Valenzuela & McNeil, 2000). Culturally relevant teaching and learning complement and complete other capacitating concepts in the practical democratic tradition outlined in the previous section.

A deluge of research, supporting culturally relevant teaching and learning, documents its effectiveness and success in reaching historically underserved populations (e.g., Cummins, 1986, 1996; Fairbanks, 1998a, 1998b; Gay, 2000; Gonzales, Moll, & Amanti, 2005; Henry, 1996; hooks, 1994; Jupp, 2004; Ladson-Billings, 1995, 2009; Moll, 1992; Moll & Gonzalez, 1994; Nee Benham, 1997; Nieto, 1999; Shor, 1987, 1992). Gloria Ladson-Billings (2009), summarizes the key role that culture plays in culturally relevant teaching and learning:

Specifically, culturally relevant teaching is a pedagogy that empowers students intellectually, socially, emotionally, and politically by using cultural referents to impart knowledge, skills, and attitudes. These cultural referents are not merely vehicles for bridging or explaining the dominant culture; they are aspects of the curriculum in their own right. (p. 20)

Additional support for teaching and learning as inherently embedded in teachers and students' identities and cultures comes from life history and teacher story research. Complementing understandings from culturally relevant teaching and learning, life history and teacher story research document that teaching and learning provide complex cultural interactions. As I read these studies through an anthropological and cultural studies lens, life history and teacher story complement insights in research on culturally relevant teaching in articulating that experiences, identities, and cultures are key in teaching and learning (Butt *et al.*, 1992; Clandinin & Connelly, 1992, 1995; Cole & Knowles, 2000, 2001; Connelly & Clandinin, 1988; Goodson, 1992, 1995; Goodson & Walker, 1991; Jupp & Slattery, 2010, 2012; Knowles, 1992; Knowles, 2001; Middleton, 1992, 1993; Xu, Connelly, He, Phillion, 2007). Completing the capacitating concepts, culturally relevant teaching and learning drives at understanding through students and teachers' lives and relevancy. As it relates to *Becoming Teachers of Inner-city Students*, teachers in this study all understood teaching and learning as culturally negotiated, integrated students' cultures and experiences into the curriculum, and through processes of reflective professionalism over time, re-thought, re-negotiated, and re-learned their professional identifications developing race-visible professional identifications.

Besides emphasizing the leveraging of students' cultures, culturally relevant teaching and learning emphasizes *teachers' relationality with students*. Culturally relevant teaching and learning's emphasis on relationality, corresponding with and supporting notions of feminist caring (Goldstein, 1997, 2002; Noddings, 1984) is also documented in a broad body of research on teaching with diverse students (e.g., Gay, 2000; Henry, 1996; hooks, 1994; Jupp, 2004; Ladson-Billings, 1995 2009; Nee Benham, 1997; Nieto, 1999; Valenzuela, 1999). Culturally relevant teaching, according to this body of research, demands teachers put skin-in-the-game with their students and that they develop relationships with communities, parents, social agencies, and the students themselves. Again, Ladson-Billings summarizes (2009) the centrality of relationality in culturally relevant teaching and learning:

> Instead of idiosyncratic and individualistic connections with certain students, these teachers work to assure each student of his or her individual importance. Although it has been suggested that teachers' unconsciously favor those students perceived to be most like themselves (or some ideal)..., culturally relevant teaching means consciously working to develop commonalities with all students. (p. 72)

Teachers' relationality with students, as all teachers in this study emphasized, was important in their ability to teach students academically. All teachers in this study, as teaching stories demonstrated, talked about developing relationships with their students. Many of them did it through assignments that made students' experiences central to the lessons, and others accomplished relationality by coaching sports or hosting afternoon clubs. Teachers' relationality with students, again reflecting Ladson-Billings' understanding, emerged as a key theme in in the teacher stories.

As a final note, culturally relevant teaching also informs capacitating concepts' recognition of critical perspectives (e.g., Giroux, 2011, 2012) yet focuses on practical commitments to teaching and learning in classrooms. Once again, Ladson-Billings (2009) informs capacitating concepts' political praxis as it relates to practical day-to-day teaching and learning: "Because of this [Giroux's critical] pedagogical view, I went into classrooms intending to examine both 'the political and the practical'" (p. 15). Capacitating concepts for practical teaching and learning, following Ladson-Billings's (2009), provide important understandings of critical content that begin to answer the question *What is to be done* in schools and classrooms right now. This recognition that practical teaching represents political praxis, perhaps more than following Giroux's remonstrative, declarative, and prescriptive voice, follows Freire's (1992/2002) understandings of tactics, strategies, and their relationships:

> Once more, then, it becomes incumbent upon them [leaders] to maintain a serious, rigorous relationship between tactics and strategy, a relationship of which I have already spoken in this book. In the last analysis, the problem facing the leaders is: they must learn through the critical reading of reality that must always be made, what actions can be tactically implemented, and on what levels they can be so implemented. In other words, *what can we do now in order to be able to do tomorrow what we are unable to do today.* (p. 125) [emphasis added]

How to write (handwritten)

Teachers in this study understood their teaching within political dimensions as life histories and teacher stories indicated. They conceived of education within political contexts, taught lessons with political-representational content, and most importantly, understood the political tactics of enabling their students now "in order to be able to do tomorrow what we are unable to do today" (Freire, 1992/2002, p. 125).

Race-Visible Curriculum Wisdom

In the second half of this chapter, I have developed capacitating concepts for practical teaching and learning in classrooms. From these capacitating concepts, a synthetic view of practical curriculum wisdom emerges that integrates progressive pragmatic educational traditions as well as understandings from anthropological and cultural studies traditions that emphasize culturally relevant teaching and learning. Following Xu, Connelly, He, and Phillion (2007) who begin to integrate narrative research, culture, and identity, I strive to develop an understanding of curriculum wisdom that integrates practical teaching and learning from the pragmatic tradition with notions of identity and learning from cultural studies and anthropological traditions.

Before advancing the term race-visible curriculum wisdom, I need to explain that the term curriculum wisdom has a long trajectory. On circulating the notion of *curriculum wisdom*, I further advance an idea that is called "wisdom of practice" (Schulman, 1987, p. 11), "wisdom through inquiry" (Clandinin & Connelly, 1992, p. 379) "wise practices" (Davis, 1997, p. 92), or directly stated "curriculum wisdom" (p. 44) from Henderson & Gornik (2007).[6] Curriculum wisdom, as I seek to advance it through pragmatic along with anthropological and cultural studies traditions, reflects Dewey's intentions to document his work in the lab school and seeks to develop a knowledge base that emerges from life histories, teaching stories, and other humanistic and qualitative research forms. Shulman (1987) summarizes what I seek to accomplish by advancing the notion of curriculum wisdom:

> It is the wisdom of practice itself, the maxims that guide (or provide reflective rationalizations for) practices of able teachers. One of the more important tasks for the research community is to work with practitioners to develop codified representations of the practical pedagogical wisdom of able teachers. (p. 11)

I understand curriculum wisdom's codified representations for guiding professional reflection as key to what Dewey (1938/1997) called "scientific method" (p. 89) in education, yet this scientific method, far from scientific "best practices," develops theory-generative, humanistic, qualitative, life history, and teacher story representations of able teachers in their work (Eisner, 1985).

Race-visible curriculum wisdom, reflected in capacitating concepts for practical teaching and learning, provides four over-arching themes that recur in all teachers stories in *Becoming Teachers of Inner-city Students*: *deliberative dialogue*, *relationality*, *synthetic teaching*, and *socio-political critique*.

1. *Deliberative dialogue*, drawing on understandings of professional deliberation and notions of students and teachers' identities from culturally relevant teaching, presents and represents teachers who work with students' experiences, interests, identities, and cultures as part of the curriculum with the intention not merely of reflecting them but of recovering, reconstructing, and critically evaluating them for advancement of students' understandings. Teachers in this study worked in deliberative dialogue with academic subject areas, colleagues' ideas and plans, professional knowledge, and students' experiences, interests, identities, and cultures.

2. *Relationality*, drawing on anthropological and cultural studies' influences, articulates teachers' need for direct relationships with students, families, communities, and social agencies that reflects feminist dictum that *the personal is the political*. Teachers in this study understood that their relationships to students and communities were key in their ability to teach students. Teachers emphasized these relationships as necessary investments in effectively functioning as a teacher.

3. *Synthetic teaching*, drawing on pragmatic understandings of reflective professionalism that rework Schwab's (1978, 1983) common places, present fluid representations of professional identifications in action that understand teaching and learning as actively synthesizing subject area knowledge, curriculum, social milieus and community contexts, students and teachers' identities in producing workable pedagogical content knowledge. Teachers in this study worked in complex synthetic ways that very much embodied reflective professionalism, and this reflective professionalism emphasized understandings of students' identities and communities' cultures.

4. *Socio-political critique*, drawing specifically on Ladson-Billings's socio-political critique, begins with understandings that education is political and that enabling students to perform academically represents a type of political praxis. Teachers in this study understood that teaching and learning took place within larger political contexts, taught politicized lessons, saw politics in the communities in which they taught, and understood academic level in their teaching as a political praxis. Part of this social political awareness included *race-visible professional identifications* developed in the first half of this section.

As this life history and teacher story research articulated in the essays, notions of synthetic teaching, deliberative dialogue, relationality, and socio-political critique provided central concepts for race-visible curriculum wisdom.

Finally, in closing the second half of this chapter on capacitating concepts for practical teaching and learning, I emphasize race visible curriculum wisdom's democratic ideals. Emerging from the US pragmatic tradition in education, the term curriculum wisdom seeks to create a language for capacitating teachers who in turn capacitate students. This notion of capacitating teachers to capacitate students irrevocably insists on democratic leadership in its ideals. Henderson & Gornik

129

(2007), in describing curriculum wisdom (2007), articulate curriculum wisdom's ideals:

> The love of democratic wisdom requires a soul-searching honesty directed toward public virtue. Do my judgments embody the democratic good life? Am I truly open to diverse others? Do I listen carefully to people with whom I disagree...? (Henderson & Gornik, 2007, p. 19)

In presenting race-visible curriculum wisdom as centerpiece for enabling teachers who morally take up notions of synthetic teaching, deliberative dialogue, relationality, and socio-political critique, *Becoming Teachers of Inner-city Students* sought to reflect teachers' practice but also integrated Dewey's vision of education with recent influences of anthropological and cultural studies.

RECAPPING CAPACITATING CONCEPTS

Reviewing and Emphasizing Second Wave White Teacher Identity Studies

These capacitating concepts, necessary for telling the stories, serve the dual purpose of *helping me narrate* life histories and teaching stories along with *seeking to inform* preservice and professional teachers' race-visible professional identifications. Capacitating concepts followed two lines of thought: White teacher identity and practical teaching and learning.

Regarding White teacher identity, I reviewed existing understandings of white teacher identity that narrated and reflected White teachers' race-evasive identities. Reaching back to Paley's (1978/2000) *White Teacher* as capacitating resource for process understandings of professional identifications, I suggested second wave White teacher identity studies that narrated the development of race-visible professional identifications. In articulating second wave White teacher identity studies, I suggested second wave *life-history-and-teacher-story-based* concepts for moving beyond static race-evasive identities in existing understandings of White teachers' identities. In developing these second wave concepts, I focused on understandings that sustain not static identities but rather articulate *professional identifications'* development and becoming over time. In addition to professional identifications, these second wave concepts included: *identifications, boundedness, race-visible profession identifications, discursive contexts*, and *progressive masculinities*. These second wave concepts, I maintain and hope, should *un*-fix White teachers' professional identifications toward understandings that emphasize on-going development and becoming that emphasize teachers' practical work.

Regarding practical teaching and learning, I emphasized the recent teacher research movement that has its roots in the long-standing pragmatic tradition in education. In this discussion on the pragmatic tradition in education, John Dewey's reflective wheel, further developed into reflective professionalism (Schön, 1983), provided an important basis for on-going reflection on teaching and learning. Additionally, notions of practical inquiry (Clandinin & Connelly, 1992; Connelly & Clandinin, 1988; Schwab, 1978, 1983), further developed into reflective professionalism (Shulman, 1987), provided pragmatic understandings for experimenting with complex tasks of teaching and learning in classrooms. Finally, anthropological and cultural studies traditions, providing understandings of culturally relevant teaching, served to recover and reconstruct an updated version of *curriculum wisdom* that integrated notions of students' cultures and identities with understandings of relationality and political praxis. *Race-visible curriculum wisdom* included key concepts of synthetic teaching, deliberative dialogue, relationality, and socio-political critique.

Capacitating concepts, as they related to White teacher identity and practical teaching and learning sought to develop progressive *race-visible professional identifications* and *race-visible curriculum wisdom* for White teachers; nonetheless, capacitating concepts reached beyond questions of White identity in education and articulated second wave White teacher identity studies.

NOTES

[1] "Evidence-based" concepts differ from scientistic "best practices" in that they embrace theoretically-driven qualitative understandings and research including autobiography, life history, and narrative among other approaches. Wresting the term back from scientistic understandings of educational research, the purpose in discussing evidence-based practices in Appendix A is to review vast qualitative evidence for capacitating concepts.

[2] According to the National Center of Education Statistics (NCES) (2004), White teachers make up 88.6% of combined elementary and secondary school teachers while children of color approach 45% of children attending public schools (NCES, 2008).

[3] Gary Howard's REACH conducts interventionist multicultural staff development and training for schools and corporations.

[4] For examples of textbooks outlining similar discussions see Bennett, 2010; Johnson, Musial, Hall, & Gollnick, 2010; Nieto & Bode, 2011; Tozer, Senese, Violas, 2009.

[5] The notion of identifications, extended into professional identifications throughout this book, *do not* assume race-transcendent positions nor race-transcendent look-alikes such as White abolitionist or race traitor positions. Further, identifications *do not* assume color blind positions, nor do identifications assume, as mass media sources felicitously proclaim, post-racial positions. Contrasting with race-transcendent, color-blind, or post-racial positions, the notion of identifications, extended into professional identifications, seeks to narrate complex race-visible professional identifications.

[6] I am sure there are more versions of variously named curriculum wisdom appearing in curriculum and pedagogy research. Nonetheless, as I stated in the outset, what I am writing is not an exhaustive review of literatures on topics in Chapter One, but rather an assembly of life-history-and-teaching-story concepts that help me recount the stories that might inform preservice and professional teachers' race-visible professional identifications.

APPENDIX B

Name: ____________________

Date: ____________________

Questionnaire for Incoming 8th Grade Students

The Purpose: The reason for doing this questionnaire, and doing it as extensively as I'm going to do it, is to learn more about YOU so that I can direct my instruction toward your interests, ideas, likes and dislikes, and overall, what you want to learn and how you want to learn it.

Please answer the following questions using three to five complete sentences.

1. What was one activity last summer that you really enjoyed doing?

I went to Huston, Texas. I visited my family there and spent a lot of time with them. Then I also went to my cousin 'Erika's graduation in Huston.

Excellent

2. What is an activity that you really enjoy?

I loved playing sports alot. My favorite sport's I loved doing is Basketball, softball and softball.

Figure 1 Questionnaire

3. One activity that I really enjoyed at school was?

Playing volleyball for the school. and making A team. Also basket ball and betball or street ? in the ?

4. What's something that you are really good at?

I am very good at play shortstop ? and every thing in the infeild in my softball game. when I go up to Bat I always hit the into the out feild.

5. What's something that you are kind of good at?

I'm kind of good at spiking the ball. And I'm kind of good of reading fast.

6. What is something at school that you do not like at all?

I dont like the way there is alot of people in lunch and not being able to eat. I dont like when people think bad in school. And I also don't like the way this school is. And the way my day here is not going to be all boring outside classes.

7. What is something about school that upsets you or makes you nervous?

What makes me nervous is reading out loud to the class. I get upset when I'm reading and I'm messing up on words.

8. What is something about school that makes you very angry?

When kids talk crap about other people. Also when kids fight for stupid reasons.

9. What is something that you think is really disgusting?

When kids spit on other kids clothes, shoes, and hair. Also what really disgusting is when we have to disect animals.

10. If you could chose anything to be when you grow up, what would that be?

I would want to be a professional basketball player. I dont know what else I want to be because I want to still look for what I can do to make a lot of money, so I can get a lambeging

11. The best movie I ever saw was?

The gladiator is the best movie I ever saw. Is the best cause now I know how prisoners in Europe got treated. they had to battle until death.

12. What do you think the purpose of school is?

to learn a lot of stuff so when
we grow up we could get and
job we want. Also so we could
an education and a better
life.

13. What do you really like about your family?

What I like about my family is
that I can never stop having fun.
Because I have a lot of cousin,
Tios, and Tias that can always
talk to me, and play a lot with
me. Al... because

14. What are some things that annoy you about your family?

My little sister annoy me a lot
because she bing me, messes with
me so we can start fighting. My
little brother annoy me because
he talks tooo much.

15. Who are your friends, and why are they important?

My friends are _____ and
Sloane. They are important because
I treat them like their own
sisters, and also because we
are _____ three _____.

16. What type of music do you like, and why?

_____ , Colombianas, cumbia
_____ salsa merecue _____
I like them I could dance
to them and have parties.

17. What's the biggest problem of your life? What's the best part of your life?

The biggest problem is trying
to get my BIG family together.
The best part is that I'm
doing well and I'm still
joining now we are great
friends.

Name: _____

Date: _____

Research Project—American Civil Rights Activists

This six weeks will be your big library research project. During this six weeks, you will research an American Civil Rights Activist, take notes on the outline provided in this packet, write a rough draft that Mr. Jupp will correct, and finally, publish your work on your internet website at www.think.com .

You will also be responsible for developing a bibliography of sources that you used while making up the project. We will visit your websites in order to learn more about civil rights activists after you have published your work.

You may choose from the civil rights activist below—

Revolutionary Figures:	**Women's Movement:**
Thomas Jefferson	Abigail Adams
George Washington	Susan B. Anthony
Alexander Hamilton	Elizabeth Cady Stanton
Benjamin Franklin	Gloria Steinham
John Adams	Betty Freidan
Andrew Jackson	Bella Abzug
	Lucrecia Mott
Mexican and Mexican American	**African American**
Miguel Hidalgo	Rosa Parks
Pancho Villa	Harriett Tubman
Emiliano Zapata	Sojouner Truth
Cesar Chavez	Nate Turner (slave rebellion)
Dolores Huerta	Fredrick Douglas
	Dr. Martin Luther King, Jr.
	Coretta Scott King (MLK's wife)
	Malcolm X

You are welcome to choose another civil rights activist so long you get your topic approved by the teacher.

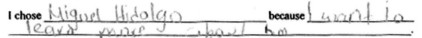

I chose Miguel Hidalgo because I want to learn more about him.

Figure 2 Research Organizer

Biographical Research Outline
Research Question: What contribution have civil rights
activists made in the United States?

I. General Information

    A.   Name of person _Hidalgo y costilla Miguel_

    B.   Date of birth _1753_

    C.   Date of death _1811_

    D.   Information about childhood

       He study at the Jesuit
       College of san Francisco
       Javier.
       He all ready know how to
       read and write

II.   A. Education

       educated in Valladolid now morelia

      B. Marriage and Children

       No marriage and no children
       because he was a priest.

C. Career

he went to the priests

was ~~~~ leader

he was a creole priest

III. Important Facts — [Use a Time Line Here]

1. 1753 Miguel Hidalgo was born

2. ~~sin~~ October 1810 they reached an agreement in Queretaro to begin a revolution.

3. 1811 Father Hidalgo fell in an ambush staged by Felix Maria Calleja and after relieved of his duties as a priest he was sentenced and shot to death

4. September 21, 1821 Mexico gain its independence.

5. September 16 1810 they were discovered and force to move up

6. Sept 16 1810 he issued el Grito de Dolores cry of dolores

IV. Accomplishments and contributions to society

Miguel Hidalgo help the people of the country site.

Miguel Hidalgo ayuda a mexico a ganar su independencia.

Hacia lavor para aprovechar los recuorse naturales

Hidalgo ysus seguidares se lanzaron ala lucha de la independencia.

Hidalgo dio su vida por mexico

To help the indigenous he built an estate where he established a pottery shop, a tanning shop, a blacksmith stable, carpentry store, and a tanning shop

V. Importance of this person to you/Conclusion
What was this person's contribution? Why was this person important in US history?

    A. How has this person been a positive influence on you?

       He was helpful to poor
       people.

    B. What was this person's big contribution to the United States—You may repeat the main points from Roman numeral IV.

       Hidalgo iba rumbo a E.U.A.
       a conseguir pertrechos
       cuando fue traicionada

RESEARCH METHODOLOGY

Life History and Teacher Story Research

OVERVIEW

For researchers and interested students, Appendix C discusses life history and teacher story research along with methodological details of *Becoming Teachers of Inner-City Students*. In this discussion, I briefly extend discussions on life history and teacher story research with particular focus on influences and purposes. In extending discussions on life history and teacher story research, I connect *identifications* within *boundedness* and *professional identifications* within *discursive contexts* explicitly to life history and teacher story methodology. After making these connections, I extend discussions of researcher positionality in Chapter One with understandings of reflexivity and relationality called "trading points" (Goodson, 1995, p. 97) important to life history as it relates to this study. After discussing reflexivity, relationality, and trading points, I provide a practical discussion on methodological details necessary for evaluating this study. This practical discussion on methodological details includes sampling strategies, data gathering, analysis, and validity. As a final note, I encourage students and future educational researchers to recover and reconstruct practical and democratic traditions of life history and teacher story research.

LIFE HISTORY AND TEACHER STORY RESEARCH

Influences, Purposes

Becoming Teachers of Inner-City Students exemplifies what is meant by life history and teacher story research. Broadly speaking, life history research recovers, reconstructs, and advances life history methodology in educational settings (e.g., Cole & Knowles, 2001; Goodson, 1992, 1995; Goodson & Sikes, 2001; Plummer, 2001). In life history methodology, the researcher transforms life stories from respondents' interviews into life histories by elaborating contexts using relevant literatures and other documents (Ivor Goodson and Pat Sikes (2001), in explaining how life histories are elaborated from life story interviews, drive at life history's purpose:

> The life history is collaboratively constructed by a life story teller and life story interviewer/researcher. Therein, the aspiration is different from that of the life story. The aim is to "locate" the life story as it operates in particular historical circumstances. A range of data is employed: documents, interviews with

relevant others, theories, texts…. These data are, so to speak, triangulated, to locate the life story as a social phenomenon existing in historical time. (p. 62)

In the researcher's transformation of life story into life history, the purpose of life history becomes historical and sociological or *the understanding of life stories in historical and social contexts.* In taking up life history, the overall purpose is to narrate a carefully contextualized story of respondents' lives and identities. Adding to literatures on life history in *Becoming Teachers of Inner-City Students*, I integrate recent narrative and process-oriented notions of identity (Bruner, 2002; Butler, 1999; Hall, 2003) as *identifications* within *boundedness*. As I narrate in Chapter One and explain in Appendix A, *identifications* and *boundedness* conceptually supplement life history research by emphasizing that life story interviews provide textually performed identifications from which the researcher constructs boundedness through semiotic analysis of life story interview transcripts (Jupp, In press).

More specifically, life history and teacher story research here elaborate on life history in educational contexts. As many life history researchers have noted, life history is particularly relevant for understanding teachers' lives and practices (Cole & Knowles, 2000, 2001; Goodson, 1992, 1995; Goodson & Sikes, 2001). As the purpose of life history is to provide a carefully contextualized story of respondents' lives, life history in educational contexts provides opportunities for careful understandings of teachers and students' lives in educational institutions including: contextualized teaching and learning, teachers' private and public understandings and aspirations, and teachers' professional identifications among other topics important for understanding teaching, learning, identity, and culture. Life history and teacher research, within this purpose of articulating lives within educational contexts, also recovers, reconstructs, and advances Clandinin and Connelly's (1992) research on *teachers-as-curriculum-makers:*

> Our initial task, then, is to listen to teachers' stories as they are told and lived out in practice. These are the teachers' stories of themselves as they engage with learners and subject matter within both the immediate and larger social, political, and cultural milieu. Some researchers are beginning to undertake the task. Although their purposes are varied, their common intention is to listen to teachers' stories as they are lived and told and to retell them in methods and languages that do justice to what they have seen. (p. 392)

Adding to literatures on teacher story research, *professional identifications* and *discursive contexts* conceptually supplement teacher story literatures by providing dynamic and narrative notions of professional identity along with careful discourse-sensitive readings of educational contexts (Jupp, 2013; Jupp & Slattery, 2012).

Reflexivity, Relationality, and Trading Points

As narratively presented and explained in Chapter One, this life history and teacher story research emerges from and is informed by my life and teacher stories as White

146

male teacher and curriculum maker of rural poor and later inner-city students. In this life history and teacher story research, I investigated what it meant for other respondents and myself to become White teachers of inner-city students during the contemporary historical period: the Conservative Restoration. The choice of investigating my own identifications and historical contexts represents a self-conscious one, a choice that corresponds with reflexivity (Foley, 2002; Lather, 1992; Goodson, 1995) in human science and educational research. Reflexivity in social science and educational research recognizes that, historically, the relation between researcher and respondents represents a colonial one, especially in research studies in which a privileged researcher investigates marginalized or less powerful participants. This choice of *reflexively studying my own identifications* adds to a growing body of research (Foley, 2002; Lather, 1991; Ladson-Billings, 1995; Valenzuela, 1999; Scheurich, 2002) that seeks equitable social relations in which researcher and respondents come from and represent the same groups.

Nonetheless, the enactment of equal social relations during the research process remains a complex task. Often, research that strives for equal social relations contains traces of the original colonial relation (Villenas, 1996, 2000) as research represents a worldly activity (Said, 1989; Said, 1993). Research exists within economies of worldly desires regarding credentialing, career, and tenure, and it remains important for consumers of research to read this worldliness along with findings. My work here, reflexively understood, exists as part of credentialing, tenure, and promotion, but as Said (1989) holds in his notion of worldliness, research and writing represent worldly activities but should not be dismissed on this basis. This research, although representing a worldly activity, also provided an opportunity for relationality with teachers that Goodson (1992, 1995) calls *trading points*.

Goodson's (1995) concept of trading points provides direction for developing relationality in negotiation relationships between researchers and respondents:

> A good deal of work now emerging on teachers' lives and careers develops insights about structure that help locate the teacher's life within the deep social structure and embedded milieu of schooling. This work and these contexts provide a prime trading point for the external researcher. One of the most valuable aspects of a collaboration between teachers as researchers and externally located researchers is that the collaboration takes place between parties that are differentially located in social structure. In this sense, each of the two collaborators sees the world through a different prism of thought and practice. This difference, far from providing a barrier to collaboration, can be valuable when trading points are sought. (p. 97)

In relation to this critical inquiry, trading points were facilitated because I was a school-based teacher and researcher that worked side-by-side with all respondents during the time data were collected. Teachers in this study and I worked together on projects, developed and shared curriculum materials, and basically shared the same space over several years.

These trading points provided an opportunity to work collaboratively and reflect sensitively on teachers' life stories as they intersected with social contexts. Although I approached teachers' stories with more cultural capital as represented in my academic training, I recognized what it was like to perform their work as I performed and continued to perform it even after the dissertation was completed as several teachers and I finished an important school project. As a reflexive researcher interested in relationality and trading points, I hoped to reveal, illuminate, and critique the teachers' life and teacher stories yet tried to avoid re-writing teachers as pathology, which is too often the case in pedagogical research on teachers in education. In sum, although this life history and teacher story research represented a worldly activity, it also allowed for my contribution to the literatures on White teachers conducted by a researcher who did the same work as the respondents for eighteen years. As very few researchers in education spent lengthy careers in public school classrooms with diverse students, my reflexivity, relationality, and trading points provided a unique opportunity that supported practical methodological details described below. Through relationality and trading points, I was able to collect the data, and by reflexively working with the data, I attempted to carefully contextualize teachers' life and teacher stories gathered in interviews thereby transforming them into life history and teacher story research.

METHDOLOGICAL DETAILS

The Sample

I initiated a purposive snowball sample starting with colleagues from my inner-city schools. After carrying out the purposive snowball sample that gathered data from seven teachers, I added my life and teacher stories taken from piloting the interview instruments. I am the eighth respondent, as I will explain below. Since life and teacher story interviews average four to six hours over a minimum of two sessions (sometimes more), the number of teacher respondents does not attempt to achieve statistical representation. Rather, life history emphasizes depth of representation within historical and social contexts (Cole & Knowles, 2001; Goodson & Sikes, 2001).

Criteria for participants in the snowball sample included being White and male, working in majority "minority" classrooms, choosing to work with inner-city students, and having worked for at least four years in inner-city settings.

1. *Being white and male* as criteria referred to teachers' status identities.
2. *Working in majority "minority" classrooms* as criterion referred to teachers who taught in schools and classrooms with a majority of "minority" students. This criterion excluded teachers who taught in classrooms with a majority of White students and focused on teachers who taught across borders of race, class, culture, language, and other differences.
3. *Choosing to work with inner-city students* as criterion referred to teachers with professional identifications that preferred and selected work with inner-city

students. *Choosing* as criterion sought to articulate teachers "commitment" referenced in the title of this book. This criterion includes teachers who originally chose to work in inner-city settings or those who, over time, developed professional identifications expressing this choice. This criterion excluded teachers who did not choose to work in inner-city settings, registered on-going complaints and dislikes regarding their work or students, or who actively sought to leave inner-city schools.

4. *Having worked for at least four years in inner-city schools* as criterion set a minimum amount of experience for participation in this study. This criterion indicated a concrete number of years for accommodation into work routines in inner-city schools and with inner-city students. Like the criterion on *choosing*, this criterion sought to articulate "commitment" referenced in the title of this book. This criterion excluded teachers who were just beginning their work in inner-city schools, who were early leavers, who were "good" with students but burned out, or others who had less stable professional commitments. The range of experience in teachers at the time of data collection ranged between seven and eighteen years.

These four criteria represented the non-negotiable starting points for this purposive snowball sample. I screened teachers along these criteria in selecting the teachers for the study. The teachers then brain-stormed subsequent respondents, and I screened teachers' suggestions applying the criteria. All teachers from the snowball sample worked with inner-city students in urban schools in Austin ISD that contained a majority of students labeled "minority," "low SES," "at risk," or "below grade level."

All teachers' and their school's names were pseudonyms. The pseudonyms of the eight respondents from the sample were Mike Taymes, Rudy Smith, Gene Johansen, Bennett Ferris, Jack Springman, Trent Cowens, David McGrady, and Frank Carmody. I, Jim Jupp, was the eighth respondent in the study, and in previous chapters, my life and teacher story interviews supplemented those of other teachers using the pseudonym of Frank Carmody. At the time of gathering the data, *Mike Taymes* worked at Eastside Middle School in Austin, Texas. Starting his teaching career at wilderness camps for "troubled" youth, he taught all subject areas in the emotionally disturbed unit at the time of this study. *Rudy Smith* worked at Southside Middle School teaching comprehensive English and Pre-AP classes at the time of this study. Additionally, he coached eighth grade basketball at Southside Middle School during this time. *Gene Johansen*, who started his career working on juvenile corrections wagon train in Arizona, worked at Southside Middle School and taught special education resource classes and remedial reading at the time of this study. Additionally, he directed several afternoon clubs including Future Teachers of America and an Art Club. *Bennett Ferris* worked at Southside Middle School teaching magnet English classes and school-wide electives at the time of this study. Additionally, he directed several afternoon clubs including the Martial Arts Club and a Gifted and Talented Club. *Jack Springman* worked at Southside Middle School at the time of this study teaching one advanced English I section, media communications electives, and comprehensive English classes. Additionally, he directed a film club during this time. *Trent Cowens* worked at Eastside Middle School at the time of this study teaching sixth grade social studies. Trent also directed several afternoon clubs including the World Garden Club and coached seventh grade girls basketball during this time. *David McGrady* worked at Eastside Middle School teaching sixth grade social studies at the time of this study. He also directed several afternoon clubs including the World Garden Club and served as an assistant coach in eighth grade football for several years.

Data Gathering

Regarding data gathering, this study used four sources: interviews, a focus group meeting, peer debriefing, and a researcher journal.

1. *Interviews.* I engaged seven teachers in a minimum of two rounds of interviews followed by member checking. In the first round of interviewing, teachers recounted their life stories. I recorded the stories for transcription and also took notes followed by member checking. In the second round of interviewing, teachers recounted their teacher stories. I again recorded the stories for transcription and took notes followed by member checking. Additional interviews followed the first two interviews, and this additional interviewing continues to date as the book is published. As for my data from my life and teacher stories, I added my piloted written responses to the data after interviewing the teachers was over.

2. *Focus group meeting.* I added the focus group meeting to the data collection methods to provide a layer of reflexivity regarding initial interviews. I recorded and transcribed the focus group meeting in the same way as the interviews. The focus group meeting began with teachers' reviewing, revising, and/or expanding on transcripts. After reviewing transcripts with teachers, I engaged teachers regarding emergent findings. When participants finished reflecting on the findings, I asked teachers to share their reflections on the research process. At the focus group meeting, the teachers were given the opportunity to comment on, revise, critique, and participate in developing research findings.

3. *Peer debriefing sessions.* I added peer debriefing as a third data source and another layer of reflexivity on emergent findings. I held peer debriefing sessions with two colleagues of color: one school-based and the other university-based. The peer debriefing sessions, in which the researcher reflected on and received collegial feedback from peers of color, provided more data and allowed for guided reflection on the findings. These peer debriefing sessions, like the interviews and focus group meetings, were recorded and transcribed for use in data analysis.[1]

4. *Researcher journal.* During the process and to date, I wrote in a journal and reflected on the research and the writing as fourth source of data. Mostly, I used the journal as a space to begin to write and make sense of the data. Additionally,

I used the journal as a means to capture additional memories of interactions and conversations with teachers as an aide in contextualizing life and teacher stories. Finally, I used the journal to contextualize life history and teacher stories by collecting documentation such as newspaper articles and mainstream research reports and copying relevant fragments into the journal. In this way, I used the journal to contextualize teachers' life and teacher stories, especially in relation to discursive contexts.

Data Analysis

Analysis for this study begins with an understanding that data are textual representations of lived experiences (Clandinin & Connelly, 2000; Denzin, 1989; Goodson & Sikes, 2001). In approaching analysis, this life history and teacher story research strives to "capture, probe, and render understandable problematic experience" (Denzin, 1989, p. 69). Although the relation between experience and data is necessarily complex in life history (Cary, 1999; Denzin, 1989; Munro, 1995), for my purposes interview data are understood as text containing traces of teachers' lived experiences.

Analysis in this critical inquiry follows a recursive and non-linear process that allows for the complexities of narrating *identifications* and *boundedness* along with *professional identifications* and *discursive contexts*. This recursive and non-linear analysis includes 1) identifying emergent patterns in interview transcripts, 2) contextualizing patterns within existing research and other documents, and 3) working reflexively through my positionality as teacher of inner-city students. In relation to these three components – identifying patterns, contextualizing patterns, and working through my positionality – all three function dialectically in detecting, analyzing, and exploring teachers' patterns of lived experience.

Identifying emergent patterns is the first component of data analysis in this life history and teacher story research (Cole & Knowles, 2001). Identifying emergent patterns necessarily requires systematic attention to the information gathered. However, identifying patterns must also be carried out with attention to "understand, in a holistic way, the connectedness and interrelatedness of human experience within complex social structures" (Cole & Knowles, 2001, p. 101). Important for holistic understanding of participants' lived experiences, identifying emergent patterns in this life history and teacher story research avoids strict and formulaic coding, categorization, and triangulation processes (Cole & Knowles, 2001; Goodson & Sikes, 2001; Plummer 2001), but rather holistic understanding follows the purposes of life history and teacher story research which holistically stories identifications within boundedness and professional identifications within discursive contexts.

Contextualizing patterns within existing research and provides a second component for the data analysis. Critical literatures on whiteness, masculinity, student difference, and difference pedagogy provide historical and social boundedness from which to question, analyze, explore, and elaborate patterns in the data. Corresponding with the purposes of life history, existing research and other documents serve to articulate, situate, and contextualize life history and teacher story research (Cole & Knowles, 2001; Goodson, 1992, 1995; Goodson & Sikes 2001; Munro, 1995; Plummer, 2001).

Working reflexively through my positionality, which provides a motive and ethic for this study, provides the third component for data analysis. Regarding interview and focus group interactions, the researcher's positionality provides a basis for empathic conversations with teachers with similar identities doing the same line of professional labor. Given that my positionality marks a starting point in these conversations, this life history and teacher story research assumes that data analysis is embedded at all levels of data generation including interviews, identifying patterns, analysis of critical literatures, and articulating participants' lived experiences (Cole & Knowles, 2001, Knowles, 2001). This life history and teacher story research, conceptualized with my positionality in mind, assumes that my experience as teacher underlies data analysis, interpretation, and findings.

Each of these components of the data analysis – identifying emergent patterns, contextualizing patterns, and working reflexively through positionality – function dialectically as analysis. Each of the components of the analysis will interact and respond to the other two.

Validity as Credibility

This life history and teacher story research works with notions of validity as credibility established the 1980s and developed in the 1990s (e.g., Bruner, 1985; Lincoln & Guba; 1985; Emihovich, 1995). As Appendix C is designed for researchers *and interested students*, I briefly outline the notion of validity as credibility.

This life history and teacher story research, corresponding generally with assumptions of qualitative and narrative research, "precludes verification as the basis for [its] 'reality' or 'meaning'" (Bruner, 1985, p. 112). Because it precludes verification for its reality or meaning, this life history and teacher story research also precludes discussions of quantitative-scientific validity (Bruner, 1985). Regarding validity, this life history and teacher story research assumes "the criteria of believability" (Brunner, 1986, p. 112) or *credibility* (Lincoln & Guba, 1985; Emihovich, 1995). Using the criterion of credibility, research validity moves toward discussions of transferability, dependability, and confirmability (Lincoln & Guba, 1985). Transferability assumes that findings of the research are relevant and transferable to readers of research in other settings. Dependability refers to the ability of other researchers working in comparable perspectives and using comparable methods to come across similarities and differences in the research conclusions. Confirmability refers to the ability of researchers working from the same epistemological assumptions to revisit evidence and find conclusions reasonable though variable. Catherine Emihovich's (1995) "Distancing Passion: Narrative in the Social Sciences" articulates the process assumed when credibility is the central measure of validity:

The key for transformation through narrative lies in collaboration, of constantly testing out meanings against those of all others, building consensus around shared meaning, and ensuring as many voices as possible are heard. (p. 45)

In short, using the criteria of credibility regarding validity, researchers measure validity through influencing a larger discussion concerning understandings of research and teaching practices.

This life history and teacher story research, in judging validity, adapts the criterion of credibility with the sub-criteria transferability, dependability, and confirmability (Lincoln & Guba, 1985). In this research, I develop a study that 1) engages my life-long struggle and preoccupation, 2) collaborates with White male teachers like myself who worked with inner-city students, 3) contains member checking during and immediately after two rounds of interviewing, 4) provides focus groups for the researcher and teachers to negotiate perspectives and meanings while reflecting on and critiquing the research process, and 5) uses peer de-briefing sessions as a form of shared reflection regarding the research process and findings.

Limits of Life History and Teacher Story Research

Life history and teacher story research, although it allows advantages of exploring identifications within boundedness and professional identifications within discursive contexts, also presents limits regarding analyses and findings. As life history research provides aesthetic representations of participants' lived experiences (Cole & Knowles, 2001; Denzin, 1989; Goodson & Sikes, 2001), it is important to bear in mind that subsequent analyses and findings remain problematic (Cary, 1999; Denzin, 1989; Munro, 1995), especially in relation to respondents' reported classroom pedagogies, which remain unconfirmed in observation. With life history and teacher story research, it remains important to bear in mind that I work with teachers' transcripts as texts (Cary, 1999; Denzin, 1989; Munro, 1995).

NOTE

[1] Even though data from the peer debriefing sessions has not emerged as a central data source used in the book, the peer debriefing sessions reflexively influenced the study at a critical point. As one example of this influence, peers of color significantly changed the direction of the analysis when they expressed incredulity to one emergent direction in the findings: teaching as subversive activity. Because of peers' incredulity before this finding (along with insufficient support in the data), I dropped this finding. In this example, I provided just one example about how peers of color played, overall, an important role regarding reflexive data analysis in the research.

REFERENCES

Allan, J. (1993). Male elementary school teachers: Experiences and perspectives. In C. L. William's (Ed.), *Doing women's work: Men in non-traditional occupations* (pp. 113–127). London: Sage Publications.

Anyon, J. (1997). *Ghetto schooling: A political economy of urban educational reform* (Chapters 1 & 2, pp. 3–38). New York, NY.: Teachers College Press.

Anyon (1995). Race, social class, and educational reform in an inner-city school. *Teachers College Record, 97*(1), 69–94.

Appelbaum, P. (2002). *Multicultural and diversity education.* Denver, CO: ABC-CLIO.

Apple, M. (1993). Constructing the "other": Rightist reconstructions of common sense. In C. McCarthy & W. Crichlow (Eds.), *Race, identity, and representation in education* (pp. 24–39). New York, NY: Routledge.

Apple, M. W. (2000). *Official knowledge: Democratic education in a conservative age.* New York, NY: Routledge.

Asher, N. (2007). Made in the (multicultural) U.S.A: Unpacking the tensions of race, culture, gender, and sexuality in education. *Educational Researcher, 36*(2), 65–73.

Bamberg, A. (2004). Considering counternarratives. In A. Bamberg & M. Andrews (Eds.), *Considering counternarratives: Narrating, resisting, and making sense* (pp. 351–371). Amsterdam: John Benjamins.

Bamberg, A., & Andrews, M. (Eds.) (2004). *Considering counternarratives: Narrating, resisting, and making sense.* Amsterdam: John Benjamins.

Bamberg, A. (2009). Identity and narration. In P. Hühn, J. P. Wolf Schmid, & J. Schönert (Eds.), *Handbook of narratology.* New York, NY: Walter de Gruyter.

Bennett, C. I. (2010). *Comprehensive multicultural education: Theory and practice* (7th ed.). Boston, MA: Allyn & Bacon.

Benton Decorse, C. J., & Vogtle, S. P. (1997). In a complex voice: The contradictions of male elementary school teachers career choice and professional identity. *Journal of Teacher Education 48*(1), 37–46.

Berlak, A. (1999). Teaching and testimony: Witnessing and bearing witness to racisms in culturally diverse classrooms. *Curriculum Inquiry, 29*(1), 99–126.

Beynon, J. (2002). *Masculinities and culture.* Philadelphia, PA: Open University Press.

Bloom, A. (1987). *The closing of the American mind.* New York, NY: Touchstone.

Bomer, R. (2011). *Building adolescent literacy in today's English classrooms.* Portsmouth, NH: Heinemann.

Burroughs, W. (2003). *Junkie.* New York, NY: Penguin Books. (Originally published in 1953.)

Bruner, J. (1990). *Acts of meaning.* Cambridge, MA: Harvard University Press.

Bruner, J. (1986). *Actual minds, possible worlds.* Cambridge, MA: Harvard University Press.

Bruner, J. (1995). *The culture of education.* Cambridge, MA: Harvard University Press.

Bruner, J. (1985). Narrative and paradigmatic modes of thought. In E. Eisner (Ed.), *Learning and teaching the ways of knowing* (pp. 97–115). Chicago, IL: University of Chicago Press.

Bruner, J. S. (2002). *Making stories: Law, literature, life.* Cambridge, MA: Harvard University Press.

Butler, J. (1999). *Gender trouble: Feminism and the inversion of identity* (2nd ed.). New York, NY: Routledge.

Butt, R., Raymond, D., McCue, G., & Yamagishi, L. (1992). Collaborative autobiography and the teacher's voice. In I. F. Goodson (Ed.), *Studying teachers' lives* (pp. 51–98). New York, NY: Teachers College Press.

Callahan, R. E. (1962). *Education and the cult of efficiency.* Chicago, IL: University of Chicago Press.

Cary, L.J. (1999). Unexpected stories: Life history and the limits of representation. *Qualitative Inquiry, 5*(3), 411–427.

Chilcot, L. (Producer), Guggenheim, D. (Director). (2010). *Waiting for superman.* United States: Paramount Vantage and Participant Media.

Clandinin, D. J., & Connelly, F. M. (2000). *Narrative inquiry.* San Francisco, CA: Jossey-Bass.

REFERENCES

Clandinin, D. J., & Connelly, F. M. (1992). *Teachers as curriculum makers*. In P. Jackson (Ed.), *Handbook of research on curriculum* (pp. 363–401). New York, NY: MacMillan.

Clandinin, D. J., & Connelly, F. M. (1995). *Teachers' professional knowledge landscapes*. New York: Teachers College Press.

Cole, A. L., & Knowles, J. G. (2001) *Lives in context: The art of life history research*. New York, NY: Altamira.

Cole, A. L., & Knowles, J. G. (2000) *Researching teaching: Exploring teacher development through reflexive inquiry*. Boston, MA: Allyn & Bacon.

Connell, R. W. (1987). *Gender and power*. Stanford, CA: Stanford University Press.

Connell, R. W. (1995). *Masculinities*. Los Angeles, CA: University of California Press.

Connelly, F. M., & Clandinin, D. J. (1988). *Teachers as curriculum planners: Narratives of experience*. New York, NY: Teachers College Press.

Counts, G. (1978). *Dare the school build a new social order*. Carbondale & Edwardsville, IL: Southern Illinois University Press. (Original work published in 1932)

Crotty, M. (2003). *The foundations of social research*. London: Sage Publications.

Cummins, J. (1986). Empowering minority students: A framework for intervention. *Harvard Educational Review 56* (1), 18–36.

Cummins, J. (1996). *Negotiating identities: Education for empowerment in a diverse society*. Ontario, Canada: California Association for Bilingual Education.

Cushman, P. (2005). It's just not a real bloke's job: Male teachers in the primary school. *Asian Pacific Journal of Teacher Education, 33*(3), 321–338.

Cushman, P. (2008). So what exactly do you want? What principals mean when they say male role model. *Gender and Education, 20*(2), 123–136.

Darling-Hammond, L., & Bransford, J. (Eds.) (2005). *Preparing teachers for a changing world: What teachers should learn and be able to do*. San Francisco, CA: Jossey Bass.

Davis, O. L. (1997). Beyond best practices toward wise practices. *Journal of Curriculum and Supervision, 13*(1), 1–5.

Delgado, R., & Stefancic, J. (Eds.) (1997). *Critical white studies: Looking behind the mirror*. Philadelphia, PA: Temple University Press.

Delpit, L. (1986). Skills and other dilemmas of a progressive Black educator. *Harvard Educational Review, 56*(4), 379–385.

Delpit, L. (1988). Power and pedagogy in teaching other people's children. *Harvard Educational Review, 58*(3), 280–298.

Denzin, N. K. (1989). *Interpretive biography*. London: Sage.

Dewey, J. (1997). *Democracy and education*. New York, NY: The Free Press. (Original work published 1916)

Dewey, J. (1997). *How we think*. New York, NY: Dover Publications, Inc. (Original work published 1910)

Dewey, J. (1997). *Education and experience*. New York, NY: Touchstone Books. (Original work published 1938)

Dewey, J. (1990). *The child and the curriculum*. Chicago, IL: The University of Chicago Press. (Original work published 1902)

Douglas, F. (1986). *Narrative of the life of Fredrick Douglas, an American slave*. New York, NY: Penguin Classics. (Original work published 1845)

Du Bois, W. E. B. (1995). *The souls of Black folk*. New York, NY: Signet Classic. (Original work published 1903)

Dyer, R. (1988). White. *Screen, 29*(4), 44–64.

Eichstedt, J. L. (2001). White identities and a search for racial justice. *Sociological Form, 16*(3), 445, 470.

Eisner, C. (1985). *The educational imagination* (2nd ed.). New York, NY: MacMillan.

Ellsworth, E. (1989). Why doesn't this feel empowering? Working through the repressive myths of critical pedagogy. *Harvard Educational Review, 59*(3), 297–324.

Emihovich, C. (1995). Distancing passion: Narratives in social science. *Qualitative Studies in Education, 8*(1), 37–48.

Emerson, R. W. (2000). *Essays first series*. In M. Oliver (Ed.), *The essential writings of Ralph Waldo Emerson* (pp. 113–274). New York, NY: The Modern Library. (Original work published 1844)

Foley, D. (2002). Critical ethnography: The reflexive turn. *Qualitative Studies in Education, 15*(5), 469–490.

Foley, D. (1990). *Learning capitalist culture deep in the heart of Tejas*. Philadelphia, PN: University of Pennsylvania Press.

Fordham Foundation. (2006). *How well are states educating our neediest children? http://www. edexcellence.net/publications/fordhamreport2006.html*. (Retrieved July 2012).

Frankenberg, R. (1993). *The social construction of whiteness: White women, race matters*. Minneapolis, MN: University of Minnesota Press.

Freeman, D. E., & Freeman, Y. S. (2004). *Essential linguistics: What you need to know to teach reading, ESL, spelling, phonics, and grammar*. Portsmouth, NH: Heinemann.

Freire, P. (2002). *Pedagogy of hope*. New York, NY: Continuum. (Original work published 1992)

Freire, P. (2002). *Pedagogy of the oppressed*. New York, NY: Continuum. (Original work published 1970)

Frith, S. (2003). *Music and identity*. In S. Hall & P. DuGay (Eds.), *Questions of cultural identity* (pp. 108–127). London: Sage.

Gay, G. (2000). *Culturally responsive teaching: Theory, research, and practice*. New York, NY: Teachers College Press.

Ginsberg, A. (1973). America. In R. Ellman & R. O'Clair (Eds.) *The Norton anthology of American poetry* (pp. 1126–1128). New York, NY: W.W. Norton & Company, Inc. (Originally published in 1956.)

Giroux, H. A. (2012). *Education and the crisis of public values*. New York, NY: Peter Lang.

Giroux, H. A. (1996). Slacking off: Border youth and postmodern education. In H. A. Giroux, C. Lankshear, P. McLaren, & M. Peters (Eds.,) *Counternarratives: Cultural studies and critical pedagogies in postmodern spaces* (pp. 59–80). New York, NY: Routledge.

Giroux, H. A. (1998). White noise: Racial politics and the pedagogy of whiteness. *Channel surfing: Youth, the media, racism, and the destruction of today's youth* (pp. 89–136). New York, NY: St. Martins.

Giroux, H. A. (2011). *Zombie politics and culture in the age of casino capitalism*. New York, NY: Peter Lang.

Gonzalez, N., Moll, L., & Amanti, C. (Eds.) (2005). *Funds of knowledge: Theorizing practices in households, communities, and classrooms*. Mahwah, NY: Lawrence Erlbaum Associates.

Goodson, I. F. (Ed.) (1992). *Studying teachers' lives*. New York, NY: Teachers College Press.

Goodson, I. F. (1995). The story so far: Personal knowledge and the political. In J. A. Hatch & R. Wisniewski (Eds.), *Life history and narrative*. New York, NY: Routledge-Falmer.

Goodson, I. F., & Sikes, P. (2001). *Life history research in educational settings*. Berkshire: McGraw Hill.

Goodson, I. F., & Walker, R. (1991). *Biography, identity & schooling*: New York, NY: The Falmer Press.

Gramsci, A. (2000). *The Gramsci reader* (Ed. D. Forgacs). New York, NY: New York University Press.

Hall S., & Jefferson T. (Eds.) *Resistance through rituals: Youth subcultures in post-war Britain* (pp. 106–118). New York, NY: Routledge. (Original work published 1975)

Hall, S. (2004). Gramsci's relevance for the study of race and ethnicity. In D. Morley & K.H. Chen's *Stuart Hall: Critical dialogues in cultural studies* (pp. 411–440). New York, NY: Routledge.

Hall, S. (1981). The whites of their eyes: Racist ideologies and the media. In G. Bridges & R. Brunt (Eds.), *Silver linings: Some strategies for the eighties* (pp. 28–52). London: Lawrence And Wishart.

Hall, S. (2003). Who needs "identity"? In S. Hall & Paul Du Guy (Eds.), *Questions of cultural identity*. London: Sage.

Henry, A. (1996). Literacy, Black self-representation, and cultural Practice in an elementary classroom: Implications for teaching children of African-Caribbean heritage. *Qualitative Studies in Education, 9*(2), 119–134.

Hinojosa, R. (1994). *Estampas del Valle*. Tempe, AZ: Bilingual Press. (Original work published 1973)

Hinojosa, R. (1977). *Generaciones y semblanzas*. Berkley, CA: Justa Publications, Inc.

Ignatiev, N. (1995). *How the Irish became white*. New York, NY: Routledge.

Hebdige, D. (1979). From culture to hegemony. In D. Hebdige (Ed.), *Subculture: The meaning of style* (pp. 5–19). New York, NY: Routledge.

Henze, R., Lucas, T. & Scott, B. (1998). Dancing with the monster: Teachers discuss racism, power, and White privilege in education. *The urban review, 30*(3), 187–210.

REFERENCES

Henderson, J., & Gornik, R. (2007). *Transformative curriculum leadership* (3rd ed.). Columbus, OH: Pearson.

Henze, R., Lucas, T., & Scott, B. (1998), Dancing with the monster: Teachers discuss racism power, and White, privilege in education, *The Urban Review, 30*, 187–210.

Hernstein, R. J., & Murray, C. (1994). *The bell curve: Intelligence and class structure in American life.* New York, NY: Free Press.

Hirsch, E. D. (1988). *Cultural literacy: What every American needs to know.* New York, NY: Vintage.

Hooks, B. (1992). *Black looks: Race and representation.* New York, Boston, MA: South End Press.

Hooks, B. (1994). *Teaching to transgress.* New York, NY: Routledge.

Howard, G. (2006). *We can't teach what we don't know.* New York, NY: Teachers College Press.

Hyten, K., & Warren, J. (2003). Engaging whiteness: how racial power gets reified in education. *Qualitative Studies in Education, 16*(1), 65–89.

Fairbanks, C. (1998a) Imagining neighborhoods: Social worlds of urban adolescents. In C. Fleischer & D. Schaafsma (Eds.), *Literacy and democracy.* Urbana, IL: National Council of Teachers of English, 136–156.

Fairbanks, C. (1998b). Nourishing conversations: Urban adolescents, literacy, and democratic society. *Journal of Language and Reading, 30*(2), 187–203.

Francis, B., & Skelton, C. (2001). Men teachers and the construction of heterosexual masculinity in the classroom. *Sex Education, 1*(1), 9–21.

Goldstein, L. (1998). More than gentle smiles and warm hugs: Applying the ethic of care to early childhood education. *Journal of Research in Early Childhood Education, 12*(2), 244–261.

Goldstein, L. (2002). *Reclaiming caring in teaching and teacher Education.* New York, NY: Peter Lang.

Jackson, P. (1968). *Life in classrooms.* New York, NY: Teachers College Press.

Johnson, J. A., Musial, D., Hall, G. E., & Gollnick, D. M. (2010). *Foundations of American education* (15th ed.). Boston, MA: Allyn & Bacon.

Julien, I., & Mercer, K. Introduction: De margin and de centre. *Screen*, 29(4), 2–10.

Jupp, J. C. (2004). Culturally relevant teaching: One teacher's journey through theory and practice. *Multicultural Review, 13*(1), 33–40.

Jupp, J. C., & Slattery, P. (2012). *Becoming* teachers of inner-city students: Identification creativity and curriculum wisdom of committed White male teachers. *Urban Education 47*(1), 280–311.

Jupp, J. C., & Slattery, P. (2010). Committed White male teachers and identities: Toward creative identifications and a "second wave" of white identity studies. *Curriculum Inquiry, 40*(3), 454–474.

Katz, M. B. (1989). *The undeserving poor: From the war on poverty to the war on welfare.* Pantheon: New York, NY.

Kaye, L. (1978). Introduction. In J. Burchill & T. Parsons (Eds.), *The boy looked at Johnny: The obituary of rock and roll* (pp. vii–x). Boston, MA: Faber & Faber.

Kerouac, J. (1995). *Desolation angles.* New York, NY: Riverhead Books. (Originally published in 1965.)

Kincheloe, J.L. (1999). The struggle to define and reinvent whiteness: A pedagogical analysis. *College Literature, 26*(Fall), 162–197.

Kincheloe, J. L., & Steinberg, S. R. (1998). Addressing the crisis of whiteness: Reconfiguring white identity in a pedagogy of whiteness. In J. L. Kincheloe, S. R. Steinberg, N. M. Rodriguez, & R. E. Chennault (Eds.), *White reign: Deploying whiteness in America* (pp. 3–30). New York, NY: St Martin's Press.

Kliebard, H. B. (1995). *The struggle for the American curriculum 1893–1958* (2nd ed.). New York, NY: Routledge.

Knowles, G. (1992). Models for understanding preservice and beginning teachers' biographies: Illustrations from case studies. In I. F. Goodson's (Ed.), *Studying teachers' lives* (pp. 99–152). New York, NY: Teachers College Press.

Knowles, G. (2001). Beginnings: Researching the professor. In A. Cole & G. Knowles (Eds.), *Lives in context: The art of life history research* (pp. 1–5). New York, NY: Altamira Press.

Kozol, J. (1991). *Savage inequalities.* New York, NY: Harper.

Kozol, J. (2005). *The Shame of a Nation.* New York, NY: Crown.

Ladson-Billings, G. (2009). *The dreamkeepers: Successful teachers of African-American students.* San Francisco, CA: Jossey-Bass.

Ladson-Billings, G. (1995). Toward a theory of culturally relevant pedagogy. *American Educational Research Journal, 32*(3), 465–491.

Lather, P. (1991). *Getting smart: Feminist research and pedagogy with/in the postmodern.* New York, NY: Routledge Press.

Leary, T. (1990). *Flashbacks: A personal and cultural history of an era.* New York, NY: Tarcher & Putnam. (Original work published 1983)

Lensmire, T. (2011). Laughing White men. *Journal of Curriculum Theorizing, 27*(3), 102–116.

Lightbown, P. M., & Spada, N. (2011). *How languages are learned* (3rd ed.). Oxford: Oxford University Press.

Lincoln, Y. S., & Guba, E. G. (1985). *Naturalistic inquiry.* London: Sage Publications.

Lortie, D. (1977). *School teacher: A sociological study.* University of Chicago Press: Chicago IL.

Lowenstein, K. (2009). The work of multicultural teacher education: Reconceptualizing White teacher candidates as learners. *Review of Educational Research, 79*(1), 163–196.

Macedo, E. (2011). Identity as the organizing principle of curriculum. Personal email communication.

Marx, S. (2008). Popular White teachers of Latino/a kids: The strengths of personal experiences and the limitations of whiteness. *Urban Education 43*(1), 29–67.

Marx, S. (2004). Confronting racism in teacher education. *Equity & excellence in education, 37,* 31–43.

Marx, S., & Pennington, J. (2003). Pedagogies of critical race theory: Experimentation with White preservice teachers. *International Journal of Qualitative Studies in Education, 16*(1), 91–110.

McCarthy, C. (2003). Contradictions of power and identity: Whiteness studies and the call of teacher education. *International Journal of Qualitative Studies in Education, 16*(1), 127–133.

McCarthy, C., & Crichlow, W. (1993). Introduction: Theories of identity, theories of representation, theories race. In C. McCarthy & W. Crichlow (Eds.), *Race, identity, and representation in education* (pp. xiii–xxix). New York, NY: Routledge.

McIntosh, P. (1988). White privilege and male privilege: A personal account of coming to see correspondences through work in women's studies. Wellesley Center for Research on Women. Wellesley, MA. Working Paper 189.

McIntyre, A. (2002). Exploring whiteness and multicultural education with prospective teachers. *Curriculum Inquiry, 32*(1).

McIntyre, A. (1998). *Making meaning of whiteness: Exploring racial identity with white teachers.* Albany, NY: SUNY.

McLaren, P. (1996). *Liberatory politics and higher education: A Freirean perspective.* In H. A. Giroux, C. Lankshear, P. McLaren, M. Peters (Eds.), *Counternarratives: Cultural studies and critical perspectives in postmodern spaces* (pp. 117–148). New York, NY: Routledge.

Middleton, S. (1992). Developing a radical pedagogy: Autobiography of a New Zealand sociologist of women's education. In I. F. Goodson (Ed.), *Studying teachers' lives* (pp. 18–50). New York, NY: Teachers College Press.

Middleton, S. (1993). *Educating feminists: Life histories and pedagogy.* New York, NY: Teachers College Press.

Miele, A. (2012a). Complicating whiteness: Identifications of veteran White teachers in multicultural settings. Unpublished manuscript.

Miele, A. (2012b). Whiteness as relational phenomena: Literature review. Unpublished manuscript.

Milam, J., Jupp, J.C., Hoyt, M., Kaufman, M., Grumbien, M., O'Mally, M. Carpenter, B. S., & Slattery, P. (In press). Autobiography, disclosure, and engaged pedagogy: A practical discussion on teaching foundations in teacher education programs. *Teacher education and practice 27* TBA.

Moll, L. C. (1992). Bilingual classroom studies and community analysis: Some recent trends. *Educational Researcher, 21*(2), 20–24.

Moll. L. C., & González, N. (1994). Lessons from research with language minority children. *Journal of Reading Behavior, 26*(4), 439–455.

Munro, P. (1995). *Subject to fiction: Women teachers' life history narratives and the cultural politics of resistance.* Philadelphia, PA: Open University Press.

National Center of Educational Statistics (NCES). (2009). *The condition of education 2009: Racial/ethnic concentration in public school.* Washington, DC: U.S. Department of Educational Statistics.

REFERENCES

National Center for Education Statistics (NCES). (2010). *Status and trends in the education of racial and ethnic groups*. Washington, DC: US Department of Educational Statistics.

National Center for Education Statistics (NCES). (2004). *Table 18. Percentage distribution of school teachers by race/ethnicity &tc.* http://nces.ed.gov/surveys/sass/tables/sass_2004_18.asp (Retrieved June 2010)

National Commission on Excellence in Education (NCEE) (1994). *Nation at risk: The full account.* Portland, OR: USA Research, Inc. (Original work published 1984)

National Council for the Accreditation of Teacher Education (NCATE). (2008). *Professional standards for the accreditation of teacher education institutions*. Washington, DC: NCATE.

Nee-Benham, M. K. P. A. (1997). The story of an African-American teacher scholar: A woman's narrative. *Qualitative Studies in Education, 10*(1), 63–83.

Nieto, S. (1999). *The light in their eyes: Creating multicultural learning communities*. New York, NY: Teachers College Press.

Noddings, N. (1984). *Caring: A feminine approach to ethics and education*. Berkley, CA: University of California Press.

Ogbu, J., & Simmons, H. D. (1998). Voluntary and involuntary minorities: A cultural-ecological theory of school performance with some implications for education. *Anthropology and Education Quarterly, 29*(2), 155–188.

Paley, V. G. (2000). *White teacher*. Cambridge MS: Harvard University Press. (Work originally published 1979)

Perry, P., & Shotwell, A. (2009). Rational understanding and white antiracist praxis. *Sociological theory, 27*(1), 33–50

Peters, M., & Lanshear, C. (1996). Postmodern counternarratives. In H. A. Giroux, C. Lankshear, P. McLaren & M. Peters (Eds.), *Counternarratives: Cultural studies and critical pedagogies in postmodern spaces* (pp. 1–40). New York, NY: Routledge.

Phillion, J. (2008). Multicultural and cross-cultural narrative inquiry into understanding immigrant students' educational experience in Hong Kong. *Compare, 38*(3), 281–293.

Pinar, W. F. (2011). Multiculturalism, nationalism, cosmopolitanism. *The character of curriculum studies: Bildung, currere, and recurring question of the subject* (pp. 49–62). New York, NY: Palgrave-MacMillan.

Pinar, W. F. (2009). *The worldliness of a cosmopolitan education: Passionate lives in public service*. New York, NY: Routledge.

Pinar, W. F. (2004). *What is curriculum theory*. Mahwah, NY: Lawrence Erlbaum Associates.

Pinar, W. F. (2012). *What is curriculum theory?* (2nd ed.). New York, NY: Routledge.

Polkinghorne, D. (1995). Narrative configuration in qualitative analysis. In J. A. Hatch & R. Wisniewski *Life history and narrative* (pp. 5–24). New York, NY: Routledge Falmer

Plummer, K. (2001). *Documents of life 2: An invitation to a critical humanism*. Sage: London.

Raible, J., & Irizarry, J. G. (2007). Transracialized selves and the emergence of post-racial identities. *Race, Ethnicity, and Education, 10*(2), 177–198.

Reynolds, W., & Webber, J. (2009). *The civic gospel: A political cartography of Christianity*. Rotterdam: Sense Publishers.

Riessman, C. K. (2008). *Narrative methods for the human sciences*. London: Sage.

Rodriguez, N. (1998). Emptying the content of whiteness: Toward an understanding of the relation between whiteness and pedagogy. In J. L. Kincheloe, S. R. Steinberg, N. M. Rodriguez & R. E. Chennault (Eds.), *White reign: Deploying whiteness in America* (pp. 31–63). New York, NY: St Martin's Press.

Roediger, D. (1994). *Toward the abolition of whiteness: Essays on race, politics, and working class history*. New York, NY: Verso.

Sargent, P. (2004). Between a rock and a hard place: Men caught in the gender bind of early childhood education. *The Journal of Men's Studies, 12*(3), 173–192.

Sargent, P. (2000). Real men or real teachers?: Contradictions in the lives of men elementary school teachers. *Men and Masculinities, 2*, 410–433.

Said, E. (1989). Representing the colonized: Anthropology's interlocutors. *Critical Inquiry, 15*(2), 205–225.

Said, E. (1993). The politics of knowledge. In C. McCarthy & W. Crichlow (Eds), *Race, identity and representation in education* (pp. 306–314). New York, NY: Routledge.

Sauvageau, J. (1989). *Stories that must not die.* Los Angeles: Pan American Publishing Company, Inc.

Scheurich, J. (2002). *Anti-racist scholarship: An advocacy.* New York: State University of New York Press.

Schön, D. (1983). *The reflective practitioner. How professionals think in action.* London: Temple Smith.

Schwab, J. J. (1978). *Science, curriculum, and the liberal tradition* (Eds. I. Westbury & N. J. Wilkof's). Chicago, IL: University of Chicago.

Schwab, J. J. (1983). The practical 4: Something for curriculum professors to do. *Curriculum inquiry, 13*(3), 240–265.

Shor, I. (1987). *Critical teaching and everyday life.* Chicago, IL: University of Chicago Press.

Shor, I. (1992) *Empowering education: Critical teaching for social change.* Chicago, IL: University of Chicago Press.

Shulman, L. (1987). Knowledge and teaching: Foundations of the new reform. *Harvard Educational Review, 57*(1), 1–22

Slattery, P. (2006). *Curriculum development in the postmodern era* (2nd ed.). New York, NY: Routledge.

Sleeter, C. (1993). How white teachers construct race. In C. McCarthy & W. Crichlow (Eds.), *Race, identity and representation in education* (pp. 157–171). New York, NY: Routledge.

Sleeter, C. (2001). Preparing teachers for culturally diverse schools. *Journal of Teacher Education, 52*(2), 94–106

Sleeter, C. (1992). Resisting racial awareness: How teachers understand the social order from their racial, gender, and social class locations. *Educational foundations, 6*(2), 7–32.

Sleeter, C. (1995). Teaching whites about racism. In R. J. Martin (Ed.), *Practicing what we teach: Confronting diversity in teacher education.* Albany, NY: State University of New York Press.

Spring, J. (2000). *The American school 1642–2000.* (5th ed.). New York, NY: McGraw Hill.

Sumsion, J. (1999). Critical reflections on the experiences of a male early childhood worker. *Gender and Education, 11*(4), 455–468.

Tozer, S. E., Senese, G., & Violas, P. (2009). *School and society: Historical and contemporary perspectives* (6th ed.). New York, NY: McGraw Hill.

Tyack, D. (1974). *The one best system: A history of American urban education.* Boston, MA: Harvard University Press.

Thoreau, H. D. (1983) *Walden.* In M. Meyer (Ed.), *Walden and civil disobedience* (pp. 43–382). New York, NY: Penguin Classics. (Original work published 1854)

Tolson, A. (1977). *The limits of masculinity: Male identity and women's liberation.* New York, NY: Harper & Row Publishers.

Valencia, R., & Solórzano, D. G. (1997). Contemporary deficit thinking. In R. Valencia (Ed.), *The evolution of deficit thinking* (pp. 160–210). London: Falmer Press.

Valenzuela, A. (1999). *Subtractive schooling: US-Mexican youth and the politics of caring.* Albany, New York: State University of New York Press.

Valenzuela, A., & McNeil, L. (2000). *The harmful impact of TAAS system testing in Texas: Beneath the accountability rhetoric.* ERIC document: 443872.

Villenas, S. (1996). The colonizer/colonized Chicana ethnographer: Identity, marginalization, and co-optation in the field. *Harvard Educational Review, 66*(4), 711–731.

Villenas, S. (2000). This ethnography called my back: Writings of the exotic gaze, "othering" Latina, and recuperating Xicanisma. In E. A. St. Pierre & W. S. Pillow (Eds.), *Working the ruins: Feminist poststructural theory and methods in education* (pp. 74–95). New York, NY: Routledge.

Watts, A. (1989). *The book: On the taboo against knowing who you are.* Vintage Books: New York, New York. (Originally published in 1966.)

Williams, C. L. (1992). The glass escalator: Hidden advantages of men in the 'female' professions. *Social Problems, 39*(3), 253–267.

Williams. C. L. (1993). Introduction. In C. L. Williams' (Ed.), *Doing women's work* (pp. 1–9). London: Sage.

Vasconcelos (1997). *The cosmic race/La raza cósmica.* Baltimore, MA: Johns Hopkins University Press. (Original work published 1925)

REFERENCES

Xu, S., Connelly, M., He, M. F., & Phillion, J. (2007). Immigrant students experience of schooling: A narrative inquiry theoretical framework. *Journal of Curriculum Studies, 39*(4), 399–422.

Yúdice, G. (1995). Neither impugning nor disavowing whiteness does a viable politics make: The limits of identity politics. In C. Newfield & R. Strickland (Eds.), *After political correctness: The humanities and society in the 1990s* (pp. 255–285). Boulder, CO: Westview Press.

Zinn, H. (2003). *A people's history of the United States: 1492-present.* New York, NY: Perennial Classics. (Original work published 1980)

The play is a representation

my practice
my teaching story

Race Visible Teaching — Theodore Taylor

Science dialogue
Chapter 8

1. Deliberative Dialogue
   Bringing Stories to the table.
   that tell stories of science not told.

2. Relationality
   Personal relationships → learn about students

Cloning 3. Synthetic Teaching ← Science topics

4. Socio Political Critique ← Science in 1951
                                Medicine "
                                Society
   Has your life been touched by
   Cancer?
   Students share their story

Learning what audience
to share   successes of work
     Ways to connect
     Can passion be mistook
          for
navigating   passion / modesty

CPSIA information can be obtained at www.ICGtesting.com
Printed in the USA
LVOW10s1630131213

365204LV00001B/50/P

9 789462 093690